D1196756

Also by Shane Peacock

The Great Farini: The High-Wire Life of William Hunt

The Dylan Maples Adventures for young readers

Bone Beds of the Badlands

The Secret of the Silver Mines

The Mystery of Ireland's Eye

Unusual Heroes

*Canada's Prime Ministers and
Fathers of Confederation*

SHANE PEACOCK

PUFFIN
CANADA

PUFFIN CANADA
Published by the Penguin Group
Penguin Books, a division of Pearson Canada, 10 Alcorn Avenue, Toronto,
Ontario, Canada M4V 3B2
Penguin Books Ltd, 80 Strand, London WC2R 0RL, England
Penguin Putnam Inc., 375 Hudson Street, New York, New York 10014, U.S.A.
Penguin Books Australia Ltd, 250 Camberwell Road, Camberwell,
Victoria 3124, Australia
Penguin Books India (P) Ltd, 11, Community Centre, Panchsheel Park,
New Delhi – 110 017, India
Penguin Books (NZ) Ltd, cnr Rosedale and Airborne Roads, Albany,
Auckland 1310, New Zealand
Penguin Books (South Africa) (Pty) Ltd, 24 Sturdee Avenue,
Rosebank 2196, South Africa

Penguin Books Ltd, Registered Offices: 80 Strand, London WC2R 0RL, England

First published 2002

1 3 5 7 9 10 8 6 4 2

Copyright © Shane Peacock, 2002

Photo credits—pp.1, 9, 14, 23, 40, 49, 56, 58, 59, 60, 80, 91, 101, 114, 126,
138, 152, 165, 177, 203, 216, 267, 317: © National Archives of Canada;
p. 30, © National Archives of Canada C264158; p. 192, © Provincial Museum
and Archives of Alberta; pp. 225, 278: © Progressive Conservative
Party of Canada; p. 229, © Gaby/National Archives of Canada/C-0023130;
p. 240, © CP Picture Archive; p. 291, © Canadian Photo Service;
p. 303, © Office of the Prime Minister/Jean-Marc Carisse

Printed and bound in Canada on acid free paper ∞

NATIONAL LIBRARY OF CANADA CATALOGUING IN PUBLICATION DATA

Peacock, Shane
Unusual heroes : Canada's prime ministers
and Fathers of Confederation / Shane Peacock.

Includes index.
ISBN 0-14-301350-5

1. Prime ministers—Canada—History—Juvenile literature. 2. Fathers of
Confederation—Juvenile literature. I. Title.

FC25.P42 2002   j971'.009'9   C2002-903264-4
F1034.3.A2P42 2002

Visit Penguin Books' website at **www.penguin.ca**

For
Jennie and Ernest Powell,
Vera and Vernon Peacock:
Liberals, Conservatives,
Canadians

Contents

Introduction: Strange Leaders in a Strange Land   ix

Part One: The Story of Confederation   1

Part Two: Our Fathers of Confederation   9

The Prophet: Thomas D'Arcy McGee   14

The Proclaimer: Sir Alexander Tilloch Galt   23

The Catalyst: George Brown   30

The Kingpin: Sir George-Étienne Cartier   40

The Class: Sir Samuel Leonard Tilley   49

The Ram: Sir Charles Tupper   56

The Man: Sir John A. Macdonald   58

Part Three: Our Prime Ministers   59

The Great One: Sir John A. Macdonald   60

Working Man: Alexander Mackenzie   80

The Great Pooh-Bah: Sir John Abbott   91

What Could Have Been: Sir John Thompson   101

Santa in Disguise: Sir Mackenzie Bowell   114

The Legendary Warhorse: Sir Charles Tupper   126

The Magnificent One (Le Magnifique):
  Sir Wilfrid Laurier   138

Salt of the Earth: Sir Robert Borden   152

The Brilliant Failure: Arthur Meighen   165

The Supernatural One: William Lyon Mackenzie King   177

A Rich Man in a Poor Man's World: R.B. Bennett   192

Uncle Louis: Louis St. Laurent   203

Canadian Dynamite: John Diefenbaker   216

International Man of Mystery: Lester B. Pearson   229

Cool!: Pierre Elliott Trudeau   240

The High River Kid: Joe Clark   254

Blue-Eyed Handsome Man: John Turner   267

Mr. Smooth: Brian Mulroney   278

Unusual Woman: Kim Campbell   291

Keeper of the Key: Jean Chrétien   303

Not the End   317

Acknowledgements   320
Index   321

"How strange I am. I really do not know myself."
—WILLIAM LYON MACKENZIE KING,
10th Prime Minister of Canada

Introduction
STRANGE LEADERS IN A STRANGE LAND

Canada is kind of a weird place. People come here from all over the world and they fit right in. It doesn't seem to matter whether you're from India, China, England, France, or Middle Earth, you can still be a Canadian. And you don't have to stop being what you were before you got here either. Pretty cool, really.

But *why* it's like that is another question, a big question. It's mostly because of the way Canada was created, and because of the weird guys who put it together and other weird people who have run the place since then. They were weird in a good way—unusual people with unusual ideas.

A whole bunch of these supposedly very serious dudes once took a break from planning the birth of the country by going to a horse race, laying their hands on some peashooters, and firing pea-missiles at the crowd. Not long before that, one of them actually joined an army of friends to fight a rebellion *against* Canada. He also nearly blew the head off a guy in a duel—he missed and put the bullet through the guy's hat. The very first Prime Minister once sat on the outside of a train engine as it sped through the Rocky Mountains, just to get a better view. Another one showed up in our government building in his slippers (he was kind of forgetful). Then there was one who talked with the dead. The current guy? He was the black sheep of his family, and an obnoxious student who kept getting booted out of school for kicking the you-know-what out of other kids. He's running the country now.

They're a pretty amazing group. And if you turn on your TV today and watch the Prime Minister and other politicians in the same Parliament where that guy wore his slippers, you'll see them yelling at each other. But that's a good thing. Everyone wants to have a say in Canada, no matter who they are, where they came from, or what they believe in. And these guys are doing just that: for us, for Canada. Unlike many other countries, our leader has to get in there with the others and argue. If you can't argue, you can't be Prime Minister.

So, these weird people have created and maintained a weird country, a place where just about anybody can feel at home. How they did that is pretty interesting.

Part One

The Story of Confederation

In the Beginning

The year everybody says it started was 1867. And they're right, in many ways. That was when the Dominion of Canada was born. But we all know that the place we now call Canada existed way, way, way before that. And some of us can trace our roots back to the people who lived here. Indians, natives, Ojibway, Cree, Blackfoot—whatever name you use, there were folks here whose descendants are now part of Canadian society. They had been living here for thousands of years before other folks came across the Atlantic Ocean from Europe and had the very strange idea that they had "discovered" Canada. Actually, they'd just seen it for the first time. Heck, they were so confused that when a native person said something about "Kan-a-ta," (meaning a little "village of small huts" nearby), they mistook it for the entire country. And that's why they called the whole kit-and-kaboodle Canada.

These new folks didn't always treat the native people very well. They came from places like France and England, where you owned your land and had money and kept trying to get ahead. The natives weren't like that. They thought everyone shared the land. But the French settled smack dab in the middle of native territory, in the area we call Quebec, in the early 1600s. Then the English showed up in big wooden sail-boats in 1759 near the capital of "New France" and climbed up an amazing cliff and beat the French in battle on a field called the Plains of Abraham. Then they took over.

They loved organizing things, and soon divided up "British North America" (as Canada was called in those days) into provinces—Upper Canada (that's now Ontario), Lower Canada (that's now Quebec), and the Maritime provinces of Newfoundland, Nova Scotia, New Brunswick, and little Prince Edward Island. To the south, something called the United States of America had come into existence after a violent revolution. They'd separated from England because they were sick of being told what to do. Then they told the world they were the freest country on earth (they still do that) and often called their land "America" (they still do that too), even though that's really the name for the whole continent. But many of their people didn't want the kind of freedom that forced them to be "Americans," and fled to British North America, sometimes after being beaten up and chased out. Those people became the founders of much of English Canada. After that first war with England, the Americans would prove to be pretty interested in wars and pretty big on themselves. England, and all its little provinces, kept an eye on them. Every now and then the Americans said they wanted Canada. In 1812 there was even a war. It turned out to be a tie, thank goodness, and they left us alone.

Canadians are supposed to be quiet folk who never rock the boat. But that's not true. We just want others to think that. In 1837, sick of not having enough say in our government, which was being run by all sorts of snobby Englishmen, we even had a couple of rebellions. One was on Yonge Street in Toronto and the other around Montreal. It was mostly pitch-forks and rocks against guns and cannons, so you can guess who won. But the English got the message, and by the early 1840s, after they changed Upper and Lower Canadas' names to Canada West and East, they started allowing us to elect a "responsible" government that actually got to run things. From then on life started to change. It wouldn't take long before we decided we wanted a country that put everyone, French and English, Maritime and West, into one big nation. That idea was called Confederation.

Threats from the South and Within

The Americans kind of pushed us into it, though they didn't mean to. By 1861 they were fighting *each other* in the Civil War. The southern half of their country had slaves and believed each of their states had all sorts of powers; the north-ern half didn't have slaves and thought the main government should have most of the power. So, they fought. Boy, did they fight. And as hundreds of thousands were killed we started to get worried. What if they turned on us when it was over? It would be like an elephant squashing a mouse. All our provinces were very different, but none of us wanted to be American.

Before Confederation we used to trade things with the United States all the time. That was called "Reciprocity." Suddenly they said they didn't want it any more. That seemed a little suspicious. So, we started trading more with each other.

There was also a group called the "Fenians" who lived in "America." They were rebels from Ireland who thought they'd like to take over Canada—a move they hoped would force the English to give them national independence back home. Soon they were coming over our border with guns. That gave us even more reason to stick together.

At the same time, England was getting kind of sick of looking after us. We cost a lot of money. We were big and cold and there weren't enough of us yet to make having us worthwhile. They started trying to persuade us to leave, like parents do sometimes with older teenagers who finish high school and keep hanging out in the house.

On top of all of this, Canada West and East were having trouble with the way things were set up. The British had insisted that both provinces be run by one combined government. They also made them officially equal to each other, giving them exactly the same number of elected members in that government, despite the fact that Canada West had more people than the mostly French Canada East. Neither province could dominate. Not much got done. There was a lot of arguing going on.

In 1864, one of the English leaders in the West, a guy by the name of George Brown, a big guy with red hair who could *really* argue, did something pretty amazing. He said he'd unite with anybody, *anybody* who'd try to change things, *and* help build a nation that went from sea to sea, all across the land that didn't belong to "America."

Wow. His idea just about floored everyone. But some of them had actually been thinking the very same thing. Soon they formed a famous government called the "Great Coalition." Their goal was to create Canada.

The Confederation Conferences

Meanwhile, the people in the Maritime provinces, who were worried about the Americans too, had been wondering about joining each other. They had a meeting scheduled for Charlottetown, Prince Edward Island, that fall. Suddenly, they got a letter from the Canadas saying they'd like to go to the meeting too. And how about us all becoming one huge country? Then it was the Maritimers' turn to be floored.

Canada East and West had some pretty big wheels—guys like John A. Macdonald, Alexander Galt, Thomas D'Arcy

McGee, George-Étienne Cartier, and the previously mentioned Brown. They zipped up the St. Lawrence River in a big boat and dropped anchor in the bay at Charlottetown. The Maritimers hardly knew what to do. They sent out a guy named William Pope to meet them, a Prince Edward Islander with a beard the size of Newfoundland. But he couldn't find a decent sized ship. So, he rowed out in a stinky little fishing boat to greet the big stars from the west.

The 1864 Charlottetown Conference itself went very well though. Very unCanadianly well. The delegates decided that they indeed liked the idea of being one big country, and worked out a plan. Unlike "America," our national government would be much stronger than the provincial governments, and be more like the British, with a Prime Minister who had to argue every day with other elected members in a "House of Commons" in a "Parliament." It would also have a "Senate," which would have a lot of power too. But their biggest idea was that everyone, French and English, Catholic and Protestant, had to have a say (though they left the native people out of things again).

Once all the "Fathers of Confederation" got home and asked each of their provinces about the plan, people started to complain. That's the Canadian way. Argue, have your say. Don't shoot. Just argue.

So, we shouted at each other for a couple of years. Meanwhile, the Fathers met again, in Quebec City in 1864. Then there was a long session in London, England, in late 1866, and finally, Ontario, Quebec, New Brunswick, and

Nova Scotia decided to become something they agreed to call "Canada" . . . or that "village of small huts." The Maritimers and the Québécois had their doubts. But the others finally convinced them that it was a good idea.

The leading guy through all of this was a rascal named John Alexander Macdonald. He was a sort of genius, and put all the very different parts of Canada together like he was jamming a super-hard jigsaw puzzle into place, amazing all the big boys in England, who had assumed they were superior to our hayseed leaders. When it was over, this "fox" was asked to be the first Prime Minister of Canada.

He was kind of a strange dude. But he had to be. Canada was a strange place. It wasn't created because of a revolution, because all of its people were the same, or because everyone was so passionate about being a nation. That's usually the way it works. Instead, Canada was created simply because it was a good idea, because it seemed right that a whole bunch of different folks should get together and see if they could work things out. You had to use your brains to solve problems in Canada. You had to argue.

And so, on July 1, 1867, it all began. There were fireworks and parties and lots of parades with bagpipes and bands. But no one was sure what they had created, or if it could survive. They were beginning a story . . . the story of Canada. Its leaders, right from the Fathers of Confederation who built it through all the Prime Ministers who have ever run it, would perform many amazing feats to keep it going.

Part Two

Our Fathers of Confederation

The Supporting Cast

At Charlottetown and Quebec City in 1864 and in London two years later, as P.E.I. and Newfoundland dropped out and four provinces hung in, 36 guys with a lot of hair on their faces put Canada together. Some of them have kind of disappeared from our history. Ever heard of Sir Ambrose Shea, Edward Palmer, Charles Fisher, Jonathan McCully, or *two* guys named John Hamilton Gray? Didn't think so. But that makes sense, because guys like that didn't play very big roles.

Thirteen other Fathers did: six near-greats and seven giants.

Near-Greats

Sir Adams George Archibald from Nova Scotia was from the first category. He bravely supported Confederation in his province, even though people threw things at him for it. He learned to duck, stood his ground, and later became Governor of the new province of Manitoba, smoothing out things with a kind of wild, rebel guy there named Louis Riel.

Alexander Campbell was important too. He was the one and only John A. Macdonald's law partner in Kingston, Ontario, and looked after their firm while the big guy was away becoming famous. Campbell was a key player in that "Great Coalition" government that united to create Canada. After Confederation, he held just about every job in the group of assistants to the Prime Minister called the "cabinet" (though it has nothing to do with furniture), each one called a "minister" (though they have nothing to do with churches).

William McDougall, also from Ontario, was important, but really a bit of a doorknob. He was a good-looking guy, kind of dashing, with great hair and big ideas about Canada. He was also a windbag, who changed his mind so often that people called him "Wandering Willie." He was against Macdonald at first, but became a Father of Confederation and cabinet minister, though Mac got sick of him blowing his own horn all the time. He really became the doorknob that history remembers him as in 1869, when he was the first guy sent to Manitoba to try to make it part of Canada. But the rebel Riel and his friends didn't like this foreign wimp becoming their leader. So they kicked him out. He got mad and caused a lot of trouble. Macdonald told "Wandering Willie" to wander back home. There he lived another 35 years, a big-time doorknob.

Sir Étienne-Paschal Taché from Quebec was the opposite. He was a nice guy and very wise. He was the oldest Father of

Confederation and boss of the Quebec Conference. By that time he had white hair and looked like someone's grandpa. But in his early days he'd been involved in the 1837 Rebellion to get better government, and once waded into a Montreal riot and shot an English guy who was causing trouble. Then he learned to compromise, and got so good at it that he became co-Premier of the Canadas (representing the French, Canada East part) and leader of the Great Coalition. But he died right in the middle of the Confederation debate in 1865. That saddened many people. This legend with the "round, friendly" face had come to believe that everyone could get along in Canada. He believed it with all his heart.

Sir Oliver Mowat was important too, though he didn't look it. He was this short, fat guy with glasses. He and Macdonald knew each other when they were kids in Kingston, where they went to the same one-room school and slim, wise-cracking Mac used to tell round little Oliver all kinds of great jokes. Later, Mac gave Mowat a job in his law firm. Then Mowat went to Toronto and joined the Reform party, against Macdonald's Conservatives. A moderately rebellious group that became the Liberal party, Reform favoured a very democratic society and closer ties with the Americans. Soon the two men were arguing about everything. One time Mac got so cheesed off he tried to punch out the little guy in Parliament. "You young pup!" he growled, "I'll slap your chops!" Luckily, another leader-guy got between them. Later Mac and Mowat were reluctant Confederation allies, but then got back to being enemies. Mowat became the longest-serving and most powerful Ontario Premier in history (running things for 24 straight years), and constantly bugged John A. for more provincial power. Who could have known what a pain in the butt that short fat kid would turn out to be!

Sir Hector-Louis Langevin from Quebec was one of the greatest Fathers. He was built like a fire hydrant and had this little goatee that hung from his chin, making him look kind of different. He had been different all his life. He was mayor of Quebec City by age 31, and by 38, a Great Coalition cabinet minister and loud voice for his people at the Confederation conferences. He knew he was a big deal. "Cartier and I, we are Nos. 2 and 3," he boasted, ranking the Fathers. Many people thought he would be our first French-Canadian Prime Minister, but he got involved in too many scandals and never made it. But if you go to Ottawa today you will find the PM's office in a building called the "Langevin Block."

Rising above these near-greats was a group of seven extra-ordinary Fathers. Wait until you get a load of these guys!

The Prophet
THOMAS D'ARCY MCGEE

Born Ireland 1825, died Ottawa 1868, Conservative

Imagine this. When Thomas D'Arcy McGee was buried, on his 43rd birthday, Easter Monday in April 1868, the Montreal streets were thronged with 100,000 people. They lined the sidewalks, hung from the windows, stood on the roof-tops, and held signs showing their sadness. "We shall never look upon his like again," read one.

There has never been a Canadian like D'Arcy McGee and may never be one again. He lived a scary life. There was violence in it, revolution, poetry, and finally, explosive pain in the blast of a Derringer pistol on a dark Ottawa street. At its core was the man himself: five feet, three inches of thunder. He was the best speaker in our history, our biggest dreamer, and our most daring leader.

Irish Dramas

Born in Ireland in 1825, the son of a sailor and an educated mother, he didn't get to go to school much but had his dad's spirit and his mom's sharp mind. Years later the Archbishop of New York said, "McGee has the biggest mind and is unquestionably the cleverest man and the greatest orator that Ireland has sent forth in our time."

Even as a teenager he was gifted with the ability to excite audiences. He spoke dramatically and with the full power of his amazing brain. And by the time he left the poverty and political problems of Ireland at the age of 17 in 1842 and passed through British North America on his way to the United States, he was ready to unleash his opinions on a bigger audience. He believed that Ireland should be a separate country from England, and that religious and racial minorities had to be treated fairly. The blood of rebellion pulsed inside him.

By the age of 19 he was an editor with the *Boston Pilot* newspaper and had published the first of many books. But he missed Ireland and soon returned to become a leader of the radical "Young Ireland" movement, writing and speaking, his passion for Irish independence growing. Famine (partly brought on by massive potato crop failures) was breaking the Irish people, and McGee, frustrated by England's lack of concern, was pushed to the breaking point himself. By 1848 he no longer believed in peaceful change, and turned to violence. He began organizing a wing of a rebel army. But the police put a price on his head, and he had to flee. He snuck north to Derry, secretly said goodbye to his young wife Mary, disguised himself as a priest, and slipped onto an ocean-going ship. Ireland would never be his home again.

To a New World

First he lived in the United States, starting two newspapers and publishing more books and passionate poetry. (McGee would eventually be elected to the Royal Irish Academy for authors.) He spoke up for the Irish and tried to help the poor when they came to America. As always, he made as many enemies as friends. But he never really became an American, and in 1857, after being invited to visit Montreal, he found his true home. It seemed his ideas might be listened to in this new place.

Before his first year in the Canadas was over he had started a newspaper *(The New Era)* and been elected to Parliament. He gave stunning speeches and began to write about a dream of his, one rarely considered by many people who had lived in the land for much longer than he. He imagined a new nation where fairness was important, where there was no slavery of any kind—a brand-new northern country stretching from sea to sea.

It became common for the galleries of Parliament in Toronto to fill when D'Arcy McGee spoke. He argued for greater democracy and powers for minority religions. To the people of the Canadas, and the eastern Maritimes where he toured to promote his idea for a new nation, he was British North America's most popular politician.

Younger than most leaders (just in his 30s), dressed in dark clothes, his black curly hair looking uncombed next to his pale Irish skin, he could hush an audience with beautiful, gentle words and then bring them to tears and thunderous applause with his explosive passion. A reporter said, "When McGee speaks I am tempted to throw down my pencil and just listen."

In 1860, seven years before Confederation, he said: "I see in the not remote distance, one great nationality, bound, like the shield of Achilles, by the blue rim of ocean. . . . I see within the round of that shield, the peaks of the Western mountains and the crests of the Eastern waves." But he warned that there must be a special spirit behind it all: a tolerance of each other's views and a real desire to be together.

In the early 1860s he joined the Liberals and became a cabinet minister. But that government was afraid of McGee's bold views, and before long he left. Then he joined John A. Macdonald and George-Étienne Cartier's Conservatives, and together they moved slowly but surely towards McGee's dream of a new nation.

He would be a prominent Father at both the Charlottetown and Quebec conferences that year, pushing his policies of cooperation and tolerance—important ideas in the big idea that would become Canada.

McGee travelled throughout the reluctant Maritimes, and was received "like a prince," lighting up people with his speeches and even taking time to throw off his jacket and play a game of leapfrog at a picnic with the proper politicians of New Brunswick and Nova Scotia. "As long as French Canadians keep their language," he told English Canadians, "they are unconquered." He vowed to help the French stay that way in his new country.

When the Confederation plan was presented to the House of Commons in 1865, it was D'Arcy McGee who brilliantly finished the proposal speech. And though he wasn't present when the London Conference opened in 1866, he was there when it ended, as the British North America Act created the Dominion of Canada.

Danger Approaches

But there was always something scary about Thomas D'Arcy McGee. Darkness and drama followed him. Because of the need for equal representation from all the regions and two main religions of Canada, he was kept out of the nation's first cabinet. With so many Quebecker and Catholic candidates (like McGee) available, he didn't fit into the mix. Instead of causing problems and seeking glory for himself, he quietly accepted this. On July 1, 1867, when celebrations across the land heralded the country's birth, the "prophet of Confederation" spent the day feeling sad and out of sight in Toronto.

Giving all his time to his country, McGee lived in near-poverty. Three of his precious children died young, and he suffered the intense pain of poor circulation in his legs, causing him to walk with a cane by the age of 40. At times he drank too much and debated in taverns, his sharp brain and tongue becoming razorlike, cutting his opponents without mercy and making enemies.

And there was trouble on other fronts. Various Irish groups in Montreal (and in Ireland and the United States too) were angry with him because he had grown critical of Irish terrorists and now believed in a new nation that tolerated everyone's views. He had turned against violence. Angry mobs began coming to his public appearances, and brawls often erupted. To hear brave D'Arcy McGee address a crowd was an entertainment unlike any other in Canadian history.

His most frightening enemies were the Fenians, who would inflict terror on anyone, even Canadians, to gain independence for Ireland. He fearlessly called them names, dared them to disturb his Canadian dream, and told the world that secret societies like theirs, that hated others, were evil. They offered $1,000 in gold for his "head" and sent him letters marked with coffins; dark visitors crept near his Montreal home. But he wouldn't give in to terror. He once told an angry Irish Montreal crowd that some Fenians "deserve death" and then stepped to the front of the stage to confront the goons who taunted him.

And then it happened.

Murder in the Street

At two o'clock in the cold morning of April 7, 1868, after McGee delivered a patriotic, midnight speech so moving that others stood and cheered, he hobbled down the big stone steps at the entrance to the magnificent new House of Commons and walked into downtown Ottawa. He turned at Sparks Street, said goodbye to a friend, and with his white silk top hat shining in the moonlight, made his way home. As he turned the key in his lock, a Derringer pistol was pointed at the back of his head and fired.

One of his poems had read:

In the time of my boyhood, I had a strange feeling
That I was to die in the noon of my day,
Not quietly into the silent grave stealing,
But torn, like a blasted oak, sudden away.

Seconds later he lay on the cold plank sidewalk, an arm pinned under his body, a pool of blood a metre wide forming nearby, remnants of his teeth embedded in the door. Prime Minister Macdonald was called from his home. He rushed over and helped lift the lifeless "prophet" onto a bed in the building. A huge crowd began gathering outside.

Hundreds would soon be arrested on suspicion of his murder throughout Canada, including the doorkeeper of the House of Commons. A Montreal tailor named Patrick James Whelan was found in Ottawa with a Derringer, accused of being a Fenian, and hanged for murder. But questions remain. Whelan insisted he was innocent. Across the street from the scene of the murder, an old man blew out his brains with a gun, taking what he knew with him to his grave. A secret society may have conducted a secret assassination, a dramatic end to a dramatic life.

That day the House of Commons plunged into sadness. Macdonald's speech, full of pain, was barely heard. "If ever a soldier fell in the front of the fight it was D'Arcy McGee," he whispered. "He deserves well of Canada. He has left us a sacred legacy." George-Étienne Cartier almost cried as he spoke, the Premier of Quebec compared McGee to Julius Caesar and Abraham Lincoln, and enemies of the Canadian dream wondered out loud if they had been wrong.

At home in Montreal, little Peggy McGee, 11 years old, was awakened by her weeping mother and told that in the night someone had killed her father.

The population of Montreal doubled on the day he was buried. Guns rang out every minute in salute, and 15,000 leaders, dignitaries, police, and common folk walked in the funeral procession that led his five-metre-long, five-metre-high carriage along the street in front of silent throngs. The people were of every sort: French, English, Irish; Catholic and Protestant; poor and wealthy; minorities and majorities. They were all Canadians to the core on that day, citizens of the now-achieved dream of Thomas D'Arcy McGee.

We will never see his like again.

The Proclaimer

SIR ALEXANDER TILLOCH GALT

More than 20 years before Canada existed, a young Alexander Galt came to Kingston to meet with the Governor General. There, he discovered that someone was laying bets that no one could cover 50 kilometres on foot in less than six hours. The young, dark-haired Galt, who stood over six feet tall with wide shoulders and a strong build, tossed off his coat, focused his deep-set eyes, and started off. Less than six hours later, he crossed the finish line in first place.

Born England 1817, died Montreal 1893, Conservative

That rugged Galt attitude helped create Canada. He not only believed in it long before most others, but was the first to proclaim it by forcing a government to make Confederation their policy.

A Running Start

Alexander Galt's connection to and love for the country began with his father. In fact, the Galts were an important family in our history. John Galt was a famous writer from Scotland who loved adventure. He came to the Ontario frontier as a young man and created "The Canada Company," which bought and sold and settled almost two-and-a-half million acres. Cutting through woods, he built roads that opened up the province and created the cities of Guelph and Galt. He believed that *all* of British North America, so raw and unfriendly, could one day be a great nation. But despite his abilities, he failed to make even a reasonable living from his schemes, and eventually crossed back over the ocean, almost penniless, to live in London. His three sons learned from his experiences. Two would rise to be knighted Canadians.

Alex grew up in England, but spent part of his boyhood at school in Chambly, Quebec, as his father pursued his adventures. He loved it there. And so in 1834 at the age of 16, when he was given the opportunity to return to Quebec, he jumped at the chance.

He went to Sherbrooke, in the Eastern Townships southeast of Montreal, to work as a lowly junior clerk for the British American Land Company, another settlement business his father had helped to found. It would eventually have more than one million acres of land and make the region thrive, but when Galt arrived he found a village of 200 people cut off from the rest of the world, with terrible roads. That wasn't the only problem. Differences between established people and newcomers, and the French and English, meant that little got done and there were lots of fights.

Galt got involved in them. In the 1837 Lower Canada Rebellion—pitting Louis-Joseph Papineau and his French-Canadian "Patriotes" against British and English-Canadian soldiers in bloody battles that left 325 dead—he confronted the rebels, gun in hand. On the other side was 24-year-old George-Étienne Cartier, fighting for French rights.

Though the rebellion was put down, it hurt the British American Land Company's business. At 26, Galt became a big wheel by suggesting smart ways to turn things around. Soon he was Chief Commissioner, and began expanding the company and getting it involved in railways. It would make his reputation and lead him to a higher calling.

Locomotive into the Future

Galt knew that Sherbrooke would have to have better communication with the world if it wanted to grow, and the best way to connect with others in the 1840s was to build a railroad. By late in that decade he was involved in the St. Lawrence and Atlantic Railway, and soon became its president. It would be the most important Canadian line of its time, connecting Montreal to Sherbrooke, and eventually expanding to Quebec City, the northeastern United States, and Toronto (when joined with the Grand Trunk Railway). All told, it was the world's largest system. Galt even had a scheme for a line that would reach all the way to British Columbia, 30 years before it actually happened.

But he was more than a businessman. His railway interests hooked him up with Cartier (the Grand Trunk's lawyer) and other budding politicians. In 1849, Galt ran for a seat in the Canadian provincial legislature and was elected. An independent member and thinker, he was almost immediately involved in controversy.

He was outraged when the Reform government of Baldwin and LaFontaine decided that they'd not only give money to the many loyal citizens who had suffered losses during the recent rebellion, but to some rebels too. He was not alone. Demonstrators gathered in the Montreal streets and one electric night surrounded Government House, attacked the Governor General, and burned the building to the ground. A long list of important Montreal men then signed a petition to join the United States. Galt, who would one day announce the dream of Canada, was one of them. The province teetered.

Things were equally exciting in his private life. By 1848 he had gotten to know John Torrance, a wealthy Montreal railway man. The Torrances lived in a mansion surrounded by a high brick wall with glass on top. It may have been there to guard his daughters. But Galt broke through and married one. When she died giving birth to their son Elliott, Galt simply married her sister Amy and took her to live in their beautiful "Rockmount" home in Sherbrooke and had 12 more children.

Announcing Canada

By then, things were going well with both his railway company and land settlement work. In politics, he stayed independent, despite many offers from all sides, especially from John A. Macdonald and his Conservatives.

Then, on July 5, 1858, at the age of 40, he rose in Parliament (in Toronto) and made a speech that would change not only his politics, but also his life and the life of his country.

He was large and dark, with eyes that looked right through people, and the others listened when he spoke. "A general Confederation of the provinces," he proclaimed, "of New Brunswick, Nova Scotia, Newfoundland and Prince Edward Island with Canada and the Western territories is most desirable." Other men, notably D'Arcy McGee, had suggested it before, but Galt insisted that the government should make it happen *now*.

The great Macdonald didn't say a word and others said only slightly more. The Toronto *Leader* wrote: "A revolution of so [grand] a character needs time." But three weeks later the clock sped up.

That happened because of the famous "double shuffle" engineered by Macdonald. He allowed his government to be unseated, let George Brown replace him as Premier, and smartly defeated Brown a mere *two* days later. Then Macdonald's government came back to power. In the midst of it all, the Governor asked Galt to lead. He refused. But the new government needed him on their side. He agreed to join them, on the condition that they adopt Confederation as their policy. They made history by accepting.

It would take nine more years for Galt's idea to become reality. There would be several fruitless trips to England to plead the case, deals made and broken, many elections, many compromises, and three legendary conferences. Galt masterminded the plan for how wealth would be shared in the new nation.

On July 1, 1867, he was named Canada's first Minister of Finance. Always restless, he left politics in 1872. Later, he was the first Canadian High Commissioner to London, and with his son Elliott, opened mines in what would be the province of Alberta. Travelling in the west in 1882, he heard the prairies called a useless "desert." He responded, "Don't you believe them. This land will one day support a great population." Just as his father had settled southern Ontario cities, he and his son would create Lethbridge, Alberta.

Alexander Tilloch Galt, like his father before him, and his son after, believed in the idea of Canada. He believed that it could be settled, that it could thrive, and that transportation could be built across its great length. He was a big man with big ambitions and emotions. But his size fit the big country he imagined.

A strong athlete, a great curler and fisherman, he loved challenges. When he took on all competitors in that race in Kingston long ago, he bet on himself to win. In 1858, long before many others believed in the greatness of their country, he bet on Canada too.

The Catalyst

GEORGE BROWN

Born Scotland 1818, died Toronto 1880, Reform/Liberal

George Brown was six feet, four inches tall in a time when the average man was eight inches shorter. He had flaming red hair, big sideburns that nearly touched his chin, and long arms that he liked to swing as he spoke. Loud and powerful, "Big Georgie" lived an aggressive life and died a violent death. Lord of the biggest newspaper in Canada, king of the Reform party, Toronto and all Ontario were his realm and none other than the great John A. Macdonald was his opponent in the most gigantic confrontation in the nation's history. Decades after their deaths, their widows wouldn't even look at each other when they passed in the street. But this tough-minded man, who had little time for compromise and took attacks personally, would be the Canadian who made the greatest compromise—the one who, in the end, allowed this country to happen.

He was born in Scotland in 1818, the son of Peter and Marianne Brown. Peter was a member of the 1832 Edinburgh city council and believed that all men should be allowed to vote and that churches shouldn't meddle in politics—people should think freely. His eldest son took on these beliefs as he moved through the best schools and then entered the family wholesale business.

But in 1837 everything came crashing down. An economic depression nearly ruined the Browns and they fled to the United States. During the difficult voyage across the ocean, tall, gangly, 19-year-old George, full of the energy that would drive him through the rest of his life, kept his father's spirits from sinking.

They opened a dry goods store on famous Broadway Avenue in New York and made it a success. But Peter Brown, the man of ideas, was more than a store owner, and before long had started a newspaper.

George often travelled on business and found no place more exciting than young, frontier Toronto. In 1843, when Reform party people invited the Brown family to relocate there, George was sure it was a good move. He convinced his more cautious father that Canada was "a rapidly rising country" with more opportunities than the United States. "There is no position a man of energy and character may not reasonably hope to attain."

George Brown, intense and anxious, was that sort of man. Toronto would be his home forever, and he would put a stamp on it and on Canada that remains to this day.

Ruler of *The Globe*

On March 5, 1844, just 25 years old, he published the first issue of *The Globe,* a four-page, weekly publication that grew to be the country's largest daily, mass-printed by the latest technology, its influence reaching across the country and beyond (today known as *The Globe and Mail,* "Canada's National Newspaper"). It would also become the official journal of the Reform (Liberal) party.

George quickly got involved in politics. It seemed to him that the two Canadian provinces needed to take a step forward by becoming more democratic, expanding to the west, and getting religion out of politics. But he was worried that French Quebec, where the Catholic Church had a big say, wouldn't change, and would try to dominate.

He was not only immediately critical of the Conservative Macdonald, but was soon at odds with fellow Reformer William McDougall. That mouthy man was a radical Liberal

who believed in American ways. Their rival newspapers
began duelling.

The Powerful Politician

Brown first tried to get elected in 1851 at age 32, but was
defeated by famous old William Lyon Mackenzie, the leader
of the 1837 Rebellion, in a dirty election. A few months later
he won a by-election, supported by his friend from Sarnia,
big-bearded Alexander Mackenzie, who would one day be
Prime Minister of Canada.

"Put plenty of work on me," he told Mackenzie, "I can
speak six or eight hours a day easily." Soon the whole country
knew about the tall, remarkable man from Toronto with the
booming voice and boundless energy.

He sat in Parliament (in Quebec City) as an independent
and loudly made his views known. One of the things he
shouted about was something he called "Representation by
Population." That meant that the province with the most
people should have the most elected members. Canada
West (Ontario) had about a million people, slightly more
than Canada East (Quebec), and the lead was growing.
"Rep by Pop" would mean that Brown's province would
have its way and not be dominated by the French. He
claimed that he also wanted the French to keep their rights,
but many feared him.

In 1854 the Conservatives joined with part of the
Liberal party and became the Liberal-Conservatives, a great
power that Macdonald and Cartier would operate for many
years. Brown responded by rebuilding the Reform party,
the true Liberals, uniting them under his ideas of free
education, western expansion, and Rep by Pop. He became
their leader.

During this period *The Globe* continued to grow and make
money. It seemed to be read by everyone, even enemies.

By 1858 Brown's party was almost the equal of the Liberal-
Conservatives, and soon defeated them on the question of
moving the capital to Ottawa. He and his Reformers didn't
want that little lumber town to become the nation's governing
city, and voted against it. When more than half of the elected
members of Parliament agreed, the Governor General
proclaimed that the Reformers had gained the "confidence" of
the House and Brown was asked to form a new government
with Quebec ally Antoine Aimé Dorion. Finally, Brown
would have his opportunity to change the nation. Then the
famous "double shuffle" happened. Macdonald tricked him by
defeating his government while he was away getting elected as
co-Premier. He was boss for just *two days!*

It was a devastating defeat. But by 1859 Brown had revived,
leading a massive Reform convention in Toronto, where he
thundered that he looked "forward with high hopes to the day
when these northern countries shall stand out among the
nations of the world as one great confederation!"

But as the pressures of politics and running his expensive newspaper grew in the early 1860s, Brown's health suffered. He missed a session of Parliament. "You have spent so much of your apparently exhaustless energy that you have over-wrought the machine," said a friend. Then he lost his seat in the 1861 election.

While he was away the Reform party gained power, but under the timid Sandfield Macdonald. Meanwhile, Brown regained his strength and returned to his old self—he said of Sandfield and company that "a greater set of jackasses was never got by accident into the government of any country."

A New Man, a New Nation

Then everything changed. In 1862 he travelled to Scotland and met Anne Nelson and fell in love. She became his wife, gave him three children, and softened his tough ways. "I am a new man in mind and body," he announced. That fact deeply affected Canada's future. Some have even said that Anne Nelson Brown deserves to be called a Mother of Confederation for the way she changed George Brown.

After he returned to the House of Commons in 1864 he was no longer the angry man who couldn't get along with others. Instead, he called for a committee to look into ways to remake the Canadas. When it met, he locked the door and took the key. "Now gentlemen," he told them, "you must talk about this matter. . . ."

One of his committee's recommendations was to investigate the idea of a grand union of the provinces. Soon Brown rose in the House and made one of the most dramatic and unselfish statements in Canadian history. He said he would change his views and work with anyone who would form a new kind of government that ignored provincial differences and got things done. The legendary tough guy was telling others to soften. That statement, more than any other, led to the creation of Canada.

Within a few days members were shocked to see Brown and Macdonald actually speaking with each other. Then Brown met with Galt, Cartier, and other opponents and agreed to gigantic changes: he and key Reform members would join the Macdonald-Cartier government, and work together to unite the British North American provinces and create a new sort of Parliament. When he announced his decision, applause exploded in the House and one short French Canadian ran across the aisle and leapt into big Brown's arms.

Brown played a crucial role at the Charlottetown and Quebec Confederation conferences, making key speeches, lecturing on his "Rep by Pop" scheme (essentially adopted for Canada), but compromising on other issues. At the many parties, Brown even tried a dance or two. "All right!!!" he wrote to his beloved wife. "Conference through at six o'clock this evening—constitution adopted—a most creditable

document—a complete reform of all the abuses and injustices
we have complained of!!"

On trips to England to speak with the Queen and the British
Prime Minister about the plan, he put his dislike of Macdonald
aside. At the Derby horse race, he even seized a peashooter and
helped naughty John A. launch peas at the crowd.

It was a temporary alliance, made for the betterment of the
country. But before the final conference in London in
1866–67, he abandoned Macdonald (though he pledged
support for Canada) and resumed his dislike for him. Many
years earlier John A. had publicly called him a liar. Brown had
never forgotten.

When July 1 came, he stayed up all night to write a long
tribute to the new country he had helped build. It appeared
on the front page of *The Globe,* loud and proud.

He lost the election in 1867. Perhaps his heart wasn't in it.
A lion in public, he was a pussycat at home. He dearly loved
his family and wanted to be near them, so he retired from
politics and returned to *The Globe.* From his office in the
famous, three-storey building in Toronto with a globe on its
roof, he fired darts at Macdonald in his articles.

He developed other businesses and bought a farm. He
got to know a chap named Alexander Graham Bell, who
happened to invent something called the telephone. Brown
even took the idea to London, England, for Bell, where he
was told it would never be of any value.

Then came the unthinkable.

A Violent End

On March 25, 1880, Brown was working in his office. It was a cloudy day, late afternoon. Suddenly a man named George Bennett appeared in the doorway. He had been fired for drinking on the job and was angry. He demanded that the great man sign something for him. Brown stood up, and in his usual brisk way, told him to leave. Bennett pulled out a gun. Brown sprang at him and wrestled him against a wall. But as he did, and as his employees came running to his rescue, the gun went off and a bullet rocketed through his right leg. Bennett was subdued. Brown seemed okay. A doctor tended to him and he walked home. But soon infection set in, and on May 9, watched over by Anne, he died.

Days earlier he had said from his deathbed, "I have enjoyed my work. . . . It's been an intense pleasure to me. . . . I've worked hard for my country, my family and myself." But, he added sadly, "I haven't accomplished what I would have liked."

He had accomplished a great deal. As the city of Toronto and the nation, now stretching from the Atlantic to the Pacific, went into mourning, Canadians were thriving.

Years earlier, in 1865, when he saw that his great moment of compromise would soon bring about the creation of the Dominion of Canada, he wrote to his wife, wondering what his eldest daughter might one day think of what he had done. "[Will she] look back with satisfaction to the share her father had in these great events?" he asked. "For great they are, dearest Anne, and history will tell the tale."

The Kingpin

SIR GEORGE-ÉTIENNE CARTIER

Born St. Antoine, Quebec 1814, died England 1873, Conservative

George-Étienne Cartier was a five-foot, six-inch Québécois dynamo with a head like a lion, a sense of fun, and a brilliant mind. Without him Canada wouldn't exist. This legendary "Lightning Striker," whom John A. Macdonald called his "other self," built many of our institutions. His life was frantic, rebellious, and marked by a fierce loyalty to both Quebec and Canada. He would fight anyone to defend both.

Legend has it that he came from noble Canadian blood.

Somewhere in his distant past an ancestor had been the brother of Jacques Cartier, the great explorer who had sailed up the St. Lawrence River in the 1530s and connected two worlds forever. His grandfather and father were named Jacques Cartier too. They were merchants who accepted the British conquest of Quebec and got to work to make their people stronger. They soon owned many mills and dominated Lower Canada's flour and grain industry.

Calm Before the Storm

Born in 1814 at the famous family home, the House of the Seven Chimneys, east of Montreal, Georges-Étienne Cartier (who preferred "George") was named after the British king. His grandfather had been elected to the Legislature and his father fought in the War of 1812, but what the boy remembered most about his youth was the family's happiness. There was laughter, political debate, and many voyageur songs sung loud and clear.

When he reached 16 he went to the big city and the Collège de Montréal. He was one of its best students, and graduated ready for a successful career as a lawyer. Louis-Hippolyte LaFontaine—the legendary politician who looked like Napoleon and would lead Quebec to true democracy as co-Premier of the Canadas—became his inspiration.

Cartier developed strong views. He worked for LaFontaine's newspaper *La Minerve* and was the first secretary of the St.

Jean Baptiste Society. It had a maple leaf as its emblem and fought for "Canadian" rights. Young Cartier wrote "O Canada, Mons Pays, Mes Amours" for its members, a song some think is the model for our national anthem.

But in the 1830s, LaFontaine's pleas for democracy had not yet won the day. English Canadians dominated business and a "Château Clique" of stuffy Brits constantly disallowed laws made by elected French Canadians. Quebeckers grew dangerously angry. Soon there were violent battles in the streets. Men attacked each other with whips and axe handles. Then, things got worse.

The 1837 Rebellion

Young George Cartier felt loyal to the British, but was bitterly disappointed in them. He chose to stand by the French Canadians, joined the "Patriotes," and readied himself for war. On November 23, 1837, it began.

Near the House of Seven Chimneys, outside St. Denis, Cartier stood his ground with rebel leader Louis-Joseph Papineau (wanted for high treason) and hundreds of others. Their muskets and pitchforks were ready. Soon the red-coated British troops appeared on the horizon. Cannonballs screamed down. Cartier fought boldly. In mid-battle, he bravely went for reinforcements. And by the end of the day, the Patriotes had won. Sixteen of their friends were killed, but even more British had fallen.

But the cause was lost in other battles, so Cartier fled across the American border to Vermont. The following year, unable to stay away from the land he loved, he slipped back to Montreal. The authorities feared arresting him: he had become a popular young man. Things had begun to change in Lower Canada anyway. After Lord Durham's report on the rebellions, the two Canadas were united. Slowly but surely democracy came and, with LaFontaine's guidance, French Canadians began to have their say.

By the mid-1840s, Cartier had matured into a powerful lawyer and Montreal political organizer, and had married Hortense Fabre. In 1848 he was elected to the Legislature.

But his hot-blooded ways were never entirely erased. After his bravery in the rebellion was questioned in the late 1840s, he challenged a journalist to a duel. Though he fired a bullet through his enemy's hat, neither man was wounded.

His influence grew quickly in politics and the railway business, the two most powerful professions in the Canadas. Soon he was chairman of the Committee on Railways, lawyer for the huge Grand Trunk Railway, and began to look like LaFontaine's successor.

He fought anyone on any issue he believed in. And he believed in many things, among them a growing sense of the value of the combined Canadas. In 1849, when important Montrealers like Alexander Galt and John Abbott signed a "manifesto" to join the United States, Cartier opposed them like a tiger. In 1855, he entered the provincial cabinet.

By then he had developed into one of the most important men in Canadian politics and was slowly moving towards the idea of joining forces with the moderate Conservatives, led by another man about his age, John A. Macdonald of Kingston.

The Two-Headed Dragon

Macdonald and Cartier were a lethal force, Canada's legendary "Siamese Twins." Cartier, the "Lightning Striker," threw thunderbolts at his foes and won French votes, and Macdonald entertained and swayed the English, "an unbeatable combination of . . . British heart and French soul . . . ." They stood for the same things: that Canada could be a great continental power, that it must join together despite language differences, oppose American ways, and be the greatest example of a democratic nation.

By 1857 Cartier and Macdonald had become co-Premiers of the Canadas. They would rule together for most of the next decade and lead the country into Confederation and beyond. They somehow bound together three-and-a-half million people of two languages and many cultures.

Cartier played a key role in the Confederation conferences. He led off the first meeting with one of his long, well-reasoned arguments for union. He sang and danced at every party, convincing the "foreign" provinces that his people were friends. They saw a brilliant leader, capable of solving the many problems ahead.

During the six years he and Macdonald dominated politics after Confederation, he helped lay the foundations of Canada. He was a driving force behind the purchase of the western prairies from the Hudson Bay Company, the creation of Manitoba and British Columbia, and the construction of the Canadian Pacific Railway from coast to coast.

Cartier had hoped that Manitoba would be a new Quebec, and helped make sure that it entered Confederation with many of the same French rights. Macdonald was ill during much of the negotiations and Cartier took over with ease, Prime Minister in his absence. He had been an idol to the Manitoba rebel Louis Riel.

Cartier brought a unique energy to Canadian politics. He spoke loudly and with feeling, and loved to laugh and sing. He once spoke in the House of Commons for 14 hours, seven in English and seven in French! His opponent George Brown commented on how long "the little wretch screetched" by saying, "They used to charge me with being long-winded, but Cartier outdoes all the world." Others were amazed when they saw him at parties. "Mr. Cartier is an oddity," said the Governor General's daughter. "His laugh is so funny, it goes rattling on so long and loud. He screams and whoops at the end of some of his Canadian songs."

Cartier also had a unique personal life. There were rumours that he was more than friends with a Montreal woman named

Luce Cuvillier. She wore pants, and liked to smoke—a wild rebel in a stuffy time, which suited Cartier just fine.

He had an incredible appetite for his work, believing so strongly in it that he rarely rested. In 1871, when British Columbian officials came to Ottawa, they were awed by his presence and stunned by his energy. They found him in shirtsleeves, sweating at duties "morning, noon and night." They hoped the government would build a railway to the edge of their province. He surprised them. "That will not do," he snapped, "ask for a railway the whole way and you will get it!" Then he took them to a cabinet meeting and forced the nation's most powerful leaders to agree. The westerners vowed that B.C. would never forget Sir George Cartier and what he had done for them.

A Painful Death

But such hard work was slowly burning him out. By late 1871 his happy, busy life became difficult. His legs were often swollen, making it painful to walk. Little did he know that he was in the early stages of Bright's disease, a fatal kidney ailment that would soon destroy him and rob Canada of his invaluable mind.

His last full year, 1872, was full of problems. During the federal election he and Macdonald accepted large amounts of money from millionaire Sir Hugh Allan at the same time that they were giving him the contract to build the Canadian Pacific Railway. Thieves working for their Liberal opponents produced telegrams that proved it. It was called the "Pacific Scandal."

Cartier, barely able to stand, was defeated in his beloved Montreal riding. And though he would soon win a by-election in Riel's Manitoba, by the fall of 1872 he was dying. He said farewell to Macdonald, distressed to leave him during difficult times, took an official salute in Quebec City, and sailed to London, England, for treatment. There, where he had many friends and knew Queen Victoria ("I am a British subject," he told her, "who happens to speak French"), he slowly descended.

"I cannot tell you how I sorrow at this," wrote Macdonald to the Governor General. "We have acted together since 1854, and have never had a serious difference."

On May 20, 1873, Cartier quietly said "I am dying," and passed away.

His body was brought back to Canada on a steamer. As it came up the St. Lawrence, the river Jacques Cartier had searched, the eerie sounds of the "Dead March" drifted into the air. Cathedral bells answered along the shoreline. At Quebec City, the army's guns saluted. Church masses gathered in Trois-Rivières, near the House of the Seven Chimneys, and in Montreal 75,000 mourners passed the casket, a bust of Jacques Cartier nearby.

Macdonald and Cartier had often visited each other. They worked and played together like they hoped the country would. Today, our busiest highway, the 401 that connects Montreal to Toronto, French to English, is called the "Macdonald-Cartier Freeway."

When the Prime Minister received word of his friend's death that dark May 20th in 1873, he sadly made his way to the House of Commons and read the announcement. His desk and Cartier's were in the front row, always together. Macdonald suddenly fell back in his chair. He buried his face in one arm and with the other reached out and hugged the empty seat of George-Étienne Cartier. For a long time he stayed that way, and couldn't stop crying.

The Class

SIR SAMUEL LEONARD TILLEY

S amuel Tilley was a class act. A clean-shaven, friendly guy in a time of loud, hard-drinking politicians, he was never involved in a scandal, rarely attacked an opponent, and didn't drink anything stronger than tea. He was even admired by his enemies. But inside his steeltrap mind, he was as tough as anyone. He never gave up on Canada, even when faced by storms of protest that threatened not only to destroy him politically, but do him real harm. He was perhaps the

Born Gagetown,
New Brunswick 1818,
died Saint John 1896,
Reform/Liberal

greatest man in New Brunswick's history and one of the most admirable in Canada's.

Tilley was born into a respectable family, at quiet Gagetown on the river between Fredericton and Saint John. He went to a little school, where the teacher often used a strap, and seldom saw much of the outside world, though one day the province's Governor appeared in town, dressed in "a fine blue coat and brass buttons," and gave him a shiny Spanish quarter-dollar.

He left Gagetown at 13 and took a job in a drugstore in the big city of Saint John. There, despite a little excitement as an excellent speaker at the Young Men's Debating Society, he continued his quiet early years. In December 1837 he even took a vow never to drink alcohol. By age 20 he was in business for himself, dealing in medical supplies, and settled into a promising but unspectacular career.

Life Speeds Up

Everything changed in 1850. While Tilley was out of town, he was nominated by others to stand for election as a Reform party candidate to the provincial legislature. Saint John elections were rowdy. Candidates were often shouted at and pelted with things, and men cast their ballots publicly, sometimes while being threatened. Young Tilley rose to the challenge and was elected with ease. Always a moral man, he resigned after a very short period, upset that several friends deserted his party to join the old Conservative government, just to gain a little power.

In 1854 he was re-elected and helped his party finally overthrow the Conservatives, who had been running things since New Brunswick began. Responsible government had finally come. Tilley became Provincial Secretary in Charles Fisher's cabinet. Then he made his biggest political mistake, a huge gamble that nearly destroyed him. But it showed his inner toughness, which he would soon need . . . just to survive.

He and his friends were "the Smashers," who believed that drinking alcohol should be totally banned. They intended to smash liquor bottles and bring down the booze business. Tilley announced the plan in the legislature and it came into effect in 1856. Now, in those days, drinking was almost a pastime in New Brunswick, believed to actually help men do more work. There was a roar of protest and the law was widely disobeyed. Before long the people voted to dump Tilley and his Reformers.

But Tilley wasn't bitter. That was his way. He just moved on, still believing in his cause, but smart enough never to try to make it law again. By 1861 he was Premier of the province, working on getting the Canadas to help New Brunswick build the Intercolonial Railway from the Maritimes to the west, his first interest in a British North American connection. Soon he favoured a union of the three Maritime provinces.

When Macdonald, Cartier, and friends suddenly asked for permission to join the union conference and showed up at

Charlottetown with a plan for Confederation, Tilley was intrigued. During that meeting and later at Quebec City he became a strong supporter. His ability in money matters was considered to be at least the equal of the great Alexander Galt. He grilled the Canadians on their plans, forced them to make changes, and then went home to convince his people.

At first, when the delegates toured New Brunswick to cheering crowds, it seemed as though Confederation would pass easily. But opposition quickly arose and Tilley called an election to let the people decide. Decide they did: they threw him and every single delegate to the Confederation conference right out of office. The union couldn't work without New Brunswick, and it appeared that the dream of a grand new Canada was dead. The quiet Tilley seemed an unlikely man to turn things around.

Laying It on the Line for Canada

But that inner toughness came roaring forward. Tilley travelled through every county in the province over the next year, addressing his people, never shouting, but making his points relentlessly and clearly. Among his opponents were some of the loudest men in politics, but Tilley faced them and the noisy crowds. He believed in Confederation, believed it was right for New Brunswick, and defended it mightily.

By late 1865 his side won a key by-election, and soon the new government fell apart. Tilley again took to the streets and halls of the province, defending Canada. He also warned that the Fenian Americans, who had recently attacked the province, could be kept away for good only if New Brunswick united with the others into a larger, stronger nation. Tilley and his party swept back into power.

Immediately he helped set up the London Confederation Conference. At that historic meeting, this rosy-cheeked man was again a key player. Liked by everyone, he still drove hard bargains, forcing others to deal honestly with every detail of the agreement. He was cool and calculating, and when he talked everyone listened.

Tilley entered Canada's first cabinet and became one of the best members the House of Commons would ever have. In February 1873, he was named Minister of Finance. But his first term in that office was short. Macdonald was dumped from office in disgrace after the Pacific Scandal was revealed. It didn't touch Tilley of course. He was, as always, totally clean. He retired to New Brunswick and became the Lieutenant Governor.

But in 1878 he was re-elected to Ottawa, returned to the Finance position and held it for seven years, some of the most important in Canadian history. It was Tilley who brought "tariffs" (taxes on things coming into Canada from other countries) into effect. This was the core of the famous "National Policy" and it allowed Canadian businesses to grow.

But his health was failing by 1885, so he retired again to the Lieutenant Governor's job at home. He would hold it for 13 years. The people of New Brunswick came to regard him as their father. He slowly turned away from political battles and never interfered in affairs. His slight, short frame grew thicker, his hair turned grey and then white. He was a smiling gentleman, a legend in his time.

Tilley's health declined throughout his later years. Even when he knew he was slowly dying, he never complained, and rarely mentioned his troubles. Every Sunday he would walk to his Anglican church in Saint John, even if he could barely get there. He didn't want anyone to hitch up horses to take him, believing that Sunday was a day of rest.

And so this famous figure could be seen struggling up hills each week on his way to church, apparently completely unaware, or at least unimpressed, by his own fame. Whether he was offering advice to the Prime Minister or visiting with the Queen in England, which he and Lady Tilley did in later years, he treated everyone the same.

One day, someone met him slowly moving up a mountainous street on the way to church. As always, he smiled at the man. "John," he cracked, "this hill has grown steeper than it used to be."

But up that hill he went, climbing it successfully, with courage, just as he had climbed many others in life and politics, admired by all who met and even fought him.

When Tilley died in 1896, the Saint John *Daily Telegraph,* which had opposed him throughout his life, said "His memory will live, not only in the hearts of all his countrymen, but enshrined in the history of this his native province, and of the great Dominion which he did so much to create, and which he so fondly loved."

Sometimes, it pays to be a good guy.

The Ram

SIR CHARLES TUPPER

*Born Amherst, Nova Scotia
1821, died England 1915,
Conservative*

If Samuel Tilley was New Brunswick, then Charles Tupper was Nova Scotia. But he was also much more. He was the biggest loudmouth in our history. He faced off against one of the most powerful forces ever in Canadian politics in Joseph Howe, slaying that fire-breathing dragon both in an election and in the Confederation debate; bullied his province into Canada; and went on to even greater victories.

He would be the most aggressive cabinet minister in

the nation, the man Macdonald knew could defeat any foe. Eventually, he would be Prime Minister of Canada. He would outlive every Father of Confederation and die in his 90s in 1915.

He had started as a small-town doctor, giving no immediate signs of his stirring future. He changed, drastically. Langevin said of him many years later, "He makes many bitter enemies for himself; he is ambitious and a gambler."

But Charles Tupper didn't care. He moved boldly forward through a huge career. He will appear again in the history of Canada's great leaders.

The Man

SIR JOHN A. MACDONALD

Born Scotland 1815, died Ottawa 1891, Conservative

John A. Macdonald was like a character from a book. He was romantic, tragic, heroic, and even sinful. He smiled on the outside but often cried inside. When it came to the creation of the Dominion of Canada, John Macdonald was simply "the man." No one—not Cartier, not Brown, McGee, Galt, Tilley, or Tupper—could touch him. And when it came to loving Canada and guiding it through truly tense and historic moments, no one has touched him either. Turn the page and see why.

Part Three

Our Prime Ministers

1st Prime Minister

The Great One

SIR JOHN A. MACDONALD

Born Scotland 1815, died Ottawa 1891, Conservative. PM: 1867–1873, 1878–1891

As Sir John A. Macdonald lay on his deathbed, still Prime Minister in the early summer of 1891 after 40 years of dominating Canada, all the steamboat whistles and taxi bells in Ottawa were silenced. The city grew quiet, and the nation listened with its breath held, afraid to face the future without him. "HE IS DYING," cried newspaper headlines. Everyone knew who HE was.

The Young Fox

Seventy-one years earlier he had been a little boy of five, sailing up the St. Lawrence River on a schooner with his parents, Helen Shaw and Hugh Macdonald of Glasgow, Scotland, anxiously watching the rugged shoreline of a new and strangely beautiful land. At the point where the river met Lake Ontario, a village of a few thousand people appeared: Kingston, Upper Canada, the place that would form him.

His father was constantly happy, occasionally tipsy from drinking, and always had money problems. He believed things would get better. They never did. He kept setting up stores and they kept closing. The couple's first baby died suddenly and a second little boy was killed by a violent slap from a family friend. Two daughters and John Alexander were left. John A. was an unusual child.

Slim, a little tall for his age, with a big nose that would grow to legendary status, his unruly black hair was parted on the side and bunched up in a great curly mass. He was a quiet kid at first, a lover of books who kept to himself, as if he were plotting. He went to a country school and then one in town, and did so well that he was sometimes bored and scribbled faces in his notebooks. One was a bizarre, severed head he called "Timothy Mudlark Toenail."

The Macdonalds were average folks, familiar with taverns and playing fields. They were respectable, but had little money to do what classy Kingston citizens did: send their son to university in England. Many of John's future opponents would own fancy degrees, but he had to leave school at 14 and study with a local lawyer.

George Mackenzie, a Conservative with political ambitions, ran the most respected law firm in town. Right away he marvelled at the abilities of young John Macdonald and groomed him for bigger things.

By the time Mackenzie died of cholera in 1834, the strange, quiet kid had become a strange, chatty 19-year-old, already manager of two branch offices and a witty joke teller who could charm anyone with the vault of stories he learned from constant reading.

When the Upper Canada Rebellion broke out in December 1837, he was part of the crowd in the streets showing loyalty to England. He even took up a musket and drilled with the ragged Commercial Bank Guard. Legend has it he went to Toronto and joined the chase up Yonge Street after the rebel William Lyon Mackenzie. Back home, John A. Macdonald, attorney, was becoming a daring force too.

On a July night in 1838, during a crashing thunderstorm, 15 prisoners escaped from nearby Fort Henry and vanished. The angry commandant rashly accused the lowly jailer of helping the criminals slip from his fortress. The charges were dropped, but the jailer turned on his boss with charges of his own. On his hopeless side was 23-year-old Macdonald. But, attacking like a smiling tiger, he won. It was soon said that he would defend anyone's rights, no matter the crime, and woe to those who took him lightly.

He even defended the ringleaders of an army of Americans who had attacked the Kingston area, hoping to exploit the unrest caused by the Rebellion. They had been defeated in a bloody battle, then roped together and paraded by torchlight in town. Despite a growing distaste for Americans, Macdonald did his job.

As the 1840s arrived, the young fox joined the Conservative party and rose in their ranks with brilliant, folksy speeches. He became a city alderman and then Member of Parliament in 1844 at age 29. On a trip to Scotland, he met Isabella Clark. They married and set up house in Kingston, where they were happy and his business grew.

But his happiness would soon fade. During his life he would be good at appearing to look at the bright side of things, but underneath there were always problems, not just political but personal. His life had a dark side.

Pain and Glory

First, Isabella got sick. As he grew to fame, she seldom left her bed. After long days in bitter political fights, he would read to her into the night as she lay in agony. She gave him two sons. The first, John Alexander, the pride of their lives who bounced on his mother's lap in her bed, died mysteriously at age one.

The second, Hugh John, born in 1850, was carefully watched, and lived. But by Christmas 1857, Isabella was dead.

Macdonald's law practice, which he could have made very profitable, instead suffered while he served his country. But almost from the moment John A. settled in Parliament, it was evident that he would be a star unlike any before (or since).

His success surprised everyone, maybe even himself. He didn't seem serious enough to be a leader. He didn't believe in long, self-important speeches and liked to tell jokes. But he solved problems like a detective and drew others to his easy, confident ways. Yes, he could be a clown, and drink as much or more than the many hard drinkers in Parliament, but like magic he became the one to follow. The ultimate Canadian, destined to define his country, he believed in compromise. His views fell between the old Conservatives and the radical Liberals—he valued differences, and felt that French Canadians or any minority should have a strong place in the nation. Known as "Old Tomorrow," he waited when attacked, let others make mistakes in a rush, and then happily sliced up their arguments. George Brown's *Globe* newspaper called him a "harmless, third-class lawyer," but he would tower over everyone, including Brown.

In 1847 he was named a cabinet minister and nine years later became co-Premier of the Canadas at the head of the powerful Liberal-Conservatives, beginning his long alliance with George-Étienne Cartier from Quebec. From that time onward, with a few breaks, John A. Macdonald ran Canada for more than 30 years.

"Some fish require to be toyed with," he cracked while letting his enemy Brown be Premier for two days in 1858, and then tricking him out of the job. During nearly half a century as a Member of Parliament he would personally lose just one election.

Though he and Brown detested each other, they eventually agreed on Confederation. In June 1864 they shocked everyone by together forming the "Great Coalition," the most amazing Canadian government ever, operated by giants to unite British North America.

Macdonald dominated the two Confederation conferences that year. No one questioned his leadership. He essentially designed our country, with its British style and its laws to protect French-Canadian rights and minority religions.

He stood out in appearance and attitude. The conference rooms were filled with serious guys with long beards and side-burns, dressed in dreary black clothes. Then there was John A. in pearl-grey trousers, clean-shaven, a smile on his face. At night, full of personal pains and overwork, he often drank to excess, and some mornings could barely walk. A few felt ashamed of him. But at work no one could match his brilliant brain.

In London in 1867, after nearly burning himself to death when he fell asleep smoking in his hotel bed while reading, he oversaw the final preparations for Canada. British official Sir Frederic Rogers watched him operate and was stunned by his "ruling genius." He forced and teased the provinces into agreement as they looked for complaints like "eager dogs watch a rat hole." There was no question he would be the first Prime Minister.

In the midst of this, while walking along a busy street he met and fell for tall, elegant Susan Agnes Bernard. She was his assistant's sister, and 20 years his junior, a companion able to be the nation's "first lady." They married on February 16 in London. Three weeks later the British North America Act was passed and Canada prepared to come into being.

Growing Pains

Despite having a lifetime of leadership behind him, this was only the beginning for "Sir John A." (Queen Victoria knighted him that year.) He would guide Canada through its difficult childhood, on an amazing adventure.

First there was the assassination of Thomas D'Arcy McGee. Called from his bed when he heard a messenger shout "McGee is murdered—lying in the street—shot through the head," Macdonald rushed to Sparks Street and lifted the little prophet of Confederation into a nearby room, the blood flowing from his wounds.

Then, under pressure from Great Britain, he bought the northwestern part of the continent from the Hudson's Bay Company for Canada. The company never considered that it wasn't fully theirs to sell. Neither did Macdonald. Natives were pushed farther west and onto small reservations by fur traders, the Métis (mixed white and native), and oncoming whites. Macdonald feared that the Americans would steal the west.

In 1869 he sent William McDougall west to become Governor of the new land. Understandably, the few thousand folks who lived there, mostly Métis, were worried about strangers deciding their future. In fact, Louis Riel, a smart, ambitious young Métis, who was anxious to control the way the land came into Canada, set up his own government. Then he and his men stopped McDougall at the border and made him turn around. Everyone got very nervous. Macdonald hoped McDougall would let things settle down so that a reasonable deal could be made. Hotter heads ruled. McDougall snuck into Manitoba, planted a flag in the snow, and then ran back over the border. Soon a group of local white men formed a posse and harassed and threatened Riel's government. The Métis, good at hunting on the prairies, captured one of them, young Thomas Scott from Ontario. They quickly held a trial and put a bullet through his head.

Macdonald was caught between sides, again. Ontario wanted Riel's head (separated from his body), but Quebec hoped negotiations could continue. John A. chose the Quebec way. Three of Riel's officials were brought to Ottawa and, despite his concern that they had changed the terms the people of the west had agreed to, Macdonald made a deal with them. The rights of Riel's French Catholics were protected and

Manitoba became part of Canada, as the Métis wanted. So, Riel, who would soon flee in fear of being charged with Scott's "murder," became the unusual father of the province.

Meanwhile, Macdonald was working his usual long hours to build Canada. Soon he was broke and wanted to return to his law practice. But he was begged to stay.

In February 1869, Lady Macdonald gave birth to a baby girl. Afterwards, John A. hugged his exhausted wife. But something wasn't right with little Mary. Though she smiled, she often lay still, and her skills developed slowly. She had mental problems and an enlarged head, and would spend her life in a wheelchair. Drained by his massive daily responsibilities, Macdonald often sat up at nights reading to his little girl.

His workload, sadness, and drinking often made him ill. Several times it was reported he was dying. But each time he'd make a miraculous recovery, like something a character might pull off in a novel. He was indeed a kind of miracle man: a larger-than-life rascal, gentleman, and genius who often left Ottawa barely able to move, recovered somewhere, and returned to cheering crowds. Then he'd plunge into work and wreck his health again.

On stage he was incredible. One day, while battling in a debate after a late night drinking, he suddenly threw up in front of everyone. The crowd went silent. Macdonald turned to them. "I'm sorry," he said. "I don't know what it is about my opponent, but every time I hear him speak it turns my stomach."

After Manitoba joined Canada, British Columbia followed in 1871 and then Prince Edward Island two years later. In between, Macdonald won another term as Prime Minister. But then big trouble came.

The Pacific Scandal

Macdonald wanted to construct a railway from coast to coast, to bind the huge, thinly populated country forever. It was one part of his famous National Policy, on which he built the nation (settling the west and developing industries were the other parts). It seemed impossible. How could a railway be built across such a huge and awesome land, and how would the money be raised to do it?

John A. wanted Canadians at the helm and decided on Montreal businessman Hugh Allan and his Canadian Pacific Railway, the CPR. At first Allan had American money backers, but Macdonald wanted them dropped. Allan agreed, or so he said. Before he officially had the job, the 1872 election took place and during it he secretly gave John A. and his Conservative candidates more than $300,000.

And that wasn't all. Before long Macdonald had a visit from a pushy American railway owner who threatened to blackmail the government. He knew that Allan was still taking U.S. money, and had used it to win the big railway contract *and* the election for the Conservatives. But Macdonald wasn't worried.

No one could prove that Allan had given him money. Or so he thought.

That spring, Allan and his lawyer, future Prime Minister John Abbott, left for London on business. While they were gone, two men broke into Abbott's Montreal office in the middle of the night. They got into the safe, found telegrams that proved Allan had indeed given money to Macdonald, and raced away with them. This evidence was then sold to the opposition Liberals to bring down John A.'s Conservative government.

It was called the "Pacific Scandal" and it was devastating to Macdonald. His dream of a grand Canada with a great railway was in trouble. He fell ill, and disappeared, amid whispers that he had committed suicide. Then he suddenly re-appeared in Parliament and made one of his greatest speeches. "I throw myself upon this House; I throw myself upon this country," he cried. "There does not exist in Canada a man who has given more of his time, more of his heart, more of his wealth, or more of his intellect and power, such as they may be, for the good of this Dominion."

But his gigantic effort was not enough. He was wrong, and even he knew it. His support began to dwindle and he had to resign. Alexander Mackenzie and the Liberals came to power and called an election. Macdonald was doomed to lose.

When he came back to Parliament in 1874 as Leader of the Opposition, he was sure he would finally be able to retire. "My fighting days are over," he said.

Another Miracle

But it was impossible to really defeat Sir John A. Macdonald. Mackenzie and his leading minister, Edward Blake, led a boring government. They were against many things, including Macdonald's CPR. Blake said that if British Columbia threatened to leave unless the railway was built, his choice was to let them go. It was something Macdonald would never have said or believed. He felt that Mackenzie was letting Canada slide. He said, "Confederation is only yet in the gristle, and it will require five years more before it hardens into bone." Those five years seemed in danger of being wasted. So he went on the attack.

In those days Parliament was a rowdy place. Canadians didn't believe in sounding flowery. Arguments were loud. They threw things at each other. They crossed the aisle to grab enemies to make them vote. Macdonald was the king of things. He used his wit, told stories, and floored opponents. Though he too disliked flowery talk (thinking it fake and American), his brains and book knowledge were on display. At times he would fight until he almost collapsed, lie in a nearby room exhausted, then return to slay more dragons.

During the Mackenzie government's reign, it became clear that Macdonald and his party could get them into trouble on many issues. Sir John began speaking at massive picnics across the land. He attacked the Liberals for not understanding how important it was for Canada to stand on its own next to the powerful United States. "A British subject I was born," he told Canadians in his thick, rich voice, "a British subject I hope to die." One day, more than 50,000 people came to hear him in Montreal.

In 1878 he swept back to power and once again the weight of work was upon him. When he went to receive the new Governor General in Halifax, it all seemed too much. He shut himself up in a room in a government house with his work, books, and a bottle. A lowly secretary was sent to fetch him, and when the shaking man arrived, Macdonald lifted his head, pointed at the door and growled, "Vamoose from this ranch!"

But he pulled himself up and got ready to build his impossible railway again. It would take eight years, nearly bankrupt the country, and almost kill him, but it was done by 1886. The country was united, geographically at least. But trouble had come, perhaps worse than the Pacific Scandal, just as the great project neared completion.

The Deadly Duel

Louis Riel, who had won a pardon, had come back to Canada from exile in the United States. The Métis in the vast land west of Manitoba had asked him to. They and the natives now felt strangled by the further advance of white people. They believed Riel was their only hope. There were rumours that he was saying weird things and beginning to lose his mind. But he could still shake things up. Macdonald and his government seemed to be doing little to make their life better.

John A., as always, wanted Canada to get its way, and worked on a compromise. But the long distance from Ottawa made the people of the prairies feel ignored and misunderstood. The buffalo were vanishing. The weather and the harvest had been terrible. Even white settlers complained.

Macdonald knew that he had to be in touch with Riel, and contacted him through frontier priests. Riel demanded Métis schools, hospitals, and good money for land. Macdonald also claimed that he asked for cash for himself.

Negotiations between the two moved slowly. Then, on March 26, 1885, it all exploded. A frustrated Riel seized a Batoche church and declared a new government. A scuffle between a Mountie and a Cree became a battle that left 18 dead—12 Mounties (and volunteers) and six Métis and natives.

Macdonald swung into action. His railway had been short on money and public support. But now the country was in war fever. Trains moved troops thousands of kilometres to the scene of the action, sent off with massive public support. Within two months the battles were over and Riel was in jail in Regina. His trial began in July.

Riel's lawyers wanted him to plead insanity, but he refused. So he was sentenced to hang for treason. Instantly, John A. was caught in the trap he had solved at Confederation and had barely escaped during his earlier duel with Riel: the eternal

Canadian problem caused by its belief in living with differences. Quebec sided with the French Riel and wanted him re-tried or pardoned; English Canada demanded his death. If Macdonald did one, he risked losing Quebec's support, and if he did the other he might lose Canada itself.

He tried to find a way out by asking the biggest British court to rule. But they returned the same verdict. So, Macdonald and his cabinet, who could have stopped the fatal sentence, decided to let it stand. Riel was hanged on November 16, 1886. Eight Plains Indians were also executed, and the great Cree chiefs Poundmaker and Big Bear were sent to jail, leading to their deaths, though few in the rest of Canada seemed to notice.

But Riel's death *was* a big deal. It was met with a storm of protest in Quebec. Crowds gathered in the streets and burned Macdonald in effigy. He had found his way out, but this time Canada paid a terrible price.

The Legend

Yet, Macdonald's status remained unquestioned. When he turned 70 in 1885, huge crowds gathered to celebrate and hear him speak. Many knew him as the only true leader the country had ever had. He had given up drinking and become respectable, decorated with honours by the Queen. But he still had a rascal's look in his eye, and loved to be out among the people, at war with his opponents. A man in one crowd shouted "You'll never die, John A.!" It seemed like the truth.

In 1886, not long after the final spike of the railway was driven into the ground near Eagle Pass in British Columbia, he and his wife boarded a train in Ottawa and headed west. He spoke to masses on the way, but his greatest thrill was seeing the land. It was the land of his dreams, which he had fought to populate and unite. In Winnipeg he told them that no one believed he would live to see the railway completed. His allies had said he would see it from heaven and his enemies said it would be from hell. "I have now disappointed both friends and foes," he quipped.

When they neared the Rockies, he got onto the cowcatcher, outside on the front of the train, and shot through the mountains, the wind blowing back his greying hair. At 71 years old, rushing past majestic mountains, over creaking bridges, and through the long tunnels of this gorgeous, gigantic land, he was young again. He had lived his life to see this.

But more trouble loomed in the late 1880s. Many favoured a business union with the Americans. Macdonald fought it. Ever since his childhood he had believed that the Americans wanted Canada. He wouldn't give it to them. And the provinces began to flex their muscles, demanding more from the national government. At times they were near revolt. Quebec remained angry about Riel, Nova Scotia voted for separation, Ontario wanted more power, and Manitoba now disliked the special rights Riel had won.

But as the 1890s approached, Macdonald kept it all together. He proclaimed that "we shall go on, as we have been going on since 1867, as one people, with one object, looking to one future, and expecting to lay the foundation of one great country." To Quebec, he said: "There is no paramount race in this country, there is no conquered race." He had believed it for half a century.

He hoped to pass his leadership to a younger man, but began to realize that Canada would need him until he was in the ground. He accepted that his country would kill him. He would have his job forever.

His bond with the people of Canada was unbreakable. He loved being with them, amusing them, using his amazing memory to recall nearly every citizen he had ever met, even if he had seen him or her just once, maybe 40 years before. Most of all, he loved children. Just before he turned 76, he received a letter from a little girl whose birthday was the same day as his, January 11. She wished him a happy birthday and told him about a problem she had: a boy was not answering her letters. He answered immediately.

My dear little friend,

I am glad to get your letter to know that next Sunday you and I will be of the same age (!) I hope and believe however that you will see many more birthdays than I shall, and I trust that every birthday may find you strong in health, and prosperous and happy.

I think it was mean of that young fellow not to answer your letter—You see, I have been longer in the world than he, and know more than he does of what is due to young ladies.

I send you a dollar with which pray buy some small keepsake to remember me by, and   Believe me,

Yours sincerely,

John A. Macdonald

In 1891, at 76, he fought his last election. And fight it he did. He still stood tall and never apologized for his beliefs. He still out-thought his opponents and pointed towards the future instead of dwelling on the past. Massive crowds came to see the living legend, defending his vision of Canada with "my latest breath . . . in this, my last effort."

He won, of course. But the election took a terrible toll on the old man. At times he was so ill he could barely see his audiences. As the votes were counted he was asleep in bed.

When Parliament opened in late April he seemed to have made another miraculous recovery. When the Leader of the Opposition, Wilfrid Laurier, tried to make fun of his victory, he held his head up proudly and said he was at his post to stay.

But he couldn't do it forever. On May 12, while meeting with Governor General Lord Stanley (of Stanley Cup fame), he had problems speaking. He bravely went on. But a series of strokes attacked him over the following three weeks, knocking him into bed at his famous "Earnscliffe" home overlooking the Ottawa River.

One night the pain was so intense he cried out in his sleep. The city was ordered quiet. The press gathered near his door. In Parliament, everyone, friend and foe, feared the end. When his condition was announced in the House, there was silence. Hector Langevin, the powerful Quebec leader, sat in his seat with tears streaming down his face. Across the nation people held their breath. "HE IS DYING," said the papers.

On the evening of June 6, 1891, his assistant Joseph Pope stepped outside the doors of Earnscliffe. "Gentlemen," he said sadly, "Sir John Macdonald is dead."

Two French Canadians stood in the House the next day and addressed a hushed audience. Laurier spoke of him at length. And then there was Langevin. "I would have wished to continue to speak of our dear departed friend," he whispered near the end, "and spoken to you about the goodness of his heart, the witness of which I have been so often, but I feel that I must stop; my heart is full of tears. I cannot proceed further."

Macdonald's body lay in state in Parliament, and the lines of Canadians, who came from all over the country to see him, seemed endless.

It was a hot day in Ottawa when they took his body in procession along the streets to the church. Mourning cloth hung from the buildings and the crowds gathered everywhere. A black cloud settled over Parliament Hill. Then a violent storm burst out.

The Ottawa train station was draped in black and purple. Every station in every province from coast to coast was just as dark. They eased him away at a slow pace. Crowds gathered at the stations. In the fields farmers looked on from a distance, their hats in their hands. The "great one" was dead.

They took him to Kingston and buried him . . . in Canadian soil.

2nd Prime Minister

Working Man

ALEXANDER MACKENZIE

*Born Scotland 1822,
died Toronto 1892, Liberal.
PM: 1873–1878*

Alexander Mackenzie had a secret staircase. And he loved to use it. Especially when he was fed up with all the people who came to him asking for favours and high-paying jobs. He was an honest leader and believed that others should earn things for themselves. So, when too many people were bothering him, he would sneak out of his office in Parliament and escape down the winding staircase into the great outdoors. That secret passageway remains to this day. So does Mackenzie's influence. He is often remembered as a dull man, but his life story proves that wasn't true. He began with almost nothing and built himself into a pretty amazing guy.

A Humble Beginning

He was born in Scotland in 1822, in a family of seven brothers, the son of working class parents. His father often moved, looking for better jobs, and young Alex, of medium height, slim and strong, was forced to leave school and become a working man too. He gained only six years of education, and almost every day of his life tried to make up for it, reading as much as he could, challenging his brain to work as hard as his hands. He was a serious teenager who didn't drink alcohol and went to a strict Baptist church.

His job was building with stones, and it was through the family of another stonemason that he met Helen Neill and fell in love. During that time Canadians often came to Scotland to attract immigrants, telling of a huge country with a great future. So, when hard times hit, the Neills decided to go. Alex, anxious to make something of himself and not wanting to lose his girlfriend, went with them.

They left Scotland in the spring of 1842 and settled in Kingston, where Alex's lifelong rival John A. Macdonald was then a rising lawyer. Mackenzie didn't have the big goals of the young swaggerer with the silver tongue. He just wanted to find a good job and marry Helen. Soon he found work as a builder, and for several years helped put up all sorts of solid buildings. In 1843 he and Helen finally married.

But their marriage was filled with sadness. Their first baby died and so did two others. Only a girl named Mary lived. Then Helen got sick and never got better.

Wanting his own business, Mackenzie moved to the frontier village of Sarnia in 1847. It was past the forests, a place of just a few hundred folks, at the southern tip of Lake Huron. But it had lots of Scottish Baptists, was anti-alcohol, and growing. There were also many Reform party people there, who had political views that interested 25-year-old Alex.

From the time he was young he believed that everyone should be treated equally—the lowliest stonemason was as good as a king. He discovered that the amazing George Brown, along with his *Globe* newspaper and his fellow Reformers, felt the same way. Mackenzie bought a subscription and settled down to work. Before long he was speaking publicly and had become the Secretary of the Reform party (soon to be the Liberals) of Kent and Lambton County.

His business began to thrive. He built a local church, the First Bank of Upper Canada, courthouses, jails, and tons of homes. But his greatest interest was politics. To state his views, he started his own newspaper, *The Lambton Shield*. It displayed his sharp tongue and stern principles. "With or without offence to friends and foes," was its motto, "I sketch your world exactly as it goes." Such was Alexander Mackenzie:

a sturdy man in dark clothing, with a long red beard, sharp features, and blue eyes like steel.

He knew he wasn't a warm sort, and felt that the mighty Brown and his own, friendly brother Hope should be the public Liberals in the region. When he ran for a local position in town and lost, it confirmed his views.

In 1851 he invited Brown to run in Sarnia. The great man won and accelerated his remarkable rise to national power. Mackenzie would remain his friend. When Brown decided to run in Toronto in the mid-1850s, Alex nominated his brother Hope locally and soon got him elected. Hope was cautious. Alex wasn't—to demonstrate his anti-alcohol views, he burned the only two barrels of liquor in Sarnia, right on the main street.

He moved swiftly in private life too. When Helen died in 1852, he quickly replaced her with Jane Sym, the daughter of a local Baptist. They married on June 17, 1853.

The Road to Fame

When his brother became ill, the local Liberals began looking for a new candidate. Alex saw himself as a simple, working guy with a mere six years of education; but others saw a good man with an incredible memory for facts, and brains galore, who had built himself into a remarkable figure. The Liberals asked him to be their man. He reluctantly accepted.

Running for election, Alex suddenly forgot his poor opinion of himself and lashed out at opponents. Calling the government "most mischievous and corrupt," he defeated their candidate and landed in Parliament in Quebec City in March 1862. Awaiting the tough Scot was that rascal John A. Macdonald and his flashy partner George-Étienne Cartier.

But "Sandy" Mackenzie immediately did well. He fought for ideas like Brown's "Rep by Pop," expansion to the west, secret voting, and equality. He was blunt and well-spoken. In a sea of pale, elegant men, he had a rough, weather-beaten face. He was a man of principles who stuck to them, his hard eyes and tight mouth signs that he would never give in to anyone, no matter who they were. Mackenzie was perfect for Parliament: his speeches well-researched, his arguments clear and accurate. He confronted his enemies.

But during the mid-1860s, as many governments came and went and the nation grew frustrated, Mackenzie came to accept Brown's idea that all sides needed to unite. Things had to be changed, and part of that involved binding the provinces into a vast new country. "I regard this scheme as a magnificent one," he said of the dream of Canada, "and I look forward to being, before I die, a citizen of an immense empire built upon our part of the North American continent."

But deep down, he hated joining the Conservatives and John A. to accomplish this feat. He took no part in the three Confederation conferences. He cheered the result, but then suited up to fight Macdonald again.

By 1867 things had changed in his party. His brother Hope had died, Brown had left Parliament, and some Liberals were supporting Macdonald. Mackenzie was now seen as a leader. That surprised him. But when times got tough, he was tougher than all the rest.

At one election meeting he stood bravely in front of a violent enemy audience. Outside he found his horses gripped by opponents and a companion beaten. Getting onto their mounts, he and his bloodied friend escaped at full gallop.

By 1872 he was "the man" in the Liberal party. And by the following year he became the official Leader of the Opposition. Worn out by his work and anxious for others to have the limelight, he had resisted at first, but accepted when it became obvious that only he commanded the party's total respect.

And then came his big opportunity. In 1873 John A. was on the ropes over the Pacific Scandal. Mackenzie appeared with a stack of evidence on his desk and tore into him, detailing his corruption. The Conservatives fell the following month.

The working man, a Scottish immigrant with little education, was Prime Minister of Canada. It was hard for Alex to believe.

On the surface, he seemed unimpressed. "It was so characteristic of him," said a friend. "He appeared no more uplifted than if he had been going out to an ordinary day's work."

But inside, he was so nervous that it made him sick to his stomach. He appointed his cabinet, called an election, whipped Macdonald, and began his reign.

The Trials of Power

Mackenzie told the country he wanted many new things: secret ballots for elections (so people could vote as they pleased and not be attacked), a CPR railway that wasn't too long or expensive, a Supreme Court, and Mounties in the west.

"What a slaughter," he said after he won. But John A. soon recovered from his down period and began plotting to unseat him. Mackenzie responded by working at his job like few have before or since, barely taking time to sleep.

Perhaps the greatest problem that faced him was the Canadian Pacific Railway. Macdonald had promised to build it to British Columbia when the province entered Canada. He had said construction would begin within two years and finish in 10. Mackenzie, against putting Canada in debt, bluntly told B.C. it was impossible, and almost caused a rebellion. His plan—to go slower, build a series of smaller lines, use water travel to join them, and allow links from the United States— never caught the public imagination and paled next to Macdonald's grand transcontinental design. It was said that the CPR would be on Mackenzie's tombstone, that it "ruined his health and damaged his reputation."

Louis Riel presented another problem. In his earlier days Mackenzie had been strongly against the Métis leader, part of the Ontario government that voted 62–1 to hunt him down. In 1874 Riel was elected from Manitoba and slipped secretly into Ottawa. While some wanted his blood, French Canadians demanded that he be accepted. Riel moved around like a ghost, never taking his Commons seat. At first, Mackenzie voted to expel him, calling him a "fugitive from justice" and an accomplice to murder. However, during his term as Prime Minister he learned about French Canada and was pleased when the Governor General forgave Riel (though he was also happy to see him kicked out of Canadian politics for good).

But the upper-crust Governor General and his sort didn't impress Mackenzie. During visits to England, Alex disliked the snobs he met. Unlike the other early Prime Ministers, he refused to be knighted, saying that he was one of a "brotherhood of man," above no one.

There were some good signs during the final years of his reign in 1877 and 1878. He saved money for Canada, which always pleased him. And Wilfrid Laurier began to rise. Mackenzie admired the young Quebecker and placed him in his cabinet.

There were several trips home to Europe with Jane. He was amazed to find himself a celebrity, sitting at the ship Captain's table and invited to elegant English dinners. In Scotland he was a hero, a working man who had become a star. On a train one day, a talkative lady, not recognizing him, began chattering about the celebrated Canadian Prime Minister who was visiting. Had he ever met Mr. Mackenzie? Yes, he replied, he had. "Is he a grand-looking man and does he really deserve all the flattering reputation which the Scottish newspapers give him for ability and stern integrity in all he does?" Mackenzie looked at her gravely. "I have always had my doubts about that," he said.

Back home, troubles mounted. "The rascals have gone, having gathered up their dead and wounded," he said after another nasty Parliament. The House was full of shouts as the economy did poorly and the CPR struggled. The Opposition saw blood.

Mackenzie looked "bone tired and alarmingly thin." The Governor General said he was "a washed-out rag and limp enough to hang upon a clothes line." In 1878 he called an election and felt he'd win: he had done a lot and, more importantly, had been honest.

Crushed

But by that year Macdonald had totally recovered. He toured the nation giving warm, funny speeches, trumpeting his National Policy of a grand railroad to B.C. and helping Canadian industries. Mackenzie looked sour, and always worried about saving money. Macdonald would smile and greet the roars of crowds with "How are you boys!" while the bearded, thinning, and ill Mackenzie would strike out with such lines as "The heart of the average [Conservative] is deceitful above all things and desperately wicked."

On September 17, 1878, John A. killed him at the polls. Alex was shocked. He muttered things about not being enough of a criminal to win and returned to Parliament to fight.

But things had changed. He had moved to Toronto and seemed distant to his Ottawa friends. He talked less and was often grumpy. At times he forgot to call the leaders of the party together. Rising young Liberal Edward Blake and others soon wanted him out.

Then came 1880, a terrible year. First there was the shock of hearing that George Brown had been shot. Then, on April 17, Alex quit as party leader. Blake, "as warm as a flake of December snow," succeeded him and became the only Liberal leader to never be Prime Minister.

Mackenzie continued to sit in Parliament. He grew frail. The long beard went grey, the face became lined. During one stretch in the early '80s he lost 22 pounds. Campaigning in his new riding in East York, Toronto, in 1882, he suffered a stroke. Enemy papers reported he was dead. Then the nation read that he was regaining strength. And somehow, he won the election.

But the stroke left him with big problems. The worst had to do with his throat. His speeches now had to be quiet and brief. One day, he steeled himself and attacked the Conservatives.

Macdonald rose. "I congratulate the honourable gentleman on the vigour with which he is able to administer these rebukes." He smiled. "Long may it be so."

The Liberal party still needed the nearly mute old leader. Each election they pleaded with him to run. In 1887 and 1891 he flattened his opponents. The last time he barely whispered a word. When he rose in Ottawa, the whole House would grow silent and listen for the faint voice of the once great leader, the distant sound of a legend.

On April 17, 1892, 10 months after Macdonald died, Alex passed away. Everywhere in the country he was hailed as an honest man with great ability. The funeral service was held at a Baptist church in Toronto and then his body was taken to Sarnia. The minister said, "The name Alexander Mackenzie, I have no hesitation in affirming, is a stainless name."

He had come from almost nothing, from a little home in Scotland. He had journeyed to Canada with a few dollars and six years of education. But he rose to the highest office in his new country. He had become an *extra*ordinary man.

The Great Pooh-Bah
SIR JOHN ABBOTT

O ver the years many people have said that Sir John Joseph Caldwell Abbott was a pretty unimportant guy. But you can bet that he did more things than all those guys put together. He may not have been a great Prime Minister, but he was right in the middle of just about every important Canadian event in the 19th century—wars, scandals, railroads, sensational trials, a famous act of treason, and even a daring robbery or two.

Born St. Andrews East, Canada East 1821, died Montreal 1893, Conservative. PM: 1891–1892

Pooh-Bah in Training

He was the first Prime Minister born in Canada. His father, Joseph Abbott, had emigrated from England to southeastern Quebec near the Ottawa River in 1818. It was a wild place and Joseph came to tame it. He was a minister, and so were John's uncle, grandfather, and father-in-law. But they weren't dull. They were adventurers and tough guys. The grandfather had been a famous sailor with explorer James Cook and had married a lady from the court of "Mad" King George III of England. John Abbott would be related to, or connected with, a ton of important people.

He was born in the minister's rough, cedar-log parsonage on March 12, 1821, at St. Andrew's East (St. André Est). In this area east of Montreal, wolves howled at night, bears and moose roamed, and raspberries and blueberries filled the woods. The talented, hard-working Reverend Abbott moved his family from one "mission" to the next, travelling by oxcart and sleeping on buffalo robes. At St. Andrew's, he built a school, wrote books about pioneer life, and gave advice on everything from law to medicine. He raised "four sledge-hammer sons and two daughters" who inherited his brains and drive. The family played chess, read, and discussed politics.

Famous English Quebec families like the Molsons and Redpaths were family friends, and young John met rebels too, like unhappy French Canadians Louis-Joseph Papineau and Victor-Louis Sicotte.

Though the Abbotts were all taught French and Joseph criticized the British for being "ignorant of the spirit and genius of the people here," they stayed loyal to the king when rebellion burst out in 1837. Cartier, Papineau, and Sicotte, peaceful politicians for years, had become convinced that the British would never give them a fair say in their affairs, and had turned to war. John Abbott, just 16, saw skies red with explosions as 70 French Canadians gave their last blood to their cause at nearby St. Eustache.

Joseph kept his sons out of harm's way. He had plans for them. Their education was important. In the 1820s he had helped create one of Canada's oldest and most respected universities, McGill in Montreal. He steered his sons its way.

But first, John wanted to make some money. At age 17, school completed, he set off for Montreal to find his fortune in business. On the way he spotted a beautiful stretch of shoreline with an old fort in ruins and vowed to one day own it. But his start in the city and at other jobs in Ontario—selling dry goods and working in a general store—didn't get him far along the road to the wealth he imagined. So he tried more education.

By 1843 McGill University had opened an Arts Building, and John was one of its first students. His father had already moved to the city to handle the school's money. John acted as his assistant and secretary to the Board of Governors. He also worked at one of Montreal's best law firms, Meredith and Bethune. It was another good connection: Bethune's father was McGill's principal, and soon John married relative Mary Bethune. In 1847 he became a lawyer in his own right.

His talented father had by now been a farmer, minister, teacher, and architect. He wrote a respected novel and made friends with the famous Canadian writers Susanna Moodie and Catherine Parr Traill. He would be McGill's first librarian, its chaplain, and professor of Ancient History. John would inherit his multi-skilled ways.

And there was rebellion in John too. In 1849, now a respected lawyer in the firm of Badgley and Abbott, he committed treason. Or sort of. It all had to do with the Rebellion Losses Bill that gave government money to some 1837 rebels. It got the Governor General pelted with rocks in Montreal and Government House burned to the ground. It also brought about The Annexation Manifesto, the shocking document that suggested union with the United States. Like Alexander Galt, John Abbott willingly signed it, a rash decision he would later regret. But it wouldn't be the last time he was in hot water.

Despite this mistake, he rose in the 1850s. By age 34 he was a professor and head of law at McGill. And when his partner Badgley was appointed Attorney General for Canada East, Abbott took over the firm. Using his big brains, ability to work long hours, and amazing attention to detail, he became one of Canada's best lawyers, a favourite of the rich and powerful. His firm grew to gigantic size and influence.

As early as 1852 he and his brothers had become involved in one of the great Canadian trends of that era—railways. He started with small companies near St. Andrew's, investing and acting as lawyer. By 1862 he was president of the Canada Central Railway and then lawyer for the granddaddy of them all, the CPR. He wrote the legal document that created it. Brother Harry would also play a key role with that historic line.

Not only was Abbott a railway man, lawyer, and professor (Wilfrid Laurier was one of his students), but also president, chairman, or director of all sorts of companies, from Standard Life Insurance to the mighty Bank of Montreal. He was the city's Harbour Commissioner, and believe it or not, in the late 1880s while in his 60s, Montreal's mayor. He also commanded his own military regiment (that patrolled the border ready to fight the Fenians), helped create the famous Royal Victoria Hospital, and operated The Fraser Institute, an arts organization that gave Montreal its first free library.

He was a well-dressed, distinguished-looking man, thick-set with a broad face, bushy eyebrows, and a whole series of serious looks. Connected up and down and sideways to all the big wheels in Montreal and the greatest railways and businesses in Canada, he had little problem launching a political career.

Adventures with John A.

It started in 1857, when he represented the St. Andrew's area. He began as a Liberal, and in 1862, barely 40, became the

Solicitor General (head lawman) of the Canadas for co-premiers Sandfield Macdonald and Victor-Louis Sicotte.

Sicotte had risen from rebel to powerful Canadian leader. His daughter Amélie was married to John's brother, Harry Abbott. After the government fell in 1863 and Sicotte left both the Liberals and politics, John, loyal to his sister-in-law's family, moved away from the party too.

Though he'd had doubts about Confederation, worrying that English Quebec would be hurt by it, he was soon a major part of Sir John A. Macdonald's Conservative team, valued by the legendary leader. Now the very government of Canada wanted him as their lawyer. By 1887 he was a cabinet minister and later, leader of the Senate.

Long before this, he'd had some amazing adventures with the rascal John A.

In October 1864, just as the North seemed about to defeat the South in the American Civil War, a group of young Southerners living in exile in Montreal struck a stunning blow for the rebel cause. They raced south on horseback through lower Quebec and then over the U.S. border, where they raided little St. Alban's, Vermont, like outlaws from the Wild West, using guns to knock over several banks, and escaping back to Canada with $200,000. The northern U.S. demanded the traitors be handed over. Otherwise, cried some newspapers, they would destroy Canada.

That was when John Abbott stepped forward. He didn't care a hoot about American threats. The raiders would have fair treatment in Canadian courts, and he would see to it personally. He defended them, and got them off. He said they were soldiers at war, not criminals. The police chief even gave them back their money. Americans just about burst their blood vessels. Prosecute those guys, they told Canada, or we are coming after you! John A. wasn't pleased either. As he tried to make the Americans back off, he considered how to defend Montreal from attack. Soon things calmed down, some money was returned to St. Albans and, luckily, the Civil War began to wind down.

In the early 1870s Abbott was involved in something not nearly as noble. It began with Montreal multi-millionaire shipping magnate Hugh Allan. He was in line to build the massive Canadian Pacific Railway. Abbott was his lawyer.

The CPR was supposed to be a Canadian firm, but Allan had shadowy U.S. backers and secretly gave big money to Macdonald, Cartier, and others in the 1872 election. Abbott was deeply involved. When the Liberals uncovered it all, it caused a sensation unlike any other and destroyed the powerful Macdonald government.

At centre stage was one of Abbott's young law clerks. On a dark Montreal night, while Abbott was away with Allan in England, he and a friend had used his key to break into the office and open secret files. The stolen goods—telegrams and letters between Allan and government leaders—were sold to the Liberals as evidence of bribery.

Death by Leadership

But by 1890, scandals and other excitements were long
behind him. He had risen again and played a key role in
getting the CPR completed. Quieter things now interested
him. He had bought that beautiful spot at the east end of
Montreal that he had vowed to own as a 17-year-old. He
called it Boisbriant and built a mansion overlooking the St.
Lawrence River where it flowed around the Island of
Montreal. He grew rare flowers, raised valuable cattle, hunted
and fished, and had famous visitors. He loved to entertain his
eight children with "hair-raising ghost stories of his own
invention."

He was tired of his many ventures, not in great health, and
ready to ride off into the sunset. He had been appointed to the
Senate and leisurely ran the government's business from that
quiet chamber, glad to be free of the angry debates and lies of
the main political ring. But on June 6, 1891, Sir John A.
Macdonald died. And John Abbott's quiet life exploded.

Macdonald had always wanted the young, politically
talented John Thompson to succeed him. But Thompson was
a Catholic, not a good thing for a national politician to be in
those prejudiced days. Macdonald knew that someone else
would have to guide the government for a while, until
Thompson was acceptable. "Old Tomorrow" came up with
the most reliable man in the Dominion—the aging, semi-
retired Abbott.

The Prime Minister's job could have easily gone to two other men: Hector Langevin or Sir Charles Tupper, both Fathers of Confederation. But Langevin was involved in too many scandals and the wealthy, aging Tupper didn't want the pressure of being PM.

So, with Macdonald lying in his coffin in Parliament, Governor General Stanley asked Abbott to be Prime Minister. He wanted it even less than Tupper did. "I hate politics," he had once snarled. Now they were asking him to be the prime politician in the country.

But he believed that working for Canada was a high calling. His country needed him, so he reluctantly accepted. He even moved into Macdonald's famous "Earnscliffe" home. In his first speech he told the truth: being PM was a great honour, but he had gotten the job because he was "not particularly obnoxious to anyone."

It would be a short reign, a strange end to his career. He achieved the highest calling in his country and didn't want it. Then he did some of his least impressive work.

He had disadvantages. He had to run the government from his seat in the Senate (while Thompson looked after the House of Commons), an economic depression had hit Canada, and there were divisions within his party and continuing scandals.

Abbott did what he could. He knew he was just a caretaker. Much of his time was spent delaying big decisions and avoiding scandals. He knew the work would likely destroy his health, and it did. By August 1892, he was suffering so badly he received visitors while lying on a couch in the Prime Minister's office.

He went to Europe to see if he could get well, not knowing he had stomach cancer. For a short while he was happy. He played cards and went to the theatre, enjoying life far from his cares. But he broke down again, and when he returned to Canada in November, he resigned and fled to Montreal and his beloved Boisbriant. He died less than a year later, on October 30, 1893, killed by his last tour of duty for his country.

There was little reaction to his funeral, just as there is little note of him in our history books. But he was an amazing man.

Today when you drive into Montreal along the Macdonald-Cartier Freeway, the first land you see, on your left, is Pointe Abbott, the land of Boisbriant. Nearby is Sir John Abbott College in St. Anne de Bellevue. In the movies and on television, you can glimpse John Abbott's face and intelligence in his great-grandson, actor Christopher Plummer.

John Abbott was at the centre of an incredible number of big Canadian events. He did just about everything. A friend once rightly called him "the Great Pooh-Bah or Lord High Everything Else."

What Could Have Been

SIR JOHN THOMPSON

I t is said that the good die young. John Thompson was good, and may have one day been great. If he had lived his name might have been remembered forever by Canadians. It might have been Thompson on our five-dollar bill, on our street signs and universities. But his life ended suddenly in a castle in front of the Queen. Then he faded into history as the great "what if" of our past, instead of being part of what we were and are.

Born Halifax 1845, died Windsor Castle 1894, Conservative. PM: 1892–1894

"I am afraid of the nights and I am afraid of the days and I am afraid of the years," his wife cried when he died, "and if it were not for the children I should long to creep away in some corner and die." Canada felt the same.

Falling in Love with John Thompson

He always hated prejudice. That decency came from his Irish father, who moved to Halifax in 1827 and loved it. John Thompson, Sr. was a newspaper editor, teacher, and post office official, an intelligent man who struggled to support his family. But he believed that being honest and educated and caring for your family was more important than fame or fortune. He and his wife Charlotte, from nearby Pictou, had seven children. John was the youngest, born in their little house on Argyle Street on November 10, 1845.

As a boy he was quiet and into books. By the time he became a teenager he was "noted for his [good looks] and good manners . . . a shrewd little fellow." Finishing school at 14, too poor to go further, he studied with a lawyer. "Thompson, you will never be able to earn your salt," said his boss. But in 1865 he passed his exams and opened a Halifax firm.

The following year he fell in love with a remarkable woman who would dominate his life. Dark-haired Annie Affleck was the beautiful daughter of a sea captain. She was smart, moody, and dramatic, and loved wild weather and swimming in the ocean. She was Catholic; he was Methodist. Marriage was impossible. But, fascinated by this brilliant, handsome young man, Annie dropped her Catholic boyfriend, and then, like the star-crossed lovers in *Romeo and Juliet,* she and John stuck together against family wishes.

He was shy and she was bold. He had brains and she had drive. Throughout his life, she would push him towards his destiny, and teach him to understand women. He controlled her emotions with his cool touch, and her spirit inspired him. She wrote him wild love letters in code, and in later years they grew fat together, and loved it.

They rushed off to Maine and married. He sacrificed everything by becoming Catholic—endangering his reputation, professional hopes, and political ambitions. They would raise a close family of three boys and two girls.

A keen follower of politics, he was a Liberal, a fan of Joseph Howe like his father. Howe had brought real democracy, "responsible government," to Nova Scotia and been a dynamic Premier. When Howe joined Macdonald and the Conservatives in 1869, young Thompson did too. He was impressed with the party's ability to change and its tolerance towards Catholics.

His reputation as a lawyer grew quickly. No challenge was too great for him, and he constantly read law books to stay ahead of his opponents. It was obvious he'd be a good leader, and in 1871, though only 25, he was invited to run for city council, and won.

At the tough council chamber, he excelled. He seemed calm and always well informed. But inside, his sharp, aggressive mind was like a volcano. All his life he worked at self-control, which made him a devastating politician—he burned with passion for his ideas, but moved them forward coolly like a chess master. When he left council in 1877 he was 32 years old . . . and popular enough to be mayor.

In court he became almost unbeatable, even when he tried cases before the Supreme Court of Nova Scotia. One day, an old judge tried to stop him by ruling that he couldn't read from a medical book to defend his client. Thompson set the book down . . . and recited the entire page from memory.

In 1877 the provincial Conservatives asked him to run in Antigonish, far from Halifax, but he wasn't sure. He loved being a lawyer and being near his family. But Annie pushed him. So, even though he hated politics so much that he wouldn't ask for votes ("When you vote on election day, remember me," was all he'd say), he ran and won. In government he quickly became a star, making perfect arguments in his clear, rich voice. "You could print his speeches as they stood," said one reporter, "friend and foe paid attention."

Before long he ruled the justice system as a 34-year-old Attorney General, the most powerful position in cabinet. He made the courts more efficient, and wasn't afraid to do unpopular things—when he believed he was right, he never gave in. His style during battle was polite. He simply cross-examined opponents until their arguments broke.

The Premier of Nova Scotia was a bit of a boob, and by 1882 party troubles forced him to resign. The brown-haired, brown-eyed, clean-shaven Thompson, aged 37, became the leader. The following year, hurt by its past record, the government lost an election and Thompson's 54-day rule ended. He wasn't upset. He could return to law—Annie had to let him. He made himself a judge, a kid among old fogies, and built another golden reputation.

Those were his sweetest days. He took the streetcar to his office and travelled to courts throughout Nova Scotia. But none other than Sir John A. Macdonald would soon come calling, wooing him as well as Annie had, and his life would change forever.

Up on the Big Stage

Macdonald was aware of the growing Maritime legend. As the old man's Conservatives aged, as he worried that no giant was available to succeed him, he sent assistants to Nova Scotia to see if Thompson might be the man.

Young John wanted to stay home. But the pressure grew from old John and from Annie. "If we don't get Thompson I don't know what to do," Macdonald said. So in July 1885 the PM sent him an offer he couldn't refuse, turning him into an overnight star by making him one of Canada's most powerful men, the Minister of Justice.

The "baby minister" entered the House of Commons and Canada became aware of him. At first the Liberal Opposition licked their lips. Who was this quiet, slightly fat, slightly short, and very young man who seemed so careful and polite? They thought they'd eat him alive. But it was Thompson who ate well, feasting on Liberals from the moment he appeared in Ottawa until the day he died.

He moved into a rented house, alone in the capital, missing Annie, and made the rounds to a few parties, impressed by the polite, "light as a bird" Macdonald, and by the Governor General because he wasn't snobby. People's money or big titles never interested Thompson. He once said, "I detest the idea of being beastly rich."

He got right to work. His employees were astounded at how quickly he learned.

A huge issue was facing the nation: the fate of Louis Riel. Thompson felt that Riel had, above all, broken Canada's laws. If you believed that Canada had good laws, and Thompson did, and if someone was judged fairly by the courts, then politics should never change a verdict. That would be unfair. Riel had caused an armed revolt in Manitoba and was responsible for many deaths. That meant, in Thompson's mind, that he had to die.

As Conservatives raged against Liberals, English against French, Macdonald gave young John the task of defending the government. They were getting pummelled. So, up stood Thompson. The galleries were filled. Everyone waited to see what he was made of.

As it turned out, a great deal. He delivered an historic speech. He said dramatically that *anyone* who pushed the natives to armed violence "takes his life in his hands, and when he appeals to me for mercy, *he will get justice.*" Many stood and cheered. He asked how Riel could go free when native Wandering Spirit was being hanged for similar charges. Was Riel's life more important that Wandering Spirit's?

"A great figure has emerged from a curious obscurity," said *The Globe* the next day.

Thompson eventually recommended that many natives involved in the rebellion be freed. He would release other people from other trials he thought unfair. But he had no sympathy if children were mistreated. When a woman who had been cruel to a two-year-old asked for freedom, he exploded. "I tell you, if you lived for a hundred years and I was still Minister of Justice, you would never get out with my consent."

He guided Canada's justice system for nine years and began creating our Criminal Code. His stature grew in Parliament. It wasn't because he was dramatic. He kept sticking to facts, careful to raise his voice only when needed. In the midst of attacks, when others would run scared, he was cool as a cucumber. Macdonald began to lean on him. In early 1888, after he defended Canada in a nasty trade dispute with the Americans, he was knighted. But he found it almost funny to be "Sir John."

In the midst of this praise, he was more concerned about his daughter Frankie, his "dizzle dazzle," confined to a hospital with bad hips. "[Annie] says you think more of your little daughter," wrote a friend, "than all the government, and I believe her!" Other daughters were at school in Quebec, becoming bilingual.

In 1890 Thompson went to England for his first trip overseas. Britain seemed stuffy. "Canada," he discovered, "is the place to live after all." His skills impressed the Brits. Back home, he kept winning elections, hoping each was his last. Annie pushed him forward. The big job was on the horizon and she knew John A. wanted him to have it.

After the 1891 election the old man's health faded. As Macdonald was dying he worried that Canada would not accept his brilliant, Catholic protégé. He put his arm around Thompson and told him sadly that old Sir John Abbott might have to have the job.

Almost every Conservative and the Governor General wanted Thompson to be Prime Minister. But he had inherited Macdonald's wise caution. He too thought Abbott should be PM for now. So, from June 1891 until December 1892 the new old man ruled, though from the Senate. Thompson ran the House of Commons and everyone knew it.

The Opposition, fronted by the elegant Laurier, feared Thompson's abilities. They knew he was "the brains of the combination." But with Abbott in the Senate it was difficult for Thompson to get much done. He did finish his Criminal Code. It was a unique act, a mark of the young nation's ability to be a leader in the world. It stated what Canada thought was right and wrong, crimes and not crimes. And it went easy on kids.

Despite his success, Thompson still yearned to leave politics behind and be with his family. In October 1892, when a Supreme Court judge's job came open, he wanted it. He was working himself into poor health, doing tough jobs others couldn't. "I am as well and fat as ever," he cracked. But he needed rest. Annie wanted him home too, but knew he could be a great Canadian, not just a great judge. She told him, "Baby . . . there will come a time soon when they cannot do without you." She was right.

Triumph . . . and Tragedy

The elderly Abbott's health declined so quickly that in the fall of 1892 he went to Europe to recover, and resigned in late November. Everyone knew who would be the next PM. "Sir John Thompson holds the keys of the future," said *The Montreal Daily Star.*

In early December, Sir John Sparrow David Thompson, all of 47 years old, and Roman Catholic, took the job. (The first Catholic U.S. president, John F. Kennedy, was elected in 1960.) The country had to have him despite his religion.

Things would be different now in Canada. They had a brilliant young Prime Minister. He wanted a "vigorous" cabinet and believed in honest, polite politics.

He did all he could to preserve Catholic rights in Manitoba, got Canada its own trade treaty with France, and kept British ties despite American pressure. He established Labour Day as a rest day for working people. And he continued to reform our laws. In Parliament he and Laurier seemed a new breed. They were seen talking in the House, laughing together. A competition of two great, honourable men seemed on the horizon.

Thompson asked Canadians to stop judging each other. They had many differences—of race, religion, and geography. Accept differences, he said, and have an amazing future.

He also believed that women should take their rightful place. He thought they had "courage and endurance." Canada needed their full participation. He spoke of giving them the vote a quarter of a century before it happened. Canada would have led the world in accepting women's rights. When the National Council of Women was formed in 1894 with the Governor General's wife, Lady Aberdeen, as president and Lady Annie Thompson as vice-president, he and Laurier were invited to speak. In those days most men didn't like to appear to be taking women's political opinions seriously. Laurier backed out, but Thompson came, and after he spoke, stayed for the meeting. Lady Aberdeen, a Liberal, adored Thompson. He had, in her mind, "a strong, elevated, trained character." She looked forward to many years of working with him.

But by the summer of 1894 Thompson started having problems. First he noticed his swollen legs. "Sometimes the warning to stop and rest comes very suddenly and sternly," he told a friend. But he said little else, and rested with his family in the beautiful Muskoka Lakes district in Ontario. They laughed and fished and sailed. Thompson put on a silly captain's hat and sat in their little boat. When cottagers saw him, cheers went up.

Fearing he had Bright's disease, which had killed Cartier, he consulted the best doctors. The first one thought he had bad kidneys and suggested rest, but two others said he was fine, so off he went to London to be made a member of the famed Privy Council by Queen Victoria. Friends pleaded with him to slow down. He had given everything to his country—Annie didn't go to London because the Prime Minister of Canada couldn't afford it.

When he arrived in England that November *The Times of London* was praising Canada's success and future. He took off with an adoring daughter (at school in Europe) for a trip to Rome. They climbed 400 feet to the dome of St. Peter's Cathedral. When he came down he was badly out of breath. The breathlessness never left him.

Back in London, he immediately went to work despite feeling rotten. Tupper saw him and made him go to an English doctor. He was told he had strained his heart. But he wouldn't stop. He had many appointments to keep.

On December 12, 1894, he dressed in fancy knee socks and britches, combed his short, greying brown hair, and went to Windsor Castle to meet the Queen. There he was sworn into the Privy Council and then happily went to eat. But he wasn't feeling well. As he sat down, he collapsed. They eased him into another room. "It seems too weak and foolish to faint like this," he said sadly, his head in his hands. He convinced them that he could go on. The Queen's personal doctor was called and seated next to him.

Back at the table, he turned to say he felt pain in his heart. He barely got it out, and fell forward onto the doctor. They felt his pulse.

John Thompson was dead, aged 49. In Canada the shock was enormous. At first government officials didn't believe it. Then they feared telling Annie. "Poor Lady Thompson," cried cabinet minister Mackenzie Bowell, and burst into tears.

At the Queen's command his body lay in state in the Marble Hall at Windsor Castle. A British battleship was brought from Gibraltar, painted black, ready to take him home. A mass was held, attended by British dignitaries and the poet Lord Tennyson.

When he arrived in Halifax they were waiting for him, lining the docks and the streets. The procession went slowly down the main avenue, past the little house where he was born. Twelve thousand flowers decorated the funeral; 7,000 dignitaries tried for the 700 seats at St. Mary's Cathedral. Annie and the family, absolutely devastated, didn't want dark colours, but the city was dressed in black.

A great opportunity was going to be missed. The wonder boy, the good man capable of pulling Canada through its great early problems, was suddenly gone.

Annie tore apart her Ottawa home and went to live in Toronto. "Just think for a moment," she had written to John years ago, as their kids gathered around her in their bed, "what would become of us without you." She died in 1913, still desperately missing her amazing man, never allowed to vote in a national election.

She remembered things no one else knew: shopkeepers could sell him anything; the sweetness of a child or its pain brought him to tears.

"God guard him along into the dark future, be it long or be it short," she had written in her diary when they married. It had been short and glorious. But oh, what could have been.

5th Prime Minister

Santa in Disguise

SIR MACKENZIE BOWELL

*Born England 1823,
died Belleville, Ontario 1917,
Conservative. PM: 1894–1896*

When Mackenzie Bowell was Prime Minister of Canada he looked a bit like Santa Claus, but without the red suit, the presents, and definitely without the laugh—being the boss was never anything like Christmas for him. It was mean and nasty, and over before he knew it.

It's amazing that he ever became PM. His start in life made that idea almost a joke. When he was born two days after Christmas in 1823 in a village in England, his mother was in disgrace. She had given birth without being married. In those days, that made others think that you were worse than a nobody, and your family and child were cursed. Three months later Elizabeth Marshall married John Bowell and eight years after that they fled to Canada. They never had much money and never sent their son to school.

Tough Guy

After a dangerous, three-week voyage across the Atlantic Ocean, they reached Montreal, then moved farther up the St. Lawrence River on steamers and a flat boat pulled by ponies, and came to the little town of Belleville, Upper Canada. It was early December 1832—the sky was probably grey, the weather cold.

There were fewer than 1,000 people there. Log homes and simple stores sat close to the shore and wild land stretched out behind them. Pigs, horses, and cows moved freely on the frozen, muddy streets.

John Bowell set up a woodworking shop and Mackenzie became his employee. Two years later, after his mother died, the boy, just 10, was apprenticed to the editor of *The Intelligencer,* a newspaper run by George Benjamin. He was a unique man: a Jew who had given up his religion to come to a conservative, English-Canadian town. Mack had to move in with the Benjamin family, but he accepted this as he did most things, with a willingness to work hard and learn. The newspaper's politics were obvious—old-fashioned Conservative stuff, loyal to British ways.

Benjamin was also part of the Loyal Orange Lodge, a group that promoted British Protestant religions and attacked others, especially Catholicism. He became an Orange leader and young Mack followed him. The group had been created in Ireland long ago, its members called Orangemen because they celebrated an ancient victory of King William of Orange, a British Protestant king, over a Catholic leader. They had secret passwords, and beat big drums as they marched down Ontario streets every 12th of July in orange-coloured parades, led by "King Billy" on a white horse.

During the 1800s the Orange Lodge grew to be powerful in Canada and played an important role in politics. Eventually, one out of every four Canadian voters belonged to it, often working men. Benjamin became its national boss.

Meanwhile, Mack worked hard at every job he was assigned, among them setting the inky type for the paper by hand, a "printer's devil" with blackened face and hands. By 18, he had more responsibility at *The Intelligencer,* and six years later he and another employee bought it. In 1847 he married his new partner's sister, Harriet Moore.

As they raised five children, he became sole owner of the paper, made it a success, and acquired a reputation as a rock-hard Conservative of clear (sometimes nasty) opinions.

With Bowell's help, Benjamin was elected to Parliament in 1856 as a Conservative. In those days of political street fights, Mack was a fighter too. He defended Benjamin in strong language. He once wrote that their Liberal opponents were "blood-thirsty" traitors who held a "cup of pollution . . . to our very lips to be forced down our throats."

His first brush with fame came in 1856, during a national Orange Lodge dispute about whether the group should be a religious or political power. Bowell thought they should be both and said so publicly. He also became Chairman of Belleville's Board of Education and helped form their Board of Trade, and in 1859 moved his family into an impressive two-storey brick home and his influential newspaper into a big downtown building.

Short, but with thick shoulders, arms and chest developed from years of work, he was a vigorous man of harsh words and thoughts. His dark eyes seemed to glare out from hooded lids on a face half covered by a very thick, very large, and very black beard, like a thundercloud hiding his mouth and cheeks.

In 1860, his Orangemen refused to lay down their banners as the Prince of Wales approached Belleville for an historic visit. The Prince stayed away, not wanting to be greeted by a group banned in England. Bowell cut quite an Orange figure, with a sword in hand, medals covering his chest, that big, black beard looking ominous.

From Loudmouth to Leader

With his power growing, he was the obvious choice to succeed Benjamin, and was elected to Parliament in 1867. It was a wonderful year for him. Though some questioned Confederation, Bowell raved about it. "Not in the history of the world," he wrote in *The Intelligencer,* "was such a scene witnessed as that which passed before the eyes of four million Canadians yesterday morning. The day dawned upon a new nation."

The Parliament that Bowell entered was tough and dramatic, filled with prejudiced feelings between Protestants and Catholics, French and English. The tolerance that Canada was built upon was not always evident. Bowell wasn't any help—he brought his Orange feelings with him. He often disagreed with Macdonald while his leader searched for compromises on tough problems. One opponent called him a "growler."

He voted against the expense of taking in the North West Territories in 1869 and of building the CPR in the early '70s, and then began a series of attacks on Louis Riel that gave him the reputation of being Protestant Canada's loudmouth.

Bowell was now Grand Master of the Loyal Orange Lodge of British North America. Thomas Scott, whom Riel and his Manitoba government executed in 1870, was an Orangeman from little Madoc, smack dab in the middle of Bowell's riding. Mack spoke angrily of Scott's death at the hands of French

Catholics and thundered demands for Riel's life. When that didn't happen, he raged, "Why is this murderer allowed to go free?" That offended many French Canadians, who thought Riel a hero.

He and his friends would be considered bigots today. But in those days he had many followers and represented a mainstream group, not a bunch of weirdos. In French Canada equally bigoted men, the "ultramontane" Catholics, were on the opposite side, just as bad as Orangemen. Compromise was the solution—sometimes neither side could see it.

But a slight change was slowly creeping into Bowell's heart and mind.

The Conservatives were kicked out in 1874 because of the Pacific Scandal. Bowell defended his party but was not personally accused of doing anything wrong (and never would be). When Macdonald spoke of retiring, Bowell's name came up.

The possibility that he might have a chance to be national leader, and the fact that he'd now spent years working with Catholics and others he had once considered enemies, began to make him more tolerant, more Canadian. He praised Riel's 1885 hanging, but on other issues his attitude would change. Before long, he actually criticized another politician for being anti-Catholic, and offered little support when the Orange Lodge tried to become an official business. He also grew more loyal to Macdonald.

In 1878 he rose to a cabinet position. As Minister of Customs, he refused to be swayed by companies or big shots who tried to sneak goods into the country without paying. No one could bribe him. A businessman once tried to get away without paying his fees. Bowell told him that if he didn't pay he would go to jail. The man complained to the Prime Minister. At first Macdonald said he was sure the Minister would let him off the hook. Then he realized who the Minister was. "My friend, you will have to settle," the PM laughed. "If Bowell said you will go to jail . . . to jail you will go."

English Canada and his old Orange friends were outraged whenever he opposed them. Macdonald, however, respected such integrity and relied on him more in his last years. In fact, the final time the grand old man left the House of Commons was with his Minister of Customs. "Well, it is late, Bowell," he had said in a tired voice. "Good night."

Mack offered his resignation to the new Prime Minister, Sir John Abbott. But he was made Minister of Militia instead. When Sir John Thompson took over the following year, Bowell became the first Minister of Trade and Commerce, a powerful position.

Though he was nearly 70 years old, he plunged into his job and did it well. He even explored new ideas, like running a telegraph cable through the ocean to Australia and expanding international trade. He lacked others' brains, but wasn't a fool. A journalist wrote that "few men in the House hit harder, quicker and more effectively; few men see the weakness in the enemy's position more keenly."

His close relationship with the brilliant Thompson, a strong Catholic, showed his maturity. They became friends, took holidays together, and trusted each other. When the younger man died, Bowell cried. He said: "A man of broader views, a man of keener intellect, or a man who dared to treat all classes of the community more equally, never, I believe, lived in Canada." He now admired people like that.

Bowell versus the Sourpusses

Thompson's cruel death created a huge problem. Sir Charles Tupper still didn't want to be Prime Minister and was disliked by many anyway. So who could take over? No one stood out. "Here we are," said Finance Minister Sir George Foster, "twelve of us, and every one of us as bad, or as good as the other." Finally the Governor General decided on . . . Mackenzie Bowell. He was 71 years old and now not even an elected Member of Parliament; instead, he sat in the Senate as leader.

He wasn't a popular choice. Though others didn't strongly dislike him, they didn't think much of him as boss either. He, of course, was thrilled, and returned home to Belleville for Christmas to adoring crowds.

But right from the beginning things went terribly wrong. His cabinet thought their new leader was full of himself, and whether that was true or they were just jealous, resentment boiled. During their first meeting it was decided that an election was needed, and Bowell agreed. Then he changed his mind and went back to Parliament to gain popularity. Cabinet felt double-crossed, and fumed.

There were all sorts of other problems: labour strikes, Newfoundland deciding against entering Canada, and the Governor General (who at first considered Bowell a "good and straight man") complaining that his old PM wasn't keeping him informed.

The biggest problem he faced was one that Macdonald, Abbott, and Thompson hadn't solved, and that Laurier later "fixed" with a Band-Aid. It was the Manitoba Schools Question. Riel and Macdonald had made a deal that protected the French language and Catholic schools in little Manitoba. But now there were 150,000 people there and only 10 percent were Catholic, so Manitoba abolished French as an official language and stopped giving money to Catholic schools. French Canada and the Catholic Church complained bitterly.

Of course, everyone thought the sour old Orangeman would put his sword into Catholic hopes. But the slowly changing Bowell surprised everyone. He decided that since his enemy Riel and his mentor Macdonald had legally given Catholics their rights, they should keep them. It was a matter of principle. He would no longer be prejudiced. He got ready to bring Catholic schools back to Manitoba.

French Catholics were overjoyed, English Canada was aghast, and Bowell's cabinet couldn't believe it. Chaos reigned in the party. As Bowell was laughed at in cartoons for siding with the enemy, Conservative heavyweights plotted against the "leader who couldn't lead." To them, Bowell was confused and in way over his head. Cabinet Minister Charles Tupper, Jr. and others secretly asked Tupper, Sr. to take control of a sinking ship. The Prime Minister didn't see the noose tightening around his neck. Then, on January 4, 1896, seven Ministers went to his office and shocked him out of his boots. They all resigned. They hoped he would too. Nothing like this had happened before. "Political Assassination!" shouted *The Toronto Star*.

The next session of Parliament was very dramatic. The galleries were packed when the Finance Minister stood in the House and told the nation that cabinet no longer had confidence in Bowell's leadership. There was dead silence. Then Bowell rose and walked over to the front row of the Opposition. He shook their hands, saying it was good to "shake hands with honest men after being in the company of traitors for months."

When he addressed the Senate he nearly broke down. He knew he wasn't a brilliant man, but had worked hard for what he had and felt betrayed. He defended his right to be Prime Minister, saying there must be "something in this grey old head of mine that justifies my rising to a position of that kind." Many were clinging to unreasonable views about religion and leadership, just as he once had. He knew it wasn't good for Canada. A nation that wants to be great, said the former bigot, "must respect individual opinions."

He resigned. But the Governor General liked him more than the "nest of traitors" who had betrayed him and asked him to stay. So he tried to hang on for a while. But on April 27, 1896, he handed the burden to Tupper. He was the only PM ever forced out.

Outliving Them All

Bowell went home to Belleville, but he didn't sulk or hold grudges. It wasn't in him to pity himself—he never had in his hard, remarkable life. He fought for the Conservatives in the Senate for another decade, finally retiring in 1906 in his 83rd year.

At home he took over *The Intelligencer* again, became involved in businesses, and grew a big garden, happy to have dirty hands once more. He was often seen working there in his wide-brimmed straw hat, as strong as ever. At age 89, an energetic, white-bearded little man, he drew a thunderous ovation when he spoke in a Masonic Hall. As late as 1911, he rushed to the Conservatives' aid during elections. He remained fit, maybe the fittest of all Prime Ministers. In his 90s he visited the north, as he'd often done before, and swam in the Yukon River.

Two-and-a-half weeks short of his 96th birthday, Mackenzie Bowell died in Belleville. It was December 10, 1917, *50 years* after Confederation.

"I hope," he said in his old age, "the time is fast approaching in Canada when we shall never hear the question raised of the place of a man's birth, or the creed he possesses." He had come a long way from the little village in England, to Belleville, through the Orange Lodge, Parliament, the Prime Minister's job, and on past. He had begun as Scrooge, but died a much better man. Canada had made him tolerant.

The Legendary Warhorse

SIR CHARLES TUPPER

Born Amherst, Nova Scotia 1821, died England 1915, Conservative. PM: May–July 1896

Sir Charles Tupper ran Canada for 10 weeks, the shortest rule ever. But that says nothing about him. He was a giant personality in Canadian history, one of the toughest and loudest this country has ever seen. No one could *really* defeat him: not a Liberal, a Conservative, a scandal, or even a two-fisted sailor. Joseph Howe? No problem. George Brown? Make me laugh. Mackenzie Bowell? Get real. Wilfrid Laurier? Bring him on! Even God took a long time to finish off Charles Tupper.

Kicking Butt as a Kid

He began life in little Amherst, Nova Scotia, on July 2, 1821, the son of a strict Baptist minister, and right from childhood had brains galore and lots of confidence. His father demanded that his two sons love learning. He paid them for every page of the Latin Reader they translated, and made Charles read the Bible through at age seven. When the boy did lessons at tough Amherst Grammar School, he towered over other kids, and knew it.

At age 12, he built a boat out of a hollowed-out log and began to pilot it down a river with his brother. It flipped over. Charles hauled himself up onto the capsized vessel, reached down, seized his brother, and threw him up on deck too. Knowing that their mother would skin them for this sin, they stripped and left their clothes in the sun to dry. Mother Tupper never suspected a thing.

He wanted to be a doctor, and by age 17 was apprenticed to Dr. Harding in Windsor. There he got to do things like watch the amputation of an Indian's leg. Then he happily experimented on it, until natives asked him to bury the severed limb because their friend might miss it in the great beyond.

In 1840, at age 19, he went to Scotland to study medicine at the University of Edinburgh, an education beyond most pastors' sons. Either an uncle or a girlfriend gave him the money. Legend says it was a beautiful young lady whom he promised to marry, but later refused. He always denied the story, but the ladies definitely had an eye for him and he for them . . . even after he married.

His ocean voyage was very much in the Tupper style. He travelled on a little boat stacked with lumber and seven passengers, most of them salty sailors. The mate, named Brown, was a tough, sea-going guy who loved to smoke. But Tupper wanted to read his Bible and asked him to butt out. Brown refused. So . . . Tupper slugged him. Brown wasn't pleased. "He sprang on me like a tiger and clinched me. He was a much heavier man than I but I brought into requisition the hip-lock . . . and brought him down on his head and shoulders under me; but as we were at the edge of the top rail of the deck, and the slightest movement would send us both overboard, I rolled over, which brought Brown on top. With my left arm around his neck, I pinned his face to the deck, and with my right fist paid attention to his ribs."

After that, he recalled, "Mr. Brown gave me a wide berth. . . ."

He spent three years in Scotland and loved it, not only getting a good education, but visiting Europe and sampling the theatre and whisky. When a businessman gave him money to visit Paris hospitals, he took the man's "very interesting" daughters to parties.

He returned to Amherst, a supremely confident, neatly dressed, stocky young doctor with brown hair parted perfectly on the side and huge sideburns growing down his cheeks.

Well-muscled, chest always out and stomach in, his big voice boomed as though it were projected through a loudspeaker. He raced around the countryside on horseback, medical bag in hand, always sure of his skill. Though there were no painkillers in those days, Tupper never shied away from extreme measures. Once he treated a woman who had cancer in her leg by cutting it off at the hip, and saving her life.

In 1846 he married Frances Morse, from a prominent Amherst family. They would have six children. Connections to noted people were important to him. In the future, he would give political jobs to his many friends. When he was attacked for it, he simply turned on his accusers and attacked them.

Getting into the Game

Tupper was interested in politics from an early age, and developed a dislike for the province's legendary Liberal politician, Joseph Howe. When that wickedly brilliant speaker came to Tupper's Cumberland County in 1852, the young man confronted him. "Let us hear the little doctor by all means," said nasty old Howe. "I would not be any more affected by anything he might say than by the mewing of yonder kitten." But he was. Tupper seemed nervous, a youth of quick movements (the first 20 years of his political career he threw up before every appearance), but once he stood, he sailed. That day in 1852, he launched cannonballs at Howe, shocking him and delighting the crowd.

Three years later Howe came back to Cumberland to get elected. He hadn't been defeated in nearly two decades of politics. But Charles Tupper, the "Warhorse of Cumberland," ran against him and crushed him.

Tupper's influence in the Nova Scotia Assembly grew from the moment he entered it. He forced his Conservatives to favour ideas like putting money into railways. But the Liberals remained in power, and after the 1859 election, Howe became Premier. Tupper fought him like a pit bull terrier. The older man could barely believe it. "When time shall have mellowed his character . . . he will come perhaps to feel that to stand up and blast the reputation of a human being is not a political virtue." But Tupper would never change his tune. And Howe should have known better, for he was an expert blaster himself.

In 1863 the Conservatives became the government, and the following year their leader retired. Into his shoes stepped Dr. Charles Tupper, Premier for the next three years, some of the most amazing in Nova Scotia history.

He went a million kilometres an hour, moving his practice to Halifax and expanding it, becoming City Medical Officer and first president of the Canadian Medical Association. But his greatest pursuit was Canada—Confederation was in the air and Tupper almost single-handedly dragged Nova Scotia into it, kicking and screaming.

He spoke favourably of a British North American federation as early as 1860, helped lead the Maritime union movement, and then played a key role at all three Confederation conferences. But many at home believed that Nova Scotia would lose tax money by joining Canada and get little in return. At the helm of the opposition was Joseph Howe.

Premier Tupper schemed, delayed a vote on Confederation, and then, on April 17, as troops marched through Halifax to board ships to fight the Fenians (invading from the United States), he acted. With fear in the air and an alliance with Canada looking temporarily attractive, he engineered a debate in the Legislature that went into the early morning, and forced through an agreement that gave him permission to negotiate Confederation. Howe screamed that it was done at "black midnight." Nevertheless it was done. Then Tupper went to London and finished the job.

In the 1867 national election, every Nova Scotian candidate who supported union lost, except Tupper. The people stayed against it for many years—it took all the efforts of Tupper, Macdonald, and a good deal of money to keep Nova Scotia in Canada.

Tupper purposely stayed out of Macdonald's first cabinet, to wait for the right time to make his mark on the national scene. Then he tackled problems for Sir John A. His style was to meet things head on with plain words. So, rather than quietly trying to persuade Howe to get on board with Canada, he simply tracked him down and argued. Howe had won a

seat in the election too, and Tupper convinced him to join the
cabinet. That was how Joseph Howe became a friend of
Confederation.

Bring It On

In 1869 he knocked on another door: Louis Riel's. Tupper's
daughter Emma and her soldier husband had gone west with
William McDougall on his trip to take Manitoba. When Riel's
armed men stopped them, they took Emma's luggage and
her husband. Most Canadians feared the Wild West, with its
gun-toting Métis and natives and wilderness, but not Charles
Tupper. Off he went in the middle of winter, first by railroad,
then dogsled, and finally on foot through snowstorms. He
scoffed at the danger. Heck, he needed his daughter's luggage
(not to mention her husband). Before long he was banging on
Riel's door at Fort Garry. Armed Métis, looking tough, let him
in. He walked up to Riel, told him who he was, and politely
asked for suitcases and son-in-law. Riel said okay. Tupper also
told a Riel advisor that if the Métis were peaceful, Canada would
negotiate a deal they would like. Later, he was informed that
the Métis had wanted to lynch him. But he advised Macdonald
to send a reasonable politician to talk with Riel and avoid
bloodshed. That might have been the solution to what turned
out to be a terrible mess. "He was in the country for about two
days," said Sir John A., "and did more good than anyone else."

Over the next two decades Tupper became the second most important Conservative. He would hold many cabinet posts, including Minister of Finance. He also spent 11 years as High Commissioner to London, a job he adored, far from political battle, living among the British elite, making more money than the PM ($10,000 compared with $8,000).

Perhaps the biggest of all his projects was the Canadian Pacific Railway. During the nasty Pacific Scandal that brought down Macdonald and helped kill Cartier, he defended his allies like a heavyweight boxer. The evidence grew in mountains against his friends, but he loudly dismissed the "Pacific slander." There was no wrongdoing that he could see! By the early 1880s, the Conservatives back in power, he was asked to complete the historic project. It was a massive undertaking and money kept running out, but bulldog Tupper forced it through. "Sir John A. Macdonald steered the ship of state," someone said, "while Tupper provided the wind."

In the House of Commons, there was no one like him. An opponent remembered him as "broad shouldered [and] vigorous looking. . . . He always spoke from a full chest and with a splendid volume of voice and wrestled with his subject as a strong man would wrestle in an amphitheatre." He never made jokes. "Sir Charles Tupper [was] the most fearless combatant that ever sat in the Parliament of Canada."

In 1884 he got into trouble for illegally holding both the London High Commissioner's job and a cabinet post, and was shipped to England for a long stay. He and Macdonald

weren't getting along then anyway. Tupper had been handing
railway cases to his son (and Macdonald's) in a Winnipeg law
office. John A. thought he should at least hide it a bit. Tupper
could care less about hiding anything.

As Macdonald aged, he kept calling Tupper back to help him
win elections. Each time, Tupper would kick some butt, help out
for a while in cabinet, and then go back to London. But finally,
in 1891, after they fought their seventh election together,
Macdonald was gone. Tupper was at the front of the line to be
Prime Minister. But he preferred his wonderful, high-paying
London job. Anyway, his rough style had made enemies.

So, he stayed away while caretaker Abbott ruled, and then
Thompson. When Thompson suddenly died, it again seemed
natural to hand the leadership to the "warhorse." But he still
wasn't interested.

So Mackenzie Bowell, ill-equipped to be Prime Minister
and with opponents in a bickering cabinet, became the boss.
He didn't last, of course, and finally, there was no other choice
but to ask the man who probably should have been leader long
before.

Taking the Throne

Oh, all right, I'll be Prime Minister, said Sir Charles. "I was
reluctantly induced to come to the rescue," he boasted. He
arrived, 74 years old but as fit as a racehorse, and whipped the

cabinet into shape and faced that young pup, Wilfrid Laurier. He still had his famous sideburns, a wide, scowling face, and a thick head of hair. First he had to defend the policy of forcing Manitoba to allow Catholic schools. It was a weird position for a Conservative, but he took it on. An election was called, featuring the English Protestant Tupper for French Catholics, and the French-Catholic Laurier against them.

Tupper fought like a battering ram, of course. One day he faced a pro-Liberal crowd at Toronto's Massey Hall, who shouted "I, I, I" at him for his legendary pride. Meanwhile, downstairs, a friend suffered a heart attack and died on a table. When told, his expression never even changed. At another crowd he snapped, "You men who are making these interruptions are the most block-headed set of cowards that I have ever looked upon."

And when the election was over, his government 20 seats behind Laurier's Liberals, he wouldn't admit to losing. Usually, the defeated PM visited the Governor General to resign. Tupper came to argue! It was his 75th birthday, July 2, 1896. "The plucky old thing," recalled Lady Aberdeen, arrived "blooming in a white waistcoat and seemingly as pleased with himself as ever. . . . Down he sat and for an hour and a half harangued His Excellency." He wanted the election recounted. But finally, on July 8, he resigned.

He stayed on as leader and fought another election. That year, 1900, he lost his own seat, his first in 13 battles. He was almost 80, one year short of his 60th year in politics.

He spent most of his remaining days in England, at his beloved Bexley Heath mansion, though he often came back to Canada. In his early 90s he lived in Victoria for a while with his son, pronouncing on politics and taking on all comers. He wrote a highly opinionated book about his life. Long since knighted, he was made a baron. A reporter who saw him in B.C. said that he was active, never dwelled on the past, and loved to "take a motor drive to enjoy the ocean breezes and survey the magic growth of Greater Vancouver."

In 1913 he bid farewell to Canada, taking a cross-country tour from west to east and, at 92, receiving a massive goodbye in Amherst. Even Prime Minister Borden came to see him off to England.

He died at his mansion two years later, age 94. He had missed his many long-dead friends. Macdonald had been gone for a quarter of a century. Around him were motor cars, flying machines, a world war, and news of a thriving Canada he had helped father.

His body was sent back to Nova Scotia and he was buried with full state honours in Halifax. Tributes came from all over. "He had courage for any crisis," said *The Times of London,* "a splendid audacity in the face of the most formidable opposition." *The Globe* called him "a thunderer in debate." Laurier said that "next to Macdonald [he was] the man who did most to bring Canada into Confederation."

Long ago, during his first speech in the Nova Scotia Assembly, he had barked, "I did not come here to play the game of follow my leader." He sure hadn't. Sir Charles Tupper, the legendary warhorse, was absolutely unique.

7th Prime Minister

The Magnificent One (Le Magnifique)

SIR WILFRID LAURIER

*Born St. Lin, Canada East
1841, died Ottawa 1919,
Liberal. PM: 1896–1911*

Laurier. It is a legendary Canadian name, in both official languages. Some say he is our greatest figure, a leader as respected in his time as any on earth. He believed that Canada could be the best nation in the world, and that English and French could live together in harmony. But others' inability to get past petty differences often disappointed him, and would today. He towers above our history like a father, showing us what we should be.

"Don't Forget That Face"

Like Cartier, the only previous French Canadian to rival him, he traced his roots back to New France. In 1642 Augustin Hébert crossed the ocean from France to settle near the abandoned Indian village of Hochelaga. Hébert was killed by the swing of an Iroquois tomahawk, but his family stayed, Montreal grew around them, and one married a man named Champlaurier, who later dropped the first five letters of his name. They moved northward, and by the early 1800s Charles Laurier was farming in the hilly, wooded St. Lin area, a horse ride north of the city.

Charles's son Carolus was a happy-go-lucky sort, who only got excited about politics. The Lauriers were "Rouges," followers of the great Papineau, who led the 1837 rebellion. They supported French rights and stood up to the powerful Catholic Church.

Carolus's wife Marcelle loved books, music, and art. When she gave birth to a boy on November 20, 1841, she named him Wilfrid, after a romantic character in a novel by Scottish writer Sir Walter Scott. It told of noble knights, which was fitting. This boy would be a Canadian hero.

His loving mother died when he was just seven, and his handsome father, who had to flee ladies who pressed near him in his church pew, married his maid Adeline.

The liberal-minded Carolus wanted his son's mind to expand, so he took an unusual step. After the boy's three years at a little Catholic school across the road, he was sent to live with a Scottish-Canadian family at nearby New Glasgow. There he learned English, which he spoke with a slight Scottish accent for the rest of his life.

The family then sent him to L'Assomption, a respected French-Catholic school, where he studied until age 19. He had to rise at five-thirty in the morning and be in bed at eight. But the discipline was good for him. He was near the top of his class in everything: a tall, slim young leader with curly brown hair, marked for an amazing future.

By 1861 Laurier was at McGill University in Montreal, studying law. He worked for a professor there and lived with Dr. Gauthier's family, where he fell in love with their piano teacher, Zoë Lafontaine, a clever young woman, small and pretty, with brown hair and big eyes. The house was open to everyone at all hours and Laurier's political friends often dropped by to debate and have fun. Among them was Antoine Dorion, once co-Premier of the Canadas. They talked about Confederation, a plan they despised—the huge new nation would swamp Quebec and drown their beloved French language.

Though he and Zoë wouldn't admit it, they drew closer every day, often sitting at the piano together, singing into the early hours of the morning.

But things began to cool when his parents moved into the city and he went to live with them. He couldn't see Zoë every day any more, a terrible cough troubled him, and his law career slowed. He had opened a firm with two college friends, then with a single partner. This new man was impressed. He told others that Laurier was a "poet, an orator, a philosopher . . . he will be heard of. Don't forget that face." But in October 1866, exhausted from work, Laurier suddenly collapsed, coughing up blood. Not yet 25, a doctor predicted that he wouldn't live 10 years.

In 1866 he moved to the little town of L'Avenir, east of Montreal, to take over the Rouge newspaper *Le Défricheur* (The Pioneer) and a law practice. But not long after, he fell for a village to the northeast named Arthabaska. He liked its beautiful homes and lazy pace, and found a little wooden building for his law office and newspaper press.

Soon he was set up there and making a reputation for himself with his paper. Writing against religion meddling in politics, and Confederation, he not only felt the scorn of George-Étienne Cartier, but also Catholic leaders. Laurier was frowned upon in the street and lectured by the local bishop. "Authority derives from God," thundered the Church.

Then, in May 1868, a telegram summoned him back to Dr. Gauthier's house in Montreal. "Come at once. A matter of urgent importance," it said. Zoë Lafontaine, who was about to wed another man, had been crying every day for Laurier. And the doctor was sick of it. Wilfrid was instructed to tend to her! Within days they were married.

Laurier had been so ill the previous year he had closed down his newspaper. But now, his new wife with him, he turned to law and politics.

The Ascension

In 1871, after an aggressive sermon from the local priest, Laurier was presented on the church lawn as the next Rouge (Liberal) candidate for the Quebec Legislature. Both the party and Laurier felt the Catholic Church was dominating Quebec. They wanted that changed. Laurier won the election, but soon found provincial politics boring. He wanted a bigger playing field, a place where he could explore the ideas he discussed with friends and read about during his hours engrossed in books.

He was sick in bed in 1873 when a Liberal committee came to ask if he would run against Sir John A. Macdonald's scandal-plagued Conservatives in the next national election. Zoë feared for his health, so he tried not to meet her eyes, and agreed.

He came to Ottawa a country boy, knowing little about life outside Quebec, a pale, slim, clean-shaven six-footer. But he would make an impressive debut that March of 1874, replying to the throne speech in French. He was quiet and serious, but eloquent.

Everyone, though, even Macdonald and Alexander Mackenzie, was overshadowed by someone else that week. Louis Riel, the Manitoba rebel, heavily bearded and wary, appeared in Ottawa, signed in as an elected Member, and then vanished. There was an uproar. The English wanted him kicked out and then hunted down; the French hoped he would take his seat. Laurier sided with Quebec. But his position wasn't simple. He had met Riel and found him informed about politics and history, but a self-centred "manipulator" who turned weird when raving about religion. However, he thought Riel's cause was just—the government had ignored and abused the Métis people and were at fault for their Manitoba rebellion. Laurier would play a role in the passionate Riel debates to come.

In Ottawa, he gained the big-bearded Mackenzie's respect, especially after a dramatic speech he delivered in Quebec City in June 1877. It shone a national spotlight on him and showed he had the stuff to be a Canadian leader. In it, he warned the Church to stay out of the country's affairs and announced that he now proudly considered himself part of "the government of the Queen of England."

Soon Laurier was elevated to the cabinet. The whole, worried force of the Conservative party turned on this rising star and defeated him in an Arthabaska election. No problem—he got himself elected in Quebec City. "I have unfurled the Liberal standard," he proclaimed, "above the ancient citadel of Quebec."

His success was short-lived. In 1878 Macdonald and the Conservatives returned to power, Mackenzie soon resigned, and Edward Blake became Liberal leader. For a time, uninspired in Opposition, Wilfred became known as "Lazy Laurier," seldom using his brilliant voice, even after he became Blake's trusted advisor and sat in the front row beside him. He fed information to the brainy Toronto lawyer from stacks of papers he kept on his desk, but rarely mounted the stage himself.

It took Riel's reappearance to light a fire in him. And a huge fire it was.

In 1885, when Riel, the Métis, and native peoples became involved in armed conflict with Canada, Laurier insisted that it should never have come to that—the fault lay with the uncaring Conservatives. And when Riel was hanged, Laurier rose in fury, angry at English Canada's inability to compromise with the French. On November 22, he shouted to masses gathered in Montreal, "Had I been born on the banks of the Saskatchewan I would myself have shouldered a musket to fight." Those words were identified with him forever. He stood by them, though at times he found them difficult to defend.

Blake was considered a genius, but he wasn't very warm or a great leader. He lost two elections to Macdonald and by 1887 wanted to resign. All sorts of successors were suggested, but when party members asked Blake what he thought, he shocked them. "There is only one possible choice," he said, "Laurier."

Becoming a Legend

Montreal's *La Minerve* said it was "the replacing of a giant with a pygmy," and for a while it seemed true. Laurier struggled to form solid Liberal positions and considered the idea of close trading ties with the United States. In the 1891 election old Macdonald tore that idea to pieces by making it seem like a move towards union with the Americans.

But there were signs of Laurier's future greatness. Against the advice of his party, he went to Toronto, in the heart of English Canada, where he silenced a loud, anti-French crowd with his eloquence and in the end made them cheer. Then Macdonald's death, followed by the quick reigns of Abbott, poor young Thompson, Bowell, and finally Tupper, played into the Liberals' hands. When 1896 came and the government still had to deal with the tricky Manitoba Catholic schools problem, Laurier saw his chance. An election loomed.

He was banking on Quebec votes. Among his many foes there, the biggest was Henri Bourassa, a former friend and editor of the powerful Montreal paper *Le Devoir*. This dark, short-haired, moustached man was tough, brilliant, and on his way to legendary status. Over the next two decades he fought Laurier at every turn, saying that he would never be silent if the French language and anything Québécois was ever in danger. "For me," Laurier replied, "the safety of the French race is not in isolation but in the struggle."

Laurier had learned how to play the game of Canadian politics. He understood that to govern this unusual, "dual" country you had to compromise and be practical, not extreme. During the election he told the Canadian public that the two sides of the Manitoba Schools Question reminded him of Aesop's fable about the wind and the sun, each trying in its own way to get a man to take off his coat. The Conservatives were being windy, while he chose "the sunny way." No one was sure what that meant. That was fine with him. It *was* clear that he wanted Catholic education in Manitoba, but wouldn't force it on anyone.

In the 1896 election he easily won Quebec, split Ontario, and marched into power. He was the first French-Canadian Prime Minister and would hold office for the longest uninterrupted reign in history. He was now a confirmed "Canadian." He opposed the extreme English with as much force as the aggressive French.

His 15 years in power stretched over three more election victories: in 1900 (when he finished off Tupper), 1904, and 1908. The country grew as never before, a nation on the verge of greatness led by an elegant man with long, flowing white hair, who became a bigger international star every year. Canada added two million people and its wealth surged. He solved the Manitoba school problem by allowing some Catholic education, then welcomed the new provinces of Saskatchewan and Alberta. Cities like Winnipeg, Edmonton, Calgary, and Vancouver ascended, and Canadian wheat, produced in the millions of bushels, was sent out to the world. He built another nationwide railway, formed the departments of Labour and External Affairs, created the Yukon Territory, watched over the gold rush, and tried to bring Canada's first navy into existence. In England he attended Imperial conferences and surprised the British by refusing to knuckle under as Canadians had in the past. He wouldn't join the Imperial Council if Canada had little power and wouldn't give up money and men to the Empire army. "For the first time on record," said the *London Daily Mail*, "a politician of our New World has been recognized as the equal of the great men of the Old Country."

At home the nation was proud of him. He toured the western provinces to see the new Canada and was met by huge crowds, drawn by the legend of Laurier. He believed that within a generation Canada could reach 60 million people, and made one of the most famous statements in our history when he said "The 20th century shall be the century of Canada." For a while it seemed as though it might be true. But of course, being Canada, no one was completely happy.

Defeat of the Giant

Throughout his career he had to fight many opponents. He stood bravely in the middle, a Canadian while others fell back on being French or English, Eastern or Western, Protestant or Catholic. He said that when the races were finally at peace, "I shall attend them bearing with me my Canadian nationality."

Extremists took turns against Laurier's national stance. And they drew great crowds to hear their narrow views. In Quebec, enemies vowed to bring him down. They said he failed to favour their interests and now spoke French with an English accent. If anything, the prejudice was worse in Ontario, where a movement tried to stop any kind of French or Catholic teaching. At times it frustrated Laurier to the point of quitting.

But he remained, sure of his middle ground. "I am branded in Quebec as a traitor to the French and in Ontario as a traitor to the English," he said. "I am neither. I am a Canadian. Canada has been the inspiration of my life."

As the years stretched on, he neared the age of 70. At times his health was in peril. On one return from Europe he looked so much like a skeleton that Robert Borden, the new Conservative leader, was shocked and had to look away. But like Macdonald, the great man he strangely resembled, he kept getting back on his feet.

In 1910, he toured the West again. There were big cheers, and moments that showed the love of this childless man for Canada and its young. Once, he was found alone playing ball with a child at a railway station. Another time, he stopped in mid-speech because he noticed a kid leaning dangerously out an upper-storey window. He pointed and asked, "Is that little one safe?" In Saskatoon he stopped to buy a paper from a newsboy and found the lad full of political ideas. He set aside his schedule to take time to talk. It was the kid who ended their chat. "Well, Mr. Prime Minister," he said, "I can't waste any more time. I have to deliver my papers." His name was John Diefenbaker.

Despite all the praise, Laurier feared his time as leader was coming to an end. He would often tell roaring English-Canadian crowds, "You cheer for me, but you don't vote for me."

He believed that Canada could now afford a closer connection with the Americans, that the old idea of free trade with them was a good policy. But it would bring him down. In the 1911 election, Borden and the Conservatives convinced the nation that free trade would mean eventual union with the dreaded Yankees. And so, finally, Laurier lost.

At first he was devastated. He didn't show it, but when he came home the day after the election, he sent Zoë off to bed, had a quiet meal, then lowered his head and cried.

But Laurier was never down for long, and for eight more years, until the age of 77, he led the Liberals. He considered handing the job to someone and had noticed young William Lyon Mackenzie King, grandson of the famous Ontario rebel. He made him Minister of Labour and predicted that he would one day be a leader. But Laurier would never quit.

In many ways it was a terrible eight years. In 1914 the First World War began, in 1916 his beloved Parliament burned down, and the nation was split by Conservative attempts to force all healthy men to fight in the war. Laurier stood tall as a defender of Canada, England, and France the minute the war was declared. Many others predicted a short conflict. But he knew that "it would stagger the world with its magnitude and horror."

As the war continued, he nobly allowed the government to stay in power without elections. The Conservatives ruled for six straight years. He toured Quebec, battling Bourassa, who considered the war a British one. Laurier opposed forced military service (called "conscription"), and tirelessly asked for more volunteers. Most Quebeckers hated the idea of being forced into the army. Many English Liberals, meanwhile, deserted Laurier to join Borden in a new wartime "Union" government that supported conscription. And so, as a December 1917 election drew near, Laurier knew, sadly, what would happen: "English will be pitted against French and French against English and there will follow years of bitterness."

The Immortal Canadian

And he was right. He was swamped in the election, taking almost all of Quebec and little else. When the government was formed not a single Québécois was in the cabinet, the country in the middle of war. "Canada is a difficult country to govern," he said.

But even past 75, he rallied the Liberals. As 1919 began and the war ended, calming things, they were re-forming, and remembering his greatness. King, always loyal, hovered nearby, the future in an unusual little fat man. "Laurier is a Liberal," said one Quebecker, "a Canadian patriot—above all, he is Laurier." He had been a Member of Parliament for 45 straight years. "The unity of the people is the secret of the future," he insisted. And they knew he was right.

But then, on a sunny February day in 1919, he was working in his office when he suddenly fainted. He struck his head on his desk as he fell. Somehow he got to his feet and took a streetcar home. There he collapsed again. Zoë stayed nervously near his bed and asked if he needed a priest to deliver last rites. He said he was fine. But a third stroke came. He took her hand, gave it a warm squeeze, said "C'est fini," and died.

The nation mourned perhaps unlike ever before. All the seats except his were removed from Parliament and his casket placed there. Fifty thousand Canadians came to see him in a long line that didn't end for 48 hours. When he was buried, more than 100,000 filled the streets, the service was read in English and French so that all could understand, and he was laid to rest, not in Quebec or Ontario proper, but in the nation's capital.

His effect on this country will be felt forever. Growing from a narrow point of view to a bigger, kinder one, he showed the world what it was to be Canadian. Not long before he died, he said in his "silvery" voice with its strange mixture of French and Scottish accents: "Let me tell you that for the solution of these problems you have a safe guide, an unfailing light, if you remember . . . love is better than hate."

8th Prime Minister

Salt of the Earth

SIR ROBERT BORDEN

*Born Grand Pré, Nova Scotia
1854, died Ottawa 1937,
Conservative. PM: 1911–1920
(L: Robert Borden,
R: Winston Churchill)*

That guy looking back at you from the $100 bill is Rob Borden. He seems awfully distinguished with his handsome face, grey-white hair parted neatly in the middle, and perfect dark moustache. But he wasn't—not always, at least. He began as a farm boy who couldn't even build a load of hay. When he made his first great speech in the House of Commons he missed the chair when he tried to sit and smashed his wire-rimmed glasses. Several times he had to hold off mutiny in his party. Yet he led the Dominion strongly through the First World War and forced the world to recognize Canada as a mature nation. His passion was for what was right as he saw it, not for fame. He was worth a hundred bucks any day.

Setting Goals

Grand Pré, Nova Scotia, is a village in one of the most beautiful parts of Canada. It overlooks the Annapolis Valley, where sweet fruit grows on rich soil and the waves of the Bay of Fundy crash against the shore. On June 26, 1854, Robert Laird Borden was born there, the son of an easygoing farmer and his energetic wife. Grandfather Laird had been the area's schoolteacher, so the boy took up that profession at age 14. He had gone to the village's private academy for just five years, a hard-working student who read all the great books in his family's library and accepted his mother's belief that discipline, sweat, and ambition would make him successful. Assistant school master wasn't a big job, but it was better than picking stones in a hay field.

He loved to write things down, noting what he had accomplished and what he hoped to do. There were many goals to be met. He was shy and knew he'd have to push himself.

At 19 he went to the United States to teach classic literature and mathematics in New Jersey. But long, boring days crept by, making him feel as though he wasn't getting where he wanted to go. So, he set his ambition on a better job. He went home, built a few more hay loads that fell apart, then headed to Halifax to become a lawyer. It was 1874.

Halifax was a grimy port town of 30,000 people. Two future prime ministers, the brilliant John Thompson and the tough Sir Charles Tupper, had begun their rise to fame there. Quiet and nervous Rob Borden, with his neatly parted brown hair, glasses, thin moustache, and wispy sideburns, hardly seemed capable of following in their footsteps. He found a position with a well-connected Liberal law firm and settled in to four years of small jobs while others got the glory and money.

But in 1878 he passed the exams that made him a full-fledged lawyer, standing first in his class (well ahead of even Charles Hibbert Tupper, son of the legend).

Eighteen years of success in the law business followed, growing slowly and built upon his belief in preparing well and using his teacher's skills to excel in court. But even with these weapons he had problems at first. Before trials, "I would be in a condition of such extreme nervous tension that I could hardly eat or sleep." Only hard-won self-control, and the drive he inherited from his mother, pushed him forward. By 1882 he had joined Thompson's firm, with C.H. Tupper, and did so well there that five years later the boss asked him to become Canada's deputy Minister of Justice. A promotion within the firm kept him from accepting.

The late '80s and early '90s brought even more success. Still young, he often took cases to the Supreme Court of Canada, and spent Ottawa days dining with cabinet ministers like young Tupper and with Prime Minister Thompson.

In the mid-'80s Borden had met Laura Bond, an attractive brunette whose father owned a Halifax hardware store. She was smart and lively, liked theatre and music, and loved to play tennis and golf, just like Rob. On September 25, 1889, they began 48 years of happy marriage. They bought a big house close to Sir Charles in a ritzy suburb and lived the good life. Rob's firm grew into the largest in the Maritimes, and he into one of eastern Canada's best lawyers. He checked off many goals set long ago.

Then everything changed. Politics was the villain. He entered that world of rogues and characters, power and fame, heartache and hatred.

The Big League Beckons

It began innocently enough, at a dinner at the Tuppers' house. It was April 27, 1896, the day Sir Mackenzie Bowell resigned as Prime Minister of Canada and Sir Charles took the helm. The great man had watched Borden maturing. He needed new blood in his party, and knew that if *he* asked, the young man could hardly refuse.

He was an unusual recruit, having rarely thought of being a politician until he was asked, and not holding strong party loyalties. In fact, he thought them unimportant. Opinions were right or wrong—it didn't matter what party held them, or what the French or English, or Catholics or Protestants, thought of them. A politician should simply do what was right.

After winning an election three days before his 42nd birthday, he became a Member of Parliament, a Conservative in Opposition. He sat on a backbench, distant from the action and from Tupper and other booming cannons of the party. Across the aisle was a friendly, growing legend, the charismatic Prime Minister Wilfrid Laurier.

Rob took a while to get going. He didn't speak much in Parliament, and when he did it was usually about his city. He worked hard behind the scenes in committees and showed skill at organization and forming ideas. He stayed at a boarding house, worried about his health (and always would), suffered from bad nerves and indigestion, and rode his bicycle through the muddy Ottawa streets to the imposing House of Commons.

Things started to change about 1899. He began speaking more, became aware of Tupper's trust in him, and moved up to a front bench to sit with rising Quebecker Frederick Monk. But never in his wildest dreams could he have anticipated what happened next.

Near the Top

On November 7, 1900, Borden was re-elected, a slightly more forceful figure on the speaking platform. The party wasn't as successful. Not only did they lose badly, but old Tupper was dumped in his own riding. So, the Conservatives needed a new leader. There were many veterans available, hard old guys who would nearly kill to get the job as the party's boss.

Tupper, who didn't care how tough anyone was, had a surprise for them. In early February 1901 he placed young Robert Borden at the head of the grand old party of Sir John A. Macdonald, and no one, despite their many doubts, dared to stop him.

Borden would suffer through a decade of leading His Majesty's Loyal Opposition. It confirmed his feeling that politics was an "infernal life." At first he moved cautiously and looked unsure, unlike a leader. He appointed Monk as his Quebec boss, then fired him. Instead of embracing tons of Canadian immigrants like Laurier, he worried about the "quality" of new citizens, even taking the racist stance that some Asians and Eastern Europeans were too foreign for our society. And yet he was a champion of rising above race. "I think we are all content to be Canadians," he said. "It is not of any importance that we should look back and say that our ancestors were English or Irish or Scotch. It only tends to keep alive ideas which really have no useful place in the life of this country."

He entered the 1904 election thinking he had turned things around and had a chance to win. He attacked the government for corruption, taking pride in his own clean political ways. But he was uninspiring, his policies lit no fires, and the

Liberals and the superb Laurier, lifted by a country growing in leaps and bounds, crushed him. Borden was not only whipped throughout Canada, but lost his own seat and was accused of being part of a scandal. He felt humiliated. How could a leader, soiled and unable to even win his own riding, be called a leader?

His party wondered the same. As he considered quitting, they whispered about him. Then he surprised everyone, as he often would. He gave up law for good, brought Laura to Ottawa to live, and totally dedicated himself to politics. He had never been a quitter and wasn't about to become one now.

But if anything, the situation worsened during the next four years. He took positions that angered the party's already small, split Quebec wing. And in 1907 he bravely put forward a "progressive" series of ideas and toured the country talking about them. He wanted Canada to respond to the many changes brought on by innovations like airplanes, cars, and telephones. He suggested totally remodelling government services to make them larger, more modern and efficient; creating a national telephone system; having mail delivered free; and building highways for automobiles. Much of it was ahead of its time. Old Conservatives worried that it wasn't Conservative enough. Liberals adopted the ideas.

So, in 1908 Borden lost again to Laurier. His party did slightly better, though, and he hoped they were gaining confidence in their new beliefs. Two years later Laurier decided to form Canada's first navy. Borden agreed with him, then changed his mind, saying that millions of dollars should instead be handed over to the British navy to handle our defence. Many English Canadians admired the idea; many French hated it. The party split again and he was criticized for changing his mind. There were attempts to fire him. But the party could never quite bring themselves to part with this practical, dedicated, and sometimes surprising man. Soon that would pay off.

Big Boss, Big War

In the 1911 election Borden finally hit his stride. His speeches became more assured, his positions stronger and more popular. Out among the people, he shouted his faith in the old British forces while Laurier campaigned for his "tinpot navy"; he proclaimed we were strong on our own while Laurier wanted free trade with the Americans. It worked. Robert Borden became Prime Minister. But he had just three seats in Quebec, none held by French Canadians. The great divide between the French and English, feared by Laurier, seemed upon the Dominion.

Rob didn't see it that way. He would help Canadians, regardless of race, deal with the changes in their lives. He set about putting his "progressive" policies into action while making Canada strong "within the British Empire."

But everything changed the third year of his reign. The assassination of a European prince in 1914 led to international tension, and by August, as Rob and Laura relaxed in Ontario's Muskoka Lakes region, word came that an ominous world war was nearing.

Borden would show his stuff during World War I. In those frightening first days he instantly gave Canada's full support to England, then bought two American submarines, ready to fight. He cared deeply for the many Canadians who went to war, and travelled to dangerous battle zones where he sat with dying men. Then he rallied Canada with his speeches. Seldom did he reveal his emotions, but later told his diary that during army hospital visits he could barely hold back his tears.

There were many political problems during the war. First, Canada had to raise an armed force overnight. Borden and Laurier took to the streets and urged Canadians to enlist. Hundreds of thousands did, but it wasn't enough. Great numbers of a whole generation of young men were shot, bombed, or gassed daily for small stretches of land in Europe. And the Empire demanded more. It was feared that Canada wasn't doing its part.

With his term as war Prime Minister allowed to extend beyond the normal five-year limit by Laurier, he considered forcing men to enlist. But Laurier wouldn't accept it and French Quebeckers couldn't, not for a "British" war.

Finally, an election came in 1917. By then, Borden had formed a new political party, the Union party, by adding to his side the many Liberals who favoured forcing military enlistment. Quebec was furious when he won. There were riots. But Borden moved on, taking Canada into the last phase of the war. The total number of soldiers rose to more than 600,000—in a nation of just eight million.

He was surprisingly strong at Empire war meetings in England. When the war began Brits had denied Canada its right to be part of decision making. But as more Canadians fell, that became ridiculous. At Ypres, as France's defences collapsed Canada's bravely held, despite suffering 6,000 casualties in three days. At Vimy Ridge, Canadian troops made history by winning an unwinnable battle. Borden saw Canadians' guts and pain and glory up close. "The memory of those visits," he said later, "has never faded and will endure as long as my life." He told the British, in a statement as blunt as any Canadian leader had ever made to the home country, that if Canada's role in decision making wasn't increased, it simply would not "put further effort into the winning of the war." Soon secret messages were sailing across the ocean for him to consider, and at war cabinets he was given as much power as anyone. His handsome face, with its snow-white hair and thick salty moustache, became a symbol of strong leadership.

Back home, where the Centre Block of Parliament had burned, he issued war bonds and tried other ways to raise money. His government gave Canada its first income tax. They also denied many citizens from enemy "alien" countries the right to vote.

Throughout the war Canadian women swung into action on the home front and surprised most men. They took to the factories, the fields, and anyplace else where help was needed; they raised funds and morale. Borden and a grateful, almost embarrassed nation gave them the vote. "I conceive that women are entitled to the franchise on their merits," he said, "and it is upon that basis that this Bill is presented to Parliament."

In 1918, as the Americans finally entered the war on our side, the Germans gave one last terrible push and Canadians held their breath. At the only secret Parliament meeting in history, Borden said things were grim. But it was the enemy's last gasp and by November 1918 the war was over. There was dancing in the streets. Today, in the fields of France and Belgium, Canadian gravestones, mostly of young men, stretch as far as the eye can see. Nearly 60,000 died and 173,000 were wounded.

As the war ended, Borden's star rose higher. The British and Americans didn't want Canada to have full votes at the Paris peace conference. Borden simply rejected the idea, then shamed them by listing Canada's war efforts. They gave in. He insisted that Canada sign the Treaty of Versailles and join the League of Nations, which he helped to form.

Back to Earth

Borden should have returned home in May 1919 a hero. But he wasn't a hero sort. And anyway, there were troubles in the Dominion. "I should be very happy to return to Canada," he said, "were it not for politics." The country was trying to adjust to the changes brought by war, and working people had had enough of low wages and poor working conditions. In June, a massive strike hit Winnipeg. Mounties were called in to end it. There was violence and death. Times were definitely changing.

But they wouldn't change with Robert Borden at the helm. He'd given everything he had to the war and was exhausted. In December his doctors recommended he retire. Others suggested a one-year holiday. Everyone in his party, except bold, brilliant young Arthur Meighen, wanted him to stay. Meighen said he feared for his leader's life.

Borden went off on a trip as a guest on a battle cruiser to gather himself for one last great effort. He went to Cuba, Jamaica, and New Zealand, and even back to England. He wrote in his diary in French. But no amount of rest helped. When he returned in May and stepped back into another cabinet argument, he almost collapsed. On July 1, Dominion Day, 1920, he resigned. Meighen was his successor.

He served quietly in Parliament for one more year, then began a happy retirement. He had invested well and was rich, living out his life in Ottawa. He and Laura travelled, he advised Canadian and world leaders, golfed, visited his cottage, made speeches, and wrote his memoirs. People were awed in his presence. But he loved to tell long, slow jokes that made fun of "Prime Minister Borden." Listeners would laugh until they cried. He also visited the local market, where he sometimes threw himself on the ground to show kids how to make snow angels.

He died on June 10, 1937, almost 83 years old. The word "Sir" did not appear on his gravestone, as he had asked. He had been a simple, hard-working man who had grown mightily during his life, and tried to do what was right. He hadn't all the time. But he had served his country bravely. And he'd accomplished a goal or two. Rob Borden, salt of the earth from Nova Scotia: remember him when you look at a $100 bill.

9th Prime Minister

The Brilliant Failure

ARTHUR MEIGHEN

A rthur Meighen once appeared in Parliament in his bedroom slippers. He wore one coat so often that his friends got sick of its dirty look and threw it out a train window. When he played golf, he only used one club—a putter, with which he could drive the ball 130 yards! You get the idea. He was a nutbar. Add to this the fact that he was Prime Minister twice, but for only 19 months altogether, and once ruled for a grand total of a few days. It seems he was kind

Born St. Mary's, Ontario 1874, died Toronto 1960, Conservative.
PM: 1920–1921, 1926

of a loser too. But . . . he was also the greatest debater and the biggest brain in Canadian political history. His role in our past, though often now forgotten, was huge. And as nutty as he was, his arch enemy, who defeated him and became the longest-serving Prime Minister ever, was even nuttier.

The Weird Kid

Arthur Meighen was born on June 16, 1874, in St. Mary's, Ontario, a little place near Stratford, where they now have a famous theatre festival dedicated to English playwright William Shakespeare. Arthur grew up to love words and literature. Shakespeare, not Macdonald or Laurier, would be his idol.

His father was a hard-working farmer who so dearly wanted a good education for his children that he moved the family, six kids and all, closer to a school. Arthur was an unusual boy, spending many days alone, curled up with a book. He was thin and frail looking, but rarely sick. Inside he was tough; his mind ate up information. His parents told him that success was up to him—no one but he would be to blame if he failed.

At age 11 he entered a contest to see who could sell the most subscriptions to a local newspaper. He won and got a watch for his efforts. The fact that it was busted didn't matter—he had worked hard and succeeded. Soon he whizzed through St. Mary's Collegiate, intrigued by everything he learned. On his long walks to school through the woods, he sometimes took time out to think . . . and left his lunchbox behind.

At home he loved to loudly debate his father. Neither cared what the subject was or who took which side. One day his mother thought he had totally lost it—he had mounted a stump in the woods to argue at the top of his lungs . . . with invisible opponents.

In 1892, at age 18, he was sent to the University of Toronto, and four years later he graduated with First Class Honours in Mathematics. A slightly flabby, flamboyant young man named William Lyon Mackenzie King, "Rex" to his friends, was in the same year. Meighen didn't have his flair and didn't care. They would later be famous foes.

After an attempt to run a general store, he became a teacher. But that didn't last long either. Early in his career he disciplined a girl for slamming her books on the floor. Her father was on the school board and a big noise in town, and objected. When the school offered weak support, Meighen instantly resigned. Refusing to enter the school, he taught students in a feed store to help them pass exams. Arthur Meighen rarely compromised.

Anxious to try something new, he decided to become a lawyer and moved to frontier Winnipeg. Restless as a mere law student, he soon relocated an hour farther west to Portage la Prairie, where he took over a branch firm.

In his early Portage days he lived in an apartment with a couple of friends, so concerned about saving money that he kept a huge bag of apples in a corner. On a trip to the Winnipeg Fair in 1902 he met Isabel Cox and fell in love, and after two years of trips on the CPR to visit her, they married. The week they tied the knot, he lost his wedding shoes. The police were called in. The precious items were soon found where he'd left them . . . in a barbershop. There was just too much going on in Arthur's brain to remember such details as his shoes.

As a lawyer he had many successes. His sharp mind when on his feet in court made him deadly. But he wanted greater challenges. So, he joined the Young Men's Conservative Club, began speaking, and in 1907 asked about being the local candidate. Bigger names feared they couldn't win this tough riding. Meighen threw himself into the struggle and travelled far and wide in wagons and buggies on bad roads, stinging the Liberals with his amazing vocabulary, sarcastic wit, and magnificent speeches. He won by 250 votes, and at age 33 went to Ottawa. His family, by then including two sons, came with him. He knew he'd be there for a while.

Arthur Slays the Liberal Dragons

It didn't take him long to make a name for himself. He loved Parliament and it loved him. Soon he was slicing up Laurier and his men, taking particular glee in demolishing newly elected "Rex" King. He could take any position and make it seem superior. In fact, he was almost too good. He believed in finishing off opponents when he had them down.

In 1910, after Meighen's first major speech, Sir Wilfrid Laurier is said to have turned to a friend and remarked, "Borden has found a man."

But despite his stunning skills in the House, he wasn't bold elsewhere. Publicly he seemed mean and tough, a skeleton-thin man with deep-set, penetrating eyes and thinning hair. But he thought little of himself and his fame, and cared deeply for a small circle of friends. Unconcerned about his appearance, he would turn up in Parliament with pants so short his ankles showed, or dressed in the long green coat that had been thrown out the train window (someone found it and mailed it to him . . . so he wore it).

In 1911 he was re-elected in Portage with an increased majority, and rose even higher in Borden's eyes. When the Conservatives had trouble getting money through Parliament to help fund the British navy, the skilled Meighen came to the rescue. He called for "closure" to stop debate and force the money through. The Liberals could barely believe how this genius manipulated things. He destroyed them without even raising his voice, and used page-long quotations from Shakespeare. Here were brains like no one had seen before. They grew to resent him.

He made enemies in Quebec too, though it wasn't just for being on the side that wanted to force men to fight in the First World War. It was because he argued for it so well. No one else could put it quite like him: "Of all the prices we must never pay for harmony in Canada, the price we must most of all decline, is national dishonour. No nation can survive a cost like that."

He enjoyed battle and had the heart of a lion. Far in the backbenches, far from cabinet ministers (he became one in 1913), the mass of his party loved to watch him slay the Liberals' big dragons. His courage gave them courage.

Borden knew his man could do the dirty work. So, during the war Meighen made the laws (which others called racist) that took away the vote from citizens born with "enemy tongues" in enemy nations. "It is abnormal," he said, "but we live in abnormal times."

By 1917, as Borden formed his "Union" wartime government, Meighen had taken on several cabinet jobs and become the most dominant politician in western Canada. As the war drew to a close, many thousands of wounded or exhausted veterans returned home without jobs. With Borden ill, Meighen (as Minister of Justice) was asked to deal with a massive Winnipeg strike. It was the most famous in Canadian history, beginning with a few thousand workers and spreading throughout the city until business ground to a halt. Meighen visited Winnipeg and cracked down. The RCMP arrested 12 leaders. Then there was a frightening, six-hour riot. The Mounties moved in again. Two people were killed.

Meighen was criticized as being pro-business, against workers. This wasn't entirely fair. He was simply the man asked to solve a terrible problem when no one else seemed capable. He believed that a general strike that froze a city had to be stopped, and stopped fast. Right or wrong, he was always brave.

King Arthur

By 1919 King was Liberal leader. Though he would rule Canada for the longest period of any PM, one-on-one he was never Meighen's match. They faced each other the rest of their lives: Meighen the brilliant speaker with the golden mind and King the rambler, as tricky as a magician. The skinny, Conservative Meighen said what he felt and felt what he said, while no one ever knew what was really on the fat, Liberal mind of Mackenzie King. Meighen intensely disliked King and said so, while King pretended to respect Meighen but deeply loathed and feared him. In combat in the House, it was almost sad to watch Meighen beat him up, but at election time, victory was usually King's.

When Borden retired in 1920, Meighen was a good bet to replace him. Other leading party candidates seemed unsure. Arthur wasn't. He had wanted to be Prime Minister since the day he stood on that stump in St. Mary's. So, in July, at age 46, he ascended to the throne, the youngest man to claim it. He had drive, brains, guts, and ideas. It seemed he had never failed and never would. But time would tell a different tale.

Though he liked the job, it took its toll; his weight once dropped to under 130 pounds. He ruled until December of the next year. People packed halls to hear his brilliant, moral speeches. His strong performance at the 1921 Imperial Conference in London gained him wider fame. And he created Armistice Day to celebrate the sacrifice of Canada's soldiers. But his old-fashioned beliefs, which included a readiness to help Britain fight even small wars, were controversial. King said his party would respond to public opinion, while the stiff Meighen replied that the Conservatives were elected to use their own brains, to do what was right and not suck up to the public.

But in the December 1921 election, King swamped him. In fact, the new Progressive party came second. Meighen, never upset by any loss in his life, just worked harder. Over the next four years he rebuilt his party, and did it so well that he defeated King in 1925. Or so he thought.

He won 116 seats, King just 99. But the Progressives, who hung on to 24, decided to support the Liberals and keep them in power. That set the stage for one of the weirdest events in Canadian history. It would be the ruin of Arthur Meighen.

The King–Byng Affair

In 1926, King's government was about to be defeated on a vote in the House. So, before that vote took place, King went to the Governor General, Lord Byng, and asked him to close Parliament and call an election. Governors General were no longer powerful figures, but still had the right to make decisions in difficult situations. Byng decided that since the government had not yet been defeated, an election was impossible. King was furious. He marched back to Parliament . . . and quit. Byng asked Meighen to form the government. Many later said that Meighen should have refused, and that he only accepted because he was anxious to be Prime Minister again. But Meighen felt he couldn't refuse: the Governor General's reputation and the reputation of Canada were on the line.

In order to take the job, he had to go through a little by-election and leave his seat in Parliament. Within a few days, King, free of his tough opponent, brought about the Conservatives' defeat by arranging another vote in the House that turned the tables. Then King went into an election saying that the new Prime Minister was a power-hungry leader, and beat him.

Meighen never recovered, at least politically. Thinkers and historians have debated who was right for many years. Controversy about the "King–Byng Affair" will never die. Meighen had no doubt as to who was the villain. He called King "the most contemptible charlatan ever to darken the annals of Canadian politics."

He soon resigned as leader and was succeeded by R.B. Bennett. Still young, he moved to Toronto and entered his fourth occupation, as a businessman. He became vice-president of a company worth five million dollars, bought a house in rich Rosedale, began to see more of his kids (for years he had forgotten to even list his daughter Lillian as one of his children in the Parliamentary Guide), and enjoyed his new life. He loved his three-mile walk to work, spoke out from time to time, and for a while served as government leader in the Senate. But he was viewed as a brilliant man whose proper place was in political power. "What a shame," people were heard to say.

At first, Meighen resisted offers to return. In 1938, when Bennett quit after a term as Prime Minister, he had to fight off requests. But in 1941, after a successor failed miserably, he was forced to take the job. Worried that at 66 his life would be shortened, he did his duty. "I have never felt so distressed as I do now," he told his son.

As King quivered at the thought of the only man who could slap him around returning to Parliament, Meighen readied himself to get re-elected. He chose a race in Toronto. King pretended to graciously help him by not running a candidate against him, but did much worse, throwing Liberal support behind the Co-operative Commonwealth Federation party (the future NDP). They claimed Meighen was a businessman placed in the race by big money, an out-of-date Conservative who didn't care about the poor. World War II had begun and Meighen again favoured forcing Canadians to fight. The Liberals, tricky on the issue, attacked him. He was defeated. During the nasty campaign,

CCF leader M.J. Caldwell actually said, "I would just as soon live under Hitler as that man." Meighen was sickened by it all. He quit again, for good. Mackenzie King was overjoyed.

Weird Until Death

Despite his scrawny appearance (he became fatter in later years), his health remained perfect for a long time. He believed in being vigorous. But then, in 1953, he contracted Ménière's disease, an inner ear affliction that left him weakened and sometimes unable to keep his balance.

For a while he kept up as brisk a pace as possible, still going to work in downtown Toronto. He liked to play golf, carrying that single putter with him; drove his car through red lights on a regular basis; and played bridge with old friends as he told jokes, imitated old foes, and endeared himself as a kindly old man. One day he was 10 cents short of his fare on a streetcar and vowed to send the little coin to the operator. He did, with an apology. The operator kept the dime as a souvenir of meeting a great man.

He was close to his friends. And in old age they were many. They came from all walks of life, religions, and political parties—he detested snobbery and shows of wealth. He gave to charities and made many visits to hospitals, his kindness unknown to those who saw only his toughness in public.

Seldom were his legendary speaking skills heard in old age. But in 1957, when Prime Minister Diefenbaker spoke at a tribute to him at Toronto's Royal York Hotel, he rose to reply. Despite his nerves, he vowed that even in his 83rd year, he would speak without notes. There was a long, nervous pause. Then he began. That voice, with its beautiful way with words, now aged, soon found itself. He spoke as he once had. And when he was finished the crowd stood and cheered until they were nearly hoarse.

On August 4, 1960, age 86, he fell asleep and never woke. The Mounties carried his casket at the state funeral in Toronto. A man who some felt possessed the greatest mind in the history of Canadian politics was laid to rest. Perhaps he had been too smart for his own good. He had been a "brilliant failure."

10th Prime Minister

The Supernatural One
WILLIAM LYON MACKENZIE KING

This one is incredible. He was boring on the outside, weird on the inside: kind of like Canada. The grandson of a famous rebel, he talked with his dead mother, discussed life with his dogs, saw dragons' faces in the clouds, and lived in one of the spookiest houses you'll ever want to hear about. He also ran the country longer than any leader ever has and likely ever will. Today, if you visit his huge Kingsmere estate east of Ottawa in the Gatineau hills of Quebec, you will see

Born Berlin, Ontario 1874, died Ottawa 1950, Liberal. PM: 1921–1926; 1926–1930; 1935–1948

something others have wondered about for many years. Ruins. Mackenzie King erected them long ago, but no one understands what they are or why they were built. They are a mystery. Just like him.

Bizarre Beginnings

His grandfather, William Lyon Mackenzie, was the first mayor of Toronto, but never part of the ruling class. He was short and bold, with red hair, burning eyes, and a sharp mind. His speeches and the articles in his newspaper were like rocks thrown at the snobby, British-backed folks who ran English Canada. He became so angry at their refusal to listen to the people that he led a group of rebels down Yonge Street in 1837 on horseback with guns and pitchforks. They were turned back by British troops. He fled, and lived in exile for many years in the United States, often poor, even in jail. His 13th child was sensitive Isabel Grace, who grew up resenting the way her father had been treated, even after he returned to Toronto and was elected to the province's legislature. He had merely wanted democracy for his people, but died, still ridiculed, in 1861.

Ghostly Isabel was not your usual sort either. She married the son of one of the soldiers who put down the rebellion: John King became a lawyer and a follower of politics but never a success, which Isabel often noted.

The family lived in Berlin, Ontario (now Kitchener). They had servants and maids and a fancy carriage, though they couldn't really afford them. Willie, the first boy of four children, born December 17, 1874, grew up a happy, chubby, mischievous kid who liked to play pranks at school and could have had better grades. Once he tied a teacher's dress to a chair so that it burst open when she stood up, and answered another's question about why he was near the bottom of his class by saying that someone had to be there.

His mother and his dead grandfather dominated his childhood, as they would his entire life. Willie adopted her feelings and memorized his grandfather's speeches and a poster offering money for his capture. Then he began a mission to avenge their past, to bring the little rebel's sense of right and wrong back to Canada.

At age 17, in 1891, he enrolled at the University of Toronto. Now focused and ambitious, known as "Rex" to friends, he played sports, loved parties, and plowed into studies with tremendous energy. He even posted lessons in his bedroom so that he could work as he dressed. Politics interested him. But most intriguing was the city and its poor. At night he went on secret trips, searching for the wretched, meeting bold, barely dressed women walking on the dark streets. He'd never known such creatures existed. This new world thrilled him. Mackenzie King would always have a double life.

Like his grandfather, he wanted to help the less fortunate. He spent hours talking to street people and giving lectures at

Toronto's Hospital for Sick Children. A brief time at the
University of Chicago, and at famous Harvard University near
Boston, completed his education and increased his interest in
politics and industries, and how they might do more for
people, especially the poor.

Back in Toronto, while writing for *The Mail and Empire*
newspaper, King stumbled upon the fact that the government
was getting its post office uniforms made at low wages, forcing
workers into poverty. Always crafty, he went to see a Laurier
cabinet minister with this secret. Before long, uniform makers
were not only getting better pay, but King was writing a
government report on factory work.

In private life he stayed a bachelor, though he often fell in
love, wrote passionate letters, and recorded details in his diary.
But his mother, obsessed by his "mission" in life, put a stop to
anything that got too serious. He had begun writing the diary
a few years earlier and continued until his death. It was not
only, as one historian wrote, "the most important single political document in twentieth century Canadian history," but a
mind-boggling story of love affairs, strange beliefs, conversations with the dead, and secret thoughts. "How strange I am,"
he wrote. "I really do not know myself."

His factory report work brought him to Ottawa by 1900,
where he climbed to the post of Deputy Minister of Labour.
He was an intense, at times shy, other times outgoing, unusual
young man. He travelled across Canada, solving problems for

the government as if by magic. If there was a strike, he was soon there and the strike was soon over. He was a bit flabby with thinning hair on his round head, but clever and ambitious. He went to church, said his prayers, and prowled the streets at night.

During this time the grand old man of Canada began noticing him. Laurier likely never dreamed that this little person would someday equal and perhaps surpass his own legend, but he recognized King's skill and wondered if he might be a leader of some sort. A frequent guest at Laurier House, King began to consider himself the great man's protégé.

In 1908 the Liberals asked King to run for Parliament in a Conservative riding (North Waterloo) near his old hometown. With Laurier's help he was elected. The following year, at just 35 years old, he became Minister of Labour.

Life seemed to be going well. He often took cycling trips into the beautiful Gatineau Hills on the Quebec side of the Ottawa River. There he spotted an old farm. Fascinated by coincidences, he loved the fact that it was called *Kings*mere, and purchased it. It was just an old farmhouse with a great view, but he would add much more land and many buildings. In Ottawa he lived in the splendid Roxborough apartments. Plans brewed in his secretive mind. One day, while embracing his dear mother, he saw a vision of his rebel grandfather's face in hers. He was sure it meant that he would be Prime Minister.

Falling and Rising

But in a six-year period beginning in 1911 everything crashed. First, both he and the Laurier government were defeated. It shocked him. He had been floating forward on his mission. Suddenly, he was on the sidelines.

Then there were three deaths, one almost impossible to bear. First his father, unable to fulfill any missions in life, then a beloved sister, and incredibly to him, his mother. She had lived in his apartment and, with medical help, he had kept her alive beyond her time. Her death devastated him. But before long he came to believe she wasn't truly dead. She had promised to give him a sign from beyond the grave. He began to look for it.

His professional life also plunged. Not only was he out of power, but now money was scarce. A wealthy British female fan soon funded him. Then, in 1914, one of the world's richest men, American John D. Rockefeller, put out a call. There were labour troubles in his businesses and King was just the inventive sort to solve them. Dressed in his three-piece suit, he went south and investigated a two-year strike in Rockefeller's Colorado mines. He got both sides to compromise and even persuaded Rockefeller to see the conditions the men had to live in.

King kept his Ottawa base. In 1917, he ran for election in his grandfather's North York riding, but was defeated, as expected. Pondering the Liberal defeat, he said mysteriously, like a mystic looking at tea leaves, "This will make me Prime Minister."

His heart remained with Laurier, and when the legend died in 1919, he was ready. He laid out his views in a book called *Industry and Humanity*. Many found it boring, just as they found him as a speaker—slow and careful, fussing as he spoke. Yet there was something important deep in these almost intentionally uninteresting words. They were never too radical, but had a certain spirit. People should always come first in business and politics, he said. They made the factories run and put governments in power. Bosses and politicians should never forget that.

When the Liberal convention to replace Laurier was called, King was in Europe. He rushed back to Ottawa and won. He was lucky: his opponents were either too old or offensive. He slipped in, championed by few, droning on about his grandfather in long speeches, but stitching together support and never offending anyone. He did make one clear point. He wanted Canada to grow—independently, but humanely.

Eliminating Enemies

The first of his many Conservative opponents was that brilliant failure, Arthur Meighen, the man of brains and ice who had disliked him at university and now liked him even less. King despised his smart-aleck enemy too.

In 1921 they faced off in a national election, Arthur pro-England, Willie favouring whatever the people wanted. King won, and all of a sudden, he was Prime Minister. His mission had begun. It would be a long, magical run.

Meighen's speeches were like surgeon's cuts and his policies were clear and hard as rocks—he didn't compromise. King compromised everywhere. He wasn't, however, what he seemed. He made decisions instantly, but like Macdonald, waited for the right time to unfold them. Even then, it wasn't always clear what he was doing. "If I try to reach that point directly," he once explained, while pointing across the Rideau Canal in Ottawa, "I shall drown. I must follow the curves of the bank and ultimately I shall get there, though at times I may seem to be going somewhere else." Problems were quietly solved, the country prospered, and the Liberals seemed to stay in power forever.

His first five years in charge weren't remarkable, or at least, didn't seem to be. He carefully watched Canada's money, helped railroads, and encouraged immigration. He realized that the public, being Canadians, were divided on free trade with the United States. So, he conjured up an idea . . . "freer trade." No one knew what it meant, but they bought it.

His party wasn't particularly fond of him. They didn't rally around speeches that seemed to say a great deal and nothing at all, nor did they love his policies. Often, he didn't like his cabinet much either. "I've always found you can control people better," he remarked, "if you don't see too much of them." He put them in power and let the good ones do their jobs. A master stroke was giving dynamic Ernest Lapointe total control of Quebec. Lapointe was his Cartier, and when Lapointe died in 1941, he snagged another in Louis St. Laurent. Quebec was handled; English Canada was happy.

Canadians didn't like King much either, this doughy boy who sat out the First World War. But he found ways to stop the divisions that had been building in Canada through the Laurier, Borden, and Meighen reigns. King vowed that East wouldn't hate West, and that French would get along with English. Through many troubles, even war, he held them together. If anything, they came to dislike him more than each other . . . and kept re-electing him.

But he almost fell from his perch in 1926. That summer the party was clinging to power when a scandal arose and Meighen got Parliament to prepare to vote down the Liberals as unfit to govern. That was the beginning of the famous King–Byng affair, in which King slipped out of power and then back in as if by magic. He quit when Governor General Byng wouldn't call an election for him, and told the House with (what appeared to be) tears in his eyes that he wasn't Prime Minister any more. Meighen was then sucked into power, and King's trap. King defeated the shaky new government, forced an election, and returned as PM. Meighen's career was over.

To this day many question the magician's tactics. But he rolled on. He told the people that no one, and certainly not the British Governor General, should tell Canada's elected Prime Minister what to do. They agreed.

His luck rose again in 1930, just as everything else crashed. It was an election year and the worst global Depression in modern times was beginning to hit Canada. Soon unemployment skyrocketed, dry seasons ravaged the West, wheat prices dropped, and people took to the streets, roads, and railway cars, searching for jobs and food. King was defeated in the election, leaving the horrible job of finding a solution to these unsolvable problems to wealthy Conservative leader R.B. Bennett. King waited out five years in Opposition, as his opponent, destined to fail in hard times, plunged in popularity.

Enter: The Dead

It would be an eventful period in King's private life. A man with an enormous inner world, often alone thinking of his mission and his mother, he took a trip to the lair of the dead. It was natural for him. Supernatural.

He had made many efforts to end his loneliness. "Marry . . . I must," he told his diary. But many candidates just didn't measure up—he wanted a smart, rich wife, who could understand him and be Canada's "first lady." That was a tall order. When he found women he wanted, they rejected him. For a while he set his sights on the daughter of American tycoon Andrew Carnegie, and later proposed to a wealthy woman he barely knew. Fascinated with married women, he grew close to an Ottawa minister's wife, 16 years his senior, then to a Mrs. Patteson. From 1919 until his death, he frequently visited the Patteson home, as if he were a member of the family. It was a strange, very private relationship. A lover of women and a bachelor, immensely powerful yet shy, elected by millions but a loner, he was indeed, as someone said, "next to a madman."

The Pattesons gave him an Irish terrier. He called it Pat and grew to love it . . . so deeply that he spoke *with* it. He prayed with Pat too, and thought him "almost human." When it died at age 17 in 1941, the PM held him in his arms and cried. The Pattesons soon sent Pat II, and there would be a third. Late in life, when the British awarded King the Order of Merit, the greatest honour ever given to a Canadian, he wrote that his dog should have been given the award, and certainly deserved it more.

But that wasn't the strangest of his ways. By then he was talking to the dead. In 1921, Sir Wilfrid's widow died and left King old Laurier House. He moved in and made it his own. To others it was a little strange, and to tourists who visit it today, it seems downright weird. It was dark and spooky, often lit by candlelight, jammed full of worn old furniture, dark rugs, and dim portraits of the dead. The Prime Minister slept on the second floor in Laurier's big brass bed, his dog in a basket near him. In the hallway hung the warrant for the arrest of his rebel grandfather William Lyon Mackenzie, dead or alive.

Up on the third floor, behind an opening in a wall, was the "dark room" where he wrote his diaries. Then there was his study. Reached by a hidden elevator, it was filled with his books, his desk, and . . . a ghostly painting of his mother. Lit by a dim glow, she gazed dreamily into a fire, looking eerily alive. The Prime Minister came here for more than 20 years to make the decisions that guided Canada. He spoke with his dead mother, and prayed to her and with her.

Here he also held seances. In 1932 he had visited a fortune teller and was fascinated. Over the following years he often brought her to Laurier House and Kingsmere. She made Laurier's ghost appear before his eyes (to predict his next election win), dead royalty, dead Edward Blake, Leonardo da Vinci, and his fiery grandfather. King used Ouija boards, made tables rap, and visited mystics on secret side-trips to England. He believed in magic numbers and in important things happening when the hands of clocks were perfectly lined up.

But when the Second World War began he suddenly stopped. He knew that if he were ever found out, he'd seem unstable. His nation couldn't afford that.

King of Canada

He had come back to power in 1935, finishing Bennett's career as he had Meighen's and as he would the next two

Conservative leaders. He slowly used some of his old ideas for sharing wealth to ease the pain of the last years of the Depression. In the late '30s he visited Germany and made friends with Adolph Hitler. He warned him, however, that if his Nazis fought Great Britain, Canada would battle him with everything it had.

And so Canada did, declaring war on its own for the first time. Mackenzie King grew to hate Hitler and everything he stood for. But Canada's unity was even more important to him than the war. He remembered Laurier's Quebec problems when men were forced to fight: it had split the country. He vowed never to let that happen. So, while Canadians fought bravely in Europe, and as opponents criticized him for lacking passion for war (he was booed when he visited troops), he quietly managed everyone's emotions.

When the Ontario Premier criticized the war effort, King called a snap election in 1940 and creamed his enemies, getting full support from the Canadian people. Then he held a national vote on forced military service (conscription). His position was "conscription if necessary, but not necessarily conscription." English Canada voted for it, Quebec against. He stalled for time. Finally, in 1944, as armies pushed to finish the war, he claimed that the military would overthrow him if he didn't use conscription, and made it law—but only for 16,000 men still at home who had already agreed to fight. It was another bit of conjuring. There were no riots in Quebec, the war was soon won, and Canada remained united.

During the war, he hadn't been nearly as popular as his good American friend President Franklin Roosevelt or that famous British windbag Prime Minister Winston Churchill. King sometimes seemed invisible. But he would rule his country much longer than either of those "great men."

By early 1945, when he announced victory to the Canadian people via radio from San Francisco (where the United Nations was being formed), his final election triumph was already planned. He was 71 years old. Three years later, his health beginning to decline, he finally decided to retire. Time was passing him by. Bright young lights of the Liberal party like Lester Pearson were interested in the new global world. He still believed in building Canada's independence.

In old age he retired to his now huge Kingsmere estate with its seven homes. He had gathered up bits of the old Canadian Parliament Buildings and the British House of Commons and built his curious "ruins." (Kingsmere and Laurier House were given to the nation, so we could all puzzle at them.) He wasn't mourned much when he quit, nor when he died in the summer of 1950. At the end, he feared a bigger, world-ending war, and saw those dragons in the sky. He had a lot of money, but didn't admit it. He walked around his estate, cane in hand, with a few close friends, spiritual as ever.

He had never taken political advice from anyone beyond the grave. He pursued them for their spirit.

King could look back on a colossal career, unmatched in Canadian history. He had been Prime Minister for an incredible

22 years, three years longer than Macdonald, more than anyone in the history of the English-speaking world! He had led his party for three decades and accomplished many missions. He brought in the old age pension and unemployment insurance, appointed the first woman to the Senate, and led Canada united through a world war. The country prospered both during the war and after. He steered the Liberals into new ways of governing, but kept them from becoming radical, demanding tolerance from them and from Canadians.

Most importantly, he established the character of the nation, or perhaps re-established it for the 20th century. Like him, it would be a tolerant, caring place that tried to look after its poor, and wasn't loud or glory seeking—a cool country, apparently not emotional, but underneath full of passions and even strange ideas.

Canada has always been a bit of a mystery, even to itself. It has a double nature: two founding races, with a conservative exterior and a progressive mind inside. Mackenzie King, that secretive, mysterious man, was much like us. It takes an unusual leader to run this unusual country. Only wizards with great ability to compromise are successful. The rebel's quiet grandson was perfect.

If John A. Macdonald is our creator and father, and Wilfrid Laurier is what we hope to be, then William Lyon Mackenzie King, in a way, *is* us.

A Rich Man in a Poor Man's World

R.B. BENNETT

*Born Hopewell Hill,
New Brunswick 1870,
died England 1947,
Conservative. PM: 1930–1935*

Viscount Richard Bedford Bennett tends to get lost in the story of the Prime Ministers of Canada. And there's good reason. He took office during the worst time the country has ever known. The problems were impossible to solve. To his credit, he tried mightily. But in the end, he just didn't fit. A millionaire, he lived in a suite of 17 rooms at the elegant Château Laurier hotel while people starved in the streets. He was a lover of everything British while his young country struggled to be itself. He was almost un-Canadian. Mackenzie King entered the afterlife in a farmhouse in the hills near the Ontario–Quebec border . . . Bennett died in a mansion in England.

Go West, Young Man

From birth, on July 3, 1870, he had something in common with King. He was deeply attached to his mother. He would also never marry, unable to find a woman to match the first in his life. Home was in New Brunswick, south of Moncton, in the beautiful village of Hopewell Cape, with its frame houses, Methodist church, and green land on the Petitcodiac River. The Bennetts had been in the province for nine generations, and his father, Henry, was in the shipbuilding business. But when the economy failed, so did he. His wife felt let down. Someone needed to build things back up.

She set her hopes on little Richard. At first he was a bit of a momma's boy, tall for his age and freckled, shy and insecure. But she filled him with a mission to be someone special. Unlike King, it wasn't spiritual: he was to be a success and make money.

By 1882, having completed Grade 8, he was pushed away from home to attend a Normal School in Fredericton to be trained as a teacher. His shyness had vanished. He did well and let others know it. They even had a rhyme about him:

194 UNUSUAL HEROES

First there came Bennett, conceited and young,
Who never quite knew when to hold his quick tongue.

Driven to get ahead, he was teaching by the age of 16. And within two years, he became principal of four schools near Chatham, a tough guy who demanded a lot.

From a young age he learned the value of good connections. He made his first with Lemeul Tweedie, a local lawyer who would rise to be Premier of the province. Tweedie liked young Dick Bennett and offered him a partnership in his firm if he could get through law school. This, of course, he did with great speed, acing things at Dalhousie University in three years and returning to join Tweedie in 1893.

He also met Max Aitkin, who would later be the legendary Lord Beaverbrook and provide the Spitfire fighter planes that helped win World War II. Their ambitions similar, they formed a lifelong friendship. In 1896, when Max was just 17, he offered up his 26-year-old buddy for election to town council and used a noisy publicity campaign to win. It was the first of many combined efforts.

Late in 1896 Bennett came in contact with James Lougheed, an ambitious frontier Calgary lawyer and young Conservative senator. He changed Dick's life simply by asking Dalhousie for the name of a talented young lawyer who could form a thriving partnership with him in the western territories. They suggested R.B. Bennett.

So, in January 1897, as he entered his 27th year, the young man boarded a train headed for the Wild West. "Lougheed and Bennett" would be a great success. Though he had grown up fast in New Brunswick, he was about to rise even faster.

Calgary, a town of 4,000 people but moving forward like a locomotive, was perfect for a brash young man on a mission to succeed. He was tall and held himself erect, aware of his appearance and manners, combing his hair to hide its thinness and dressing in elegant suits. In New Brunswick he had told a friend "Someday I'm going to be Prime Minister of Canada," and at times repeated it now. He worked hard, but could be moody and had little time for wimps. His temper could explode when he was challenged in court.

His brains were never in question. A booming speaker, sharp on attack, he had above all an awesome memory. He often dictated two letters to two secretaries at once, giving each a paragraph at a time. He could refer to a paper buried in the middle of a towering stack and remember everything that was on it.

With his boss often in Ottawa, Bennett soon became the dominant power in his law firm. He also gained political power, winning followers by speaking on subjects like his beloved British Empire and challenging the federal Liberal member at public meetings. In 1898 he was elected to the North West Territories Assembly. Within a decade (the territory by then the province of Alberta) he had made a name for himself.

He and Max Aitkin (who was living in Alberta too) had formed the Calgary Power Company (which provided electricity), and as its president he'd made a start on his fortune. He lived famously at the swanky Pallisar Hotel, where the "Bennett table" of important men debated important things. As the 1911 national election neared, he was the natural choice to be a Conservative candidate in Calgary.

Rich and Nearly Powerful

When he won his seat in Parliament and headed for Ottawa, he was sure he'd be useful to Prime Minister Borden and rise quickly. Others had different views. Lougheed was already an Alberta cabinet minister, and Arthur Meighen, with brains even bigger than Bennett's, had seized the role of Conservative star of the prairies. And so, R.B. struggled. Without power and outshone by Meighen, he was a grumpy independent voice from the back row. When Meighen jabbed at him for criticizing a party policy, he thundered: "I will not be diverted from my argument by the impertinent interruptions of this young man." Meighen scared many men—but he just annoyed Bennett.

When the 1917 election came around, Bennett quit. Back in Calgary, nearing 50, he went at his law practice and businesses full time. He soon had his hands in mining, and in the rich, new Alberta oil industry. In 1921, with the death of his old New Brunswick friend Jenny Sherreff Eddy, he inherited a chunk of the huge Eddy Match Company. In five years he controlled it and was a very rich man.

There was disappointment too. He and new Prime Minister Meighen had slowly patched up their differences, and he'd briefly been "acting" Minister of Justice. But in the 1921 election Calgary rejected him by 16 votes. Then, Lougheed broke up their law firm. Bennett ripped their names off the office door, sued Lougheed, and never forgave him. Then he worked even harder. That was his style.

In 1925 he got back into the political game. He won his Calgary seat and became Meighen's top man. He even learned to control his temper, and to carefully make friendships with powerful men who might otherwise have been his enemies. And then, a big door opened wide for him.

It happened because of the famous King–Byng affair of 1926. Prime Minister King lost his job, let Meighen have it for three days, then grabbed it back. With Meighen away in a Prime Minister's by-election, and Bennett tied to a Calgary speaking engagement, King had his way with the weakened Conservatives in Ottawa. Bennett always claimed he would have stopped King's fatal attack on the new government with a bold counter-attack. Instead, Meighen fell and Bennett rose.

He was chosen the new Conservative leader at the party convention in Winnipeg in October 1927 and immediately threw himself into rebuilding the party. Some thought he was a bad choice. *The Vancouver Sun* called him a "cool, aloof intellectual." Cool or not, in three years he won the Prime Minister's job.

It would prove, however, to be more like a loss. His luck was horrible. Canada's was even worse. The Great Depression had just begun.

The Fat PM

Bennett believed it wouldn't last, that it was just a bump on the modern road of success. Canadians, reeling from the start of hard times, were intrigued by the idea of a large, commanding man who had become fat and wealthy showing them the way. But it was soon obvious that his ideas were outdated; his orders to simply work harder so things would get better were useless. By 1934 a million-and-a-half out of 10 million Canadians were out of work, the prairies were a dustbowl, cities were jammed with the unemployed, and desperation was all around. Letters to the Prime Minister were heartbreaking. One woman pleaded for money to buy her husband a single pair of underwear.

In the midst of all this was the tall, plump man wearing a silk hat, elegant waistcoat, striped grey pants, and white gloves, living in luxury on an entire floor of Ottawa's classy Château Laurier hotel. The public heard he loved to eat, especially big boxes of chocolates. He was like a cruel cartoon of an uncaring, rich guy.

Actually, he cared deeply. Despite his tough personality he performed many private acts of kindness, like funding poor students and sending out thousands of gifts to strangers. But that was never seen. People knew only that they were caught in desperate times that begged for a big change to the old ways. And their rich leader seemed incapable of it.

He soon became the butt of jokes. The "Bennett Buggy" was a car pulled by horses because its owner couldn't afford gas. A "Bennett Barnyard" was a deserted farm. They laughed about his style of leadership too. It was said he worked 14-hour days and gave his party little to do. A stranger, one popular gag ran, saw the PM walking towards him and asked "Why is he talking to himself?" The reply: "He's holding a cabinet meeting."

On the national scene, he wanted Canada to build its own industries, and not be dependent on the United States. He thought the nation should be run like a business. A business, replied Mackenzie King, is made of money . . . a country is made of people.

Bennett had the government send out millions of dollars to help farmers. He also set up relief camps that paid unemployed men small wages to work. But things just kept tumbling. And across the river from Parliament his Eddy Match Company just kept on belching out smoke, making his fortune while Canada burned.

In the United States, President Franklin Roosevelt was trying something called the "New Deal." It was a massive program of government help. But the Prime Minister couldn't grasp such innovation. He had many other concerns anyway. New political forces were rising against him. The Communists, Alberta's Social Credit party, and Saskatchewan's CCF party were all building strong movements and demanding change.

Take the Money and Run

Finally, in January 1935, as another election loomed and things kept sinking, he had what King called "a deathbed conversion." It was one of the most remarkable U-turns in Canadian political history and for it Bennett deserves a great deal of credit. It took extraordinary courage. In a radio talk to the nation, in the strong, reassuring voice that had once won him so many votes, he announced that he was totally changing Canada. "The old order is gone," he said. "It will not return." He planned to dismantle great chunks of the system that he and many others had believed in for years. He wanted things like unemployment insurance, minimum wages, new limits on work hours, and huge money for farmers. He would make government the big boss, not businesses. In a few strokes, he set the table for Canadian politics for the rest of the 20th century.

Everyone was shocked. Including Mackenzie King, who had kept such ideas for many years in secret compartments in his brain. He called it "too little, too late."

And it was. The sudden changes made Bennett look unstable. Why hadn't he made these efforts before? The dying Conservatives were doomed. In the election that October, an incredible 75 percent of eligible voters cast ballots. They knocked out the government.

His party plunged to 39 seats, its greatest loss in history. A bitter Bennett felt he had done his best, even betrayed his old beliefs to fix an impossible problem, and had been rejected and ridiculed.

Within a few years he went to England and stayed, living out his days on a big estate next to Max Aitkin (by then Lord Beaverbrook and in England's war cabinet). Even as bombs fell around him, he refused to live in Canada. Then, one evening in 1947, his butler prepared his bed and wished him good night. Before the sun rose, he died, alone.

So bad is his reputation today that it's surprising to see that he actually accomplished a great deal. He created the CBC, the Canadian Wheat Board, and the Bank of Canada, and had the guts to change his thinking. With that change he offered a plan that would soon be used and enlarged by Mackenzie King and every Prime Minister since.

But by any measure, he failed. And in the end he left in anger. Canada is a cold, unforgiving place to govern, a continuing experiment run only by leaders capable of taking blows and bouncing back. R.B. Bennett, for all his big, gutsy ways, gave up on Canada for England. Unique among Prime Ministers, he was buried on foreign soil, as he wished. He loved the British Empire—its ceremonies, its snobbery, and its titles (and was made a Viscount, as he requested). He even served in the English House of Lords in old age. His love for his own country was incomplete.

Perhaps he was just too loud and too rich for our blood. His style was once described in American terms: "the manners of a Chicago policeman, and the temperament of a Hollywood actor." Dick Bennett took his money and fled. Canada could have forgiven him a great deal, but they would never forgive him that. It sealed his reputation.

12th Prime Minister

Uncle Louis

LOUIS ST. LAURENT

His name was the same as the St. Lawrence River, the water of life that flows through our land, connecting the Maritimes to Quebec and the French to the English. He was one part Montcalm and the other part Wolfe, two sides united in a proud Canadian. Taking office at age 66, he ruled until he was 75. No one else governed with such class and efficiency. Louis St. Laurent: as Canadian as the St. Lawrence River.

Born Compton, Quebec 1882, died Quebec City 1973, Liberal. PM: 1948–1957

Canadian Childhood

He was descended from Nicola Huot, who landed at Quebec City in 1660 and adopted the family name, perhaps after seeing the great river. Two centuries later Louis-Étienne St. Laurent kept a store at Trois-Rivières, married to a woman whose Scottish forefather had been one of the first farmers in Canada on what became the Plains of Abraham.

Louis-Étienne's son, the dark, handsome Jean-Baptiste-Moise, opened a general store in the village of Compton in an English area just south of Sherbrooke in 1879. The local schoolteacher, a red-haired Irish Catholic named Mary Ann Broderick, who couldn't speak a word of French, was fascinated by him. J.B.M.'s quiet, intelligent ways made him irresistible, and by the following year they were married.

They would have six children. Louis was the first, born on February 1, 1882. At the dinner table, getting the potatoes passed from Father meant asking in French, and beans from Mother could only be obtained in English. They had English Christmases with lots of presents and loud French New Years. People discussed life and politics in both languages around the pot-bellied stove at the St. Laurent store. J.B.M., a Liberal, insisted that equal respect be given to all views. Young Louis listened closely.

"I learned in that small community . . . ," he once said, "that it is possible for people of goodwill to live and let live without being called upon to sacrifice any of those essentials to which any group desires to hold firm."

He grew up tall, dark, and handsome like his father. For the most part he was shy and bookish, but he had thin streaks of devilry. Once he buried his sister in a pile of sand and nearly suffocated her, just to see what it was like.

His mother, strict about manners and education, kept him home until he was eight, teaching him to read and write English. He would always be as good at it as French and speak with a slight Irish lilt. Addicted to reading, he took books to bed and stayed up late. When his father rigged a switch in the master bedroom to turn off his lights, the boy held a candle beneath the covers.

He zoomed through school, showing such promise that teachers groomed him for bigger things. At age 14, in 1896, he left home for a six-year stay at Sherbrooke's St. Charles Seminary, a tough, bilingual Catholic school. His mother hoped he'd be a priest. There, where everyone wore dark uniforms and was up before five and in bed by seven, he moved to the front of the class in almost everything but athletics. He was still shy, but gaining confidence as he devoured more knowledge.

He was also a budding Liberal. When he was 12 his father had tried for the party nomination in a provincial election, and two years later they both went to see the great Laurier speak at a local meeting. As the boy trembled with awe, the legend approached his father, called him by name, and then took the young boy's hand in his.

By the time Louis reached his late teens he knew he would never be a priest. There were just too many things to do. After he graduated as the school's top scholar, he was off to Laval University in Quebec City to study law. Though he joined the student Parliament and debated well, he chose a quiet university life, spending his time reading or strolling on the Plains of Abraham. When he graduated with "great distinction" and won every scholarly prize available, one official said "young St. Laurent will go far."

In the audience that day was beautiful, dark-haired Jeanne Renault, the daughter of a wealthy store owner from Beauceville south of the city. She felt for him when, tall and awkward, he strode across the podium to get his medal from the Governor General of Canada, caught the sleeve of his gown on a chair, and nearly fell on his face.

Then, in 1906, he went to a party and found himself playing cards opposite Mademoiselle Renault. Immediately, he promised himself he would marry her. On her way home that night, the smitten Jeanne promised herself the very same thing.

The Good Life

She was a spirited woman who had vowed that she would marry a handsome and successful man. So, St. Laurent set about to make himself exactly that. It was his fate anyway.

With his brains, honesty, and perfect knowledge of the two languages, the world was his to conquer. He had a lofty view of law and never apologized for it. He saw it not simply as rules, but as guides for behaviour. He believed in justice. A lawyer's job was to help decide between right and wrong. He studied Quebec's and English Canada's laws with equal interest and mastered both.

By the time he married Jeanne in 1908 at the age of 26, he had begun a steady climb to the heights of the law business in Quebec. His easy way with English helped him immensely. By 1911 he was arguing his first case before the Supreme Court of Canada, the following year he won against the mighty CPR, and soon American companies were employing him regularly. He would also make an incredible 60 appearances before the Privy Council of London, the final court of appeal in the British Empire. Before long it was said that he was one of the greatest lawyers in Quebec. He was calm, well informed, and always fair. Laval University made him a Doctor of Law and he was invited into the best social clubs in the city.

Life was good. The family purchased land near the Plains of Abraham and built a large, 15-room, three-storey house. There were servants and a cook, and by 1917, five children. They were ruled strictly, forbidden to fight, and made to speak both languages. The first tongue of the house was French, but not a single negative word about the English was allowed and the words "French Canadian" and "English

Canadian" were banned—citizens were simply Canadians. Though he worked long hours, he valued family life and often took the whole clan on fishing trips. They bought a farm with a beach and tennis court. The only real danger was when Father was driving the car. He insisted on dead silence while he sat intensely behind the wheel, and crashed into so many cars and knocked down so many poles that the family finally made him hire a chauffeur.

Politics remained an interest, but not a profession. In fact, he kept his political views so private that he was asked by Meighen's Conservatives to join them in 1926 and by the Quebec Liberal party to be a cabinet minister in 1930.

He sounded like a statesman in public, his speeches often about Canadian unity. At age 38 in 1920 he addressed a national audience for the first time at the Canadian Bar Association, speaking of the need for lawyers from English and French Canada to work together. In 1930, when R.B. Bennett became Prime Minister, St. Laurent succeeded him as president of the Association. Still a slim, handsome man, with greying hair and salt-and-pepper moustache, he possessed "old-world charm and dignity and [a] sincere, straightforward manner." His pleas for Canadian unity, not through blending everyone but by accepting one another's differences, attracted attention. "Let us not be preoccupied with building walls around the Province of Quebec," he told his people.

He kept rejecting offers to enter politics. Things were going too well to change. And by the late 1930s he was nearing 60.

Only something extraordinary, or *someone* extraordinary, could change his mind. Both appeared, on the telephone, in December 1941.

The Call

It was that wizard Prime Minister, Mackenzie King, calling. The family had just settled down to a typically happy dinner. Overseas, the Second World War was raging, with Hitler menacing Great Britain. King's great Quebec leader, Ernest Lapointe, had died of cancer and he was desperate to have a French Canadian of stature replace him, especially as pressure grew to force men to join the army. King had candidates, among them the Premier of Quebec, but they lacked something—desire, or guts, to lead in this terrible time. Louis St. Laurent's name kept coming up. King was told he was a proud Canadian, brilliant, and brave. He also had a great sense of duty.

Jeanne St. Laurent cried the day he left for Ottawa, though he told her he would say a final no to King. But she suspected something big was about to happen. Within a week Louis was the Minister of Justice, placed right beside the Prime Minister in the cabinet room, in Ernest Lapointe's chair.

He had accepted because he could not say no while young Canadian men and women lost their lives on distant battlefields. He had a condition: he would stay only until the war was over. Okay, said Mackenzie King, his secret mind thinking something else.

St. Laurent fought and won his by-election in Lapointe's Quebec East riding as his 60th birthday passed. Many Québécois saw him as a friend of the English, with fat American clients. Some vowed that if he agreed to forced military service (called conscription), they would riot in the streets, just as in World War I. But one night, in a hall in the very district where the riots had taken place, he surprised them. He stood in front of a tough crowd in his pressed suit and read a statement of his basic political views while looking through his little pince-nez glasses. Then he set it down and looked out at the packed hall. "And now I want you to know what Louis St. Laurent is made of," he said with feeling. He was against laws that brought riots, but backed his Prime Minister. He would return to ask them to give the government the right to request military service. It would be a free vote. And you, he told them, should vote according to what you believe is right.

There was silence, then applause, and then it grew. "It takes a brave man to say that," remarked someone. They had seen an honest politician and they knew it.

Several months later the conscription vote brought mixed results, perhaps what Mackenzie King wanted. The people of English Canada and Quebec still held opposite views. So, King stalled for time, waiting for the right moment to move on the issue.

It would take two more years for that battle to come to boil. Meanwhile St. Laurent took up his post as Minister of Justice and began to make his mark in the House of Commons. He was not a dynamic speaker, but careful and intelligent. His opponents found him difficult to beat because he made so much sense and sometimes agreed with them. He played few political games.

Mackenzie King was soon convinced that this elegant man who worked 15-hour days was not only as able as Lapointe, but a possible successor to the throne. He was "the best man in the cabinet . . ." according to the PM, "and I don't exclude myself in making that statement."

When King finally, and cleverly, brought in a form of conscription in 1944, St. Laurent really showed his heart. Throughout the fights in cabinet over the issue—the resignation of Quebec ministers that left St. Laurent the only French leader, the firing of the Defence Minister, and the fear of a military revolt—King's Justice Minister stood by him. In the end, though armed guards were posted outside St. Laurent's Quebec home, he defended Canada's right to have *some* forced service. Dictators were attempting to destroy what was dear to his nation, and Canadians were dying at the war front and not being properly reinforced. Conscription was the right thing to do, so he stuck with it, regardless of the opposition. Quebec seethed, but didn't explode. They weren't with him, but many respected him. And before long, with the help of Canada's strengthened forces, the war was won. "The more I see of St. Laurent," wrote King in his diary, "the nobler soul I believe him to be. One of God's gentlemen if ever there was one."

The Prime Minister was now certain who his successor would be. It was going to be very tough for St. Laurent to return to his Quebec law practice.

King showered him with responsibilities. He took him to San Francisco for the creation of the United Nations in 1945 and had him broadcast the war victory address to French Canada. And as tensions between the big, Communist Soviet Union and our democratic Western world began to grow into the frightening buildup of weapons called the Cold War, King made him Minister of External Affairs to handle the international scene. St. Laurent ascended.

Uncle Television

By 1948, after more good work on provincial relations and getting Newfoundland into Canada, he was the obvious choice to replace King. Many times he told his boss that he wanted to return to his law practice, but each time the old wizard would stall, invite him to Kingsmere for a meal, and work on him. Appeals were made to his sense of duty and the importance of a French Canadian becoming the next leader. Finally, St. Laurent gave in. In 1948 he succeeded King and became the 12th Prime Minister of Canada.

It would be one of the smoothest runs in history. Perhaps only Laurier did better. In 1949 he led the party to the greatest election victory up to that time, amassing 190 seats out of 262. And in 1953, at age 71, he led them to another huge win.

St. Laurent's accomplishments were many. He passed the Trans-Canada Highway Act to send a highway across the nation, put Canada in the North Atlantic Treaty Organization to hold off the Soviets, helped poorer provinces, and named Vincent Massey the first Canadian-born Governor General. And, of course, he championed the idea of a united Canada.

During St. Laurent's time, television became popular. Canadians began seeing their Prime Minister on a regular basis, and they liked what they saw: a white-haired gentleman with a white moustache and a kindly smile, who seemed fair-minded and spoke to them in their own languages. The Liberal party used every chance they could to have him filmed or photographed with a child. "Uncle Louis" was born—the friendly politician with Canadian kids on his knee. He loved them anyway.

But even his smooth run got a little bumpy. After a gruelling 1954 world tour, he returned worn out. Then he had duels with Quebec's strong Premier Duplessis, and in 1956, two bigger problems came along.

First there was the ugly pipeline debate. It began because C.D. Howe, King's famous old war supply minister who had used special powers to run Canadian industry during the war, thought he still had them in peacetime. He made a deal to send a pipeline from Alberta across Canada to bring natural gas to everyone. Then he pushed the debate through the House as if the Opposition shouldn't argue, using all his powers to limit discussion. There were storms of protest. All heck broke loose. Members stood on their desks and shook their fists while the press watched with their mouths open. St. Laurent sat quietly reading a book. The Conservatives told the country it was obvious that the Liberals had been in power too long.

The Suez Crisis of 1956 was almost as bad, though St. Laurent likely did the right thing that time. It came about after Egypt seized the international Suez Canal that ran through their country. Great Britain and its snobby PM, Anthony Eden, were spitting mad about it. They demanded that Canada help stop Egypt, with force. St. Laurent did something rather bold. He said no. And when Britain went ahead with an attack, he officially told Eden that he "regretted" the mother country's actions. Canada split on the question. Some believed we had to stick by our old ally; others felt it was time to stand up for what *we* thought was right. Eventually the crisis passed, largely due to External Affairs Minister Lester B. Pearson's plan for a peacekeeping force (for which he won a Nobel Prize). Canada gained a reputation as a voice for peace. But the whole issue made some voters wonder if Uncle Louis was perfect after all.

In the June 1957 election they squeezed him out, just barely. They had a new and younger hero, a fire-breather from Saskatchewan named John Diefenbaker.

St. Laurent, though 75 years old, had expected to win. He was hurt, but hid it. He stuck around into 1958, then handed the Liberal reins over to Pearson and went back to his Quebec law practice. He had left it 17 years earlier, expecting to be home within months.

He ruled in an exciting time—a time that saw the birth of rock'n'roll, international spies, and Rocket Richard's rushes down the ice at the Montreal Forum. Some critics today say that St. Laurent, by comparison, was boring. But sometimes it's better to be ruled so smoothly that we barely notice.

He would live until the age of 91, a grand old man right up to his death in 1973. His secretary once wrote that he was the only Prime Minister in history who made governing Canada look "easy and effortless." Uncle Louis was as steady as the St. Lawrence River and just as Canadian.

13th Prime Minister

Canadian Dynamite

JOHN DIEFENBAKER

*Born Neustadt, Ontario 1895,
died Ottawa 1979,
Progressive Conservative.
PM: 1957–1963*

I magine a man with gleaming blue eyes of steel, hair of grey ocean waves on a massive head, jowls that shake with emotion, and a voice like a grizzly's growl. Imagine a man who lived in a shack on the freezing prairie frontier, defended murderers in courtroom dramas, and stood up for the underdog against all odds. Imagine huge crowds packing halls throughout Canada, surging like dangerous mobs to hear his electric speeches of love for his country. Imagine Canadians reaching out to touch his coat.

But they would grow to hate him as much as they loved him; he would fail as monumentally as he succeeded. He was suspicious and theatrical, a character of unmatched colour. This was Diefenbaker—Canadian dynamite!

Lightning from the West

He was born in tiny Neustadt in southwestern Ontario, on September 18, 1895, descended from immigrant German wagon makers and Scottish adventurers. His father, William, was a quiet teacher who often moved his family about in pursuit of a living. In 1903 he took his wife, Mary, John (seven), and a younger son out to the northern Saskatchewan frontier, where many other people with unusual names were settling. They built a homestead on the flat land between Saskatoon and Prince Albert and set down roots. Here, 20 years before, natives and Métis had gone to war with Canada for their rights.

John helped build the schoolhouse, clear the land, till the fields, and chop wood. In the bitter winters they stoked the stove to keep indoor temperatures above zero. Caught in a blizzard as a child, he nearly lost both legs. Neighbours helped each other: sharing freshly shot wildfowl and raising barns. They were underdogs fighting the odds.

Mary Diefenbaker, like many Prime Ministers' mothers, was the dominant member of the family. Unimpressed with her modest husband and hardened by her tough life, she pushed John to become someone and fight for the rights of hard-working Canadians.

He did all right in school but didn't show signs of future greatness. Other kids made fun of his strange name and appearance. In his 15th year the family moved to Saskatoon, population 10,000 and growing. There, at a railway station on July 29, 1910, arriving early to pick up newspapers for his route, he met an elegant, white-haired man, standing alone in the prairie air. They spoke, the man paid for his paper, and the boy explained that he was busy and had to go. He was always busy. He didn't tell Sir Wilfrid Laurier what he often told others. Someday he would be Prime Minister too.

By 1919 he had graduated from the new University of Saskatchewan and passed his law exams, "an ambitious romantic, who quietly nurtured his dreams." Those dreams included building a successful law practice and then entering the lion's den of politics. He spent summers teaching and selling religious books, doing so well that his company said he "made the most remarkable record ever made by anyone."

His first practice was in little Wakaw, near the old homestead. There, in a place dominated by three looming grain elevators, he thrived. The only other lawyer packed up and left. In 1924 he went north to bigger Prince Albert to increase his business.

There he acquired a reputation and loosened up. Edna May Brower, the Saskatoon teacher who became his girlfriend and in 1929 his wife, deserved much of the credit. She was energetic and flirty, a red-haired personality next to a serious young man in a double-breasted suit. Her warm ways at his side made life much easier for him in public. The new John Diefenbaker even held hands and kissed in broad daylight.

His Prince Albert courtroom days established him as a dynamic murder trial lawyer. He would defend 20 accused murderers and lose only two to the gallows. Many of his cases seemed hopeless: loners, tough guys, abused wives, and poor immigrants caught with smoking guns or confessions. But Diefenbaker loved to gamble. Often he didn't use witnesses, but relied on his ability to sway juries with magnetic performances. Perfecting a style that would mature in the House of Commons, in arenas, and on television, he would throw back his gown, place a hand on a hip, and thrust demanding fingers at opponents, his deep voice rising and lowering, pausing and pouncing. "He can take an out-and-out rascal and describe him with such wonderful oratory," said a lawyer, "that one may almost see a halo around the rogue's head." He would fix blue eyes that "bored right through you" on jury members, swaying one at a time. While questioning witnesses, he would turn his back, then swing around to make dramatic accusations. Once he showed how a murder took place by racing across a courtroom and sliding under a table. Crowds came to see him. Newspapers loved his cases.

The Will to Win

He wasn't nearly as successful in politics. Uninspired by the Liberals, who dominated the province, he joined the Conservatives. He was attracted to their colourful, pro-British show in the 1911 election, sure that it was with the underdogs that he could make his reputation, project his views, and stay independent from big business and the establishment.

He threw himself into long-shot campaigns, and kept coming out the loser. In 1925 he ran federally for Meighen's Conservatives and lost badly, only to get up and be defeated again the next year. In 1929 he chased a provincial seat and was rejected. In 1938 he was squashed again. He missed becoming Prince Albert mayor by 48 votes, then rose to be leader of the weakling Saskatchewan Conservatives, but couldn't get them a single seat.

He suspected that Establishment forces worked against him. Often he was right. Here was an unusual Conservative, fighting for the little guy, opposing his party if he thought it was wrong and believing that government should give money to farmers and the poor. He took his case to the people, and met them everywhere, on farms, on streets, and unleashed his amazing speaking style. "He was tall, lean, almost skeletal," recalled a reporter, "his bodily motions jerky and spasmodic, his face pinched and white, his pallor emphasized by metallic black curls and sunken, hypnotic eyes. But from this frail, wraithlike person, so deceptive in his look of physical infirmity, a voice of vehement power and rude health blared like a trombone."

A maturing Diefenbaker finally won in 1940, one of only three Conservatives elected to Parliament on the Canadian prairies. Soon he and Edna were on a cross-country train to Ottawa. Over the years he would make many similar journeys. On the way, his wife greeted people then introduced her brilliant husband. It was a deadly combination.

He took to Parliament like a piranha to water, his speaking style a sensation. His accusing fingers, torrents of words, and cold stares were turned on Liberals. Mackenzie King, finally free of Arthur Meighen, couldn't believe it. He shrank in his seat when Diefenbaker attacked. The wit was overwhelming, the words applied like needles and twisted. His weapons included an enormous memory and the ability to absorb a page of facts at a glance. He tore into the government for being out of touch with Canadians.

Within two years he tried for the party leadership. But he was still a bit of a loner and often suspicious of the powers that be. He ran a distant third to new leader John Bracken (a Progressive, so the party name changed to Progressive Conservative).

He won his seat in 1945 and took another run at the leadership three years later. But "Gorgeous" George Drew, the well-established Ontario Premier, crushed him. Again John was bitter. The big boys didn't like him—the common people did. Drew was a bust for two straight national elections, failing to unseat the Liberals, while in the West, Diefenbaker, the man with passion, kept winning. He barely mentioned his party's name and threw their election pamphlets into a lake. But in 1956 Drew resigned. This time, John might finally make it.

The Whirlwind

Even as he drew close to winning the Ottawa convention, he doubted they would let him have it. But "Dief" became "the Chief" by a huge margin.

He did it without Edna. For several years she had been ill and depressed, and died in 1951, John by her hospital bed in Prince Albert. At the funeral, he ran his hand through her hair as she lay in her coffin and tears dripped down his face.

After Edna's death he began dating Olive Freeman, who had first charmed him long ago in Saskatoon when he was a university student and she just 15 years old. In 1953 they were married. Intelligent and confident, this elegant Mrs. Diefenbaker became a famous Canadian, her husband's advisor, always at his side, his toughest defender.

When Louis St. Laurent went to the polls in 1957, he had no idea what he was in for. The Liberals had 22 straight government years behind them and the nation was strong. A loss was impossible. But they underestimated their dynamic 61-year-old opponent. Diefenbaker stalked across the country and gave Canadians a style of campaigning they had never seen before. He was in his element, speaking directly to the people, a bizarre-looking man with a strange name and absolute lightning in his speeches, as upset with old ways as they were. "For the first time since John A. Macdonald," wrote an historian, "a personality was running, or rather stomping, against mere humanoids." He spoke of a new Canada: strong, and ready to look after its poor, its immigrants, and native people. Phrases like "appointment with destiny" and "sacred trust" trumpeted from his lips. His energy was endless. "It is time for a Diefenbaker Government!" cried his slogan. And it was. The grand St. Laurent fell with a stunned thud and bounced right out of politics.

"My fellow Canadians," Dief proclaimed, "I have one love . . . Canada; one purpose: Canada's greatness; one aim: Canadian unity from the Atlantic to the Pacific!"

Back in the House he was a new kind of Prime Minister, with a charisma not seen since his heroes, Macdonald and Laurier. On the attack, he would shove back his chair and pace "like a caged lion." He loved it. "What a life it is to be Prime Minister!" he wrote.

But he had won by only a few seats and wanted more. He felt he could smother the Liberals in another election. Then their new leader, diplomat Lester Pearson, quiet and wearing a bow tie, gave him his chance. Pearson rashly questioned the Conservatives' authority to govern. Diefenbaker seized his opportunity. He waved secret Liberal documents in his hand, proving their government had told lies. He shook them like "they were a rattlesnake he was trying to strangle." Then he called his election.

It would be the most stunning political performance in our past and his crowning moment. It inspired U.S. Vice-President Richard Nixon to call him "one of the truly great political campaigners of our time," achieving a victory "seldom . . . equalled in history."

That was the year mobs came out to greet him everywhere he went, when they surged to touch his coat, when he spoke like a raging evangelist of Canadian pride and hope. Even in Quebec, where Conservatives hadn't won since 1887, crowds thundered when he appeared. They "just tore the roof off in a frenzy" said a politician about a huge gathering in Montreal. And they sat in awe in Winnipeg, listening to "this magnificent flurry of eloquence." "Follow John" said the posters. Everyone did. "This is the vision, One Canada!" he cried. Canada was on the move: Diefenbaker would lead. He spoke of a nation that would develop northward, as Macdonald had gone west.

In the end he won 208 seats, the Liberals 48. It was unbelievable devastation.

But almost immediately he had problems. He failed to include Quebec as much as he should have in cabinet; he unrealistically promised more trade with Great Britain. It seemed his words were greater than his actions. The development northward stalled.

There were many reasons why things didn't work the way they might have. He remained a suspicious man, and too apt to delay and then act without consulting others. The economy began to go bad. He liked to spend, mostly to help the poor, and soon the government's debt rose. The Canadian dollar, the "Diefendollar," dropped in worth.

"The Chief" could be disorganized, unpredictable, and temperamental. In 1959 he killed the production of the Avro Arrow jet, a Canadian-built fighter ahead of its time. The loss of jobs was bad enough, but even more depressing was the sudden end of a grand opportunity for Canada to be a world leader.

On the international scene he had his troubles too. Sometimes it was because he had the courage to do what was right. At the 1961 Commonwealth Conference he insisted that the newly independent South Africa be barred from membership until they agreed to give black Africans equal rights. The other leaders wanted South Africa admitted: it was good business. But Dief would not back down, and made enemies.

Then he had troubles with the United States, especially with its young President John F. Kennedy. Kennedy is remembered as a cool, peace-loving leader, but was actually ready to risk almost anything for American interests during those Cold War days—in 1962 he scared the world by confronting the Soviet Union in a showdown over nuclear weapons. The Chief wanted peace and was slow to support him. The two men grew to hate each other. Kennedy wanted nuclear tips put on U.S. missiles placed in Canada to protect America from Soviet attack, and the right to have Americans fire them. Diefenbaker resisted.

Many in his cabinet began to doubt him, worrying about his supposedly anti-American stance. When he lost more than 90 seats in the 1962 election and his magic faded, rebellion erupted in cabinet. The suspicious Chief, now 67 years old, faced them down. But many deserted him and he entered the 1963 election almost alone.

Defiant of Americans and pro-Canada, he took to the trains and travelled the nation, giving fire-breathing speeches again and meeting the people on the streets. The election was close: without him the Conservatives might have been wiped out. He lost gloriously.

For three years he was on the attack as the Leader of the Opposition. He often overmatched the quieter Pearson. Their battles, like those of Macdonald and Brown, Meighen and King, were dramatic.

The Long Goodbye

And then, as he always suspected, his own party's big guns turned on him. In 1967, Canada's centennial year, the Conservatives' president called for a review of the 72-year-old's leadership. He ran for his own job, but finished a sad fifth, and the tears ran down Olive's face. They had kicked him out.

He would hold on for another 12 years, returning to Prince Albert each election, almost pleased by the party's losses elsewhere. His wit remained sharp, his words quotable. He kept up a brisk pace and travelled widely to talk to the people.

At age 83, he was elected for a final time. Then, in August of 1979, still an energetic Member of Parliament for almost his 40th year, he died in Ottawa. His funeral, which he had carefully planned, was amazing. A train took his flag-draped casket across the country to Saskatchewan, while television broadcast its progress. As with Macdonald, the people stood at each train stop and bowed their heads. In the prairies the farmers, the average Canadians far from the towers of power, shed tears.

He had done much for them. He tried to protect them by creating a Bill of Rights, corrected a terrible wrong by giving the vote to aboriginal people, appointed our first native senator, put the first woman and first citizen of "foreign" descent into cabinet. "One Canada," to him, wasn't just French and English, but a much larger family. He once spoke of the many nationalities in his Parliament, then thundered, *". . . and they are all Canadians."*

But his rule had been shorter than it should have been. Many policies seemed muddled. He hadn't lived up to his promise.

Or had he? He never forgot his vow to help the underdog. He had the courage to be a rebel Conservative. He faced the

Americans without fear. Diefenbaker was the greatest actor our political stage had ever seen. He gave us spirit. And sometimes, when all the details fade into history, that is sufficient. There has not been enough "Canadian Dynamite."

14th Prime Minister

International Man of Mystery

LESTER B. PEARSON

Across the aisle from John Diefenbaker in the House of Commons was this nice, decent man wearing a bow tie. He had a round face, a smile, and a slight lisp. Not once in his childhood had he told himself he just had to be Prime Minister. He wasn't big and bold, his eyes didn't bore holes into people, nor did his voice thunder across the nation. In fact, he seemed too nice to be where he was. But many things about Lester Bowles Pearson were deceiving. Long before he

Born Newtonbrook, Ontario 1897, died Ottawa 1972, Liberal. PM: 1963–1968

appeared in Parliament, and without having done anything dramatic, he had been the most admired public figure in Canada. He went places and got things done, while apparently doing nothing. His influence on our history would have been substantial even if he'd never been Prime Minister.

Zigzagging

The story of Lester Pearson is really the story of a guy named Mike—that's what his friends called him—an ordinary guy who grew up to do extraordinary things. He started life on April 23, 1897, in little Newtonbrook north of Toronto. Both sides of his family were Irish Canadians. His mother, Annie Bowles (another of those strong-minded Prime Minister moms), and his father, Edwin Pearson, both grew up children of Methodist preachers. Edwin, who also became a minister, met Annie in 1890 in church. Faith dominated their lives. They believed in right and wrong: people needed to treat one another with love and respect.

As a kid, Lester was always in motion. While their father moved from church to church, he and his brothers, Duke and Vaughan, skated, ran, and bodychecked their way across hockey rinks, ball diamonds, and lacrosse fields in towns like Peterborough, Chatham, and Hamilton. Lester wasn't big, but he was quick and inventive and burned to win. In school he did well too, though he made fun of his high marks and leadership roles in order to stay popular. The boys lived happy lives. That right-and-wrong thing was a big deal to them, but their spirits were never smothered by it.

His dad was a humble sort, but also knew many rich churchgoers, and that, combined with his mother's constant push, got Lester enrolled in the famous University of Toronto at age 16. But he didn't have much ambition and spent most of his time having fun with friends and pretty girls. His success in sports continued. Then, his life shattered.

When the First World War broke out in 1914, he was only 17, but desperate to be involved. It seemed a romantic struggle about right and wrong. On his 18th birthday he enlisted and went overseas. His hospital unit landed in northern Greece. There the romance faded. The wounded cried at night, evil "Zeppelin" airships droned overhead like waiting death, and time dragged. He led his hockey team to the championship of the Greek unit and wished he were with his brothers fighting at the war front in France. Finally, after a year and a half of waiting, he was sent to England to train.

His dream was to be a flying ace like the great Canadian Billy Bishop, a dangerous and heroic role. But he never made it. He crashed during training, and then he was involved in a London bus accident. Pearson came home to Canada with wrecked nerves and a lifelong belief that war was wrong and to be avoided at all costs. "I got hurt before I got a chance to get killed," he later said. "That's about what it amounts to."

It took him a while to get going again at university. Sports helped. He was soon a hockey and basketball star and quarterback of the Royal Air Force football team. Opposing fans in big crowds at the famous Varsity Stadium shouted, "Will we get the Pearson boy? Sure we will, and then, oh joy. Goodbye RAF!"

He tried stuffing sausages and working in the fertilizer department of a food company in Chicago, but hated it. So back to school he went, first at historic Oxford University in England. He played for its hockey team, a nearly all-Canadian club that toured Europe, creaming top Swiss clubs and even the Belgian national team. (The Swiss called him "Herr Zigzag" for his fancy moves.) Then Pearson returned to the U of T, where he taught history, and almost became the coach of the football team and the university's first Athletics Director.

Almost. He still wasn't sure he had found his calling in university life. He married one of his students in 1925, the beautiful, brainy Maryon Moody from Winnipeg. She had a free spirit, loved the arts and rebel politics, and planned to be a "new woman" who wouldn't simply be a wife. She had lots of male admirers. But Mike was a boyish guy with brown hair and green eyes, full of great stories that made people laugh.

They lived in downtown Toronto and enjoyed the things it offered. A son was born in 1927. But despite their happiness, Mike wanted more excitement. During a trip to Ottawa he visited the House of Commons and saw the dramatic battle between Meighen and King during the King–Byng affair.

Intrigued, he decided to write an exam to see if he could become part of Canada's growing External Affairs Department. At university others thought he was bright, but not a heavyweight—he just seemed too happy-go-lucky, too much a jock. Mike Pearson fooled many people many times. He scored 86 percent on his test, the number one candidate in the nation, way ahead of the "intellectuals."

The Best-Known Canadian in the World

By 1928 the family (including a daughter now) had moved to Ottawa and he had begun his new job. He quickly knew that he'd found his calling. His bosses, including Mackenzie King, noticed how inventive and hard working he was. He was charming, quick-witted, a good listener, and friendly too—all perfect skills for a diplomat.

Unlike some, Pearson was willing to take on any job. Soon he was making many contacts and gaining a reputation for helping opponents agree. He started travelling to international conferences, and did so well that he was recommended by Prime Minister Bennett for the Order of the British Empire. He didn't want the medal, but one day, while he was playing tennis, someone came by and tossed it to him. It was the perfect way to honour Mike Pearson.

By the mid-1930s he was posted to London as an assistant in High Commissioner Vincent Massey's office. The famous

Massey was an old-fashioned Empire man and liked to wear fancy uniforms. Mike found them ridiculous. But he and Maryon loved the fast-paced life of the Empire's capital. He became an important part of Canada's international relations team and his opinion was valued at conferences. His boss, who seldom said flattering things, remarked, "He has marked ability in . . . developing friendly relations with representatives of other governments without losing his distinctive Canadian point of view."

He believed that the future depended on nations reaching out to one another, not turning inward. He still feared wars, knowing they solved nothing, and worried about nations arming. But by the late 1930s even he had to advise England and Canada to prepare to defend themselves, big time. He knew the Second World War was coming. He hated German dictator Adolph Hitler—his lust for war, his treatment of Jews, and all that he stood for.

Mike was in London when it was bombed, when the heroic Battle of Britain was fought and as the tide turned against Germany. Then in 1942 he was sent to Washington. Within three years he was Canadian Ambassador to the United States. The timing was perfect, since Canada was growing closer to the U.S. As the war came to an end, Pearson was a big part of international efforts to create a lasting peace. Among the greatest of these was the United Nations. He was one of its creators.

As worldwide respect for him grew, he led various international associations. One was the Food and Agriculture

Organization, formed to attempt a fairer distribution of food throughout the world.

Just after the Americans dropped the atomic bomb on Japan, President Truman asked for his views on that horrible weapon of destruction. Pearson told him that he was concerned about big weapons and superpowers. He thought the United States was too emotional about everything, too self-centred and unreasonable about the Soviet Union and communism, and that the Soviets were just as stubborn.

Pearson was appearing on radio talk shows and giving public speeches, becoming known to average Canadians. His opinions were in tune with the modern, international world and the need for understanding in the age of the frightening new bombs. In Ottawa, the old man in the Prime Minister's chair was eyeing him. Mackenzie King even told his diary that Mike Pearson would make a perfect successor.

In 1946 he was brought back to Canada to become the number two man in External Affairs. King had handed over the Minister's job to a new guy, Louis St. Laurent.

St. Laurent ran Ottawa's fastest-growing department. By 1948 it had 1,200 employees, more than twice as many as when the war ended. His favourite was Pearson. So, Mike could do almost anything he wanted. He flew around the world, trying to keep it peaceful.

When King retired in 1948, Prime Minister St. Laurent pushed Pearson into politics. Mike was 51 years old and ready: behind his happy exterior lurked an ambitious guy who wanted to rise to the top. St. Laurent made him Minister of External Affairs.

He ran in a popular Liberal riding in Algoma East, a huge area in northern Ontario. The folks there weren't always impressed with "Pearsonian diplomacy," as the world called it. He had just finished signing the NATO pact (a military plan to protect the "free world" from the Soviets), but a voter in a northern village told him, "Yes, that was a fine thing you did down there in Washington, a fine thing for Canada, but it won't help you much around here if you don't get us a new post office."

They elected him anyway. And kept on electing him. He charmed them like he charmed the big wheels and told them great stories and took off his jacket and played ball. And out in the world, he was an External Affairs Minister unlike Canada had ever seen before. Honours poured in. He became the Chancellor of the University of Toronto in 1951, the President of the United Nations General Assembly in 1952 (and would have been its Secretary General had the Soviets not stopped him), and world leaders asked his advice.

The few times he got into trouble only made him a bigger star. When he went to the Soviet Union, his tense, face-to-face defence of democracies against Communist leader Khrushchev made headlines.

For the most part that wasn't his way. He believed in finding quiet solutions. Like in 1956, when his idea of sending a peacekeeping force to Egypt avoided an explosive war. That was the high point in his diplomatic career, and for it he was awarded the Nobel Peace Prize. When officials phoned him in his Ottawa home he said that he must have been merely nominated. They said no. He said "Gosh."

He had become the best-known Canadian in the world. No one had had such impact outside our borders. People proudly saw him as a symbol of the country's growth.

The Maple Leaf Forever

It was almost inevitable that he would become the Liberal leader when St. Laurent left in 1957. Mike was in his 60th year, but many predicted a great future. It got off to a rocky start when Diefenbaker, his opposite in many ways, just about tore him apart in Parliament when he demanded that the Conservatives resign. Then the Chief whipped him harder than any Liberal had ever been whipped at the polls.

Pearson slowly rebuilt his party by bringing in more Québécois members and other new recruits. It would take him two more elections to become PM, and even then, in 1963, he barely won. In 1965 he won again, but by exactly the same margin.

Though his time as Prime Minister lasted just five years and was plagued with scandals, indecision, and mistakes (including an attempt to shrink American control over our businesses), it also jammed in many accomplishments and set the pace for the future.

He started the ball rolling on bilingualism, making Quebec's language a true part of the nation (when he was first at External Affairs there were no French Canadians, nor did anyone speak French). He told Charles de Gaulle that he wasn't welcome in Canada when the legendary French president supported Quebec separatism on a visit to Montreal. He brought in the Canada Pension Plan and Medicare, ensuring that no Canadian was denied medical care. He reached an historic trade agreement for cars (the "Auto Pact") with the U.S., increased aid to poor countries, and ran Canada's 100th birthday celebration and Expo 67 in Montreal, which drew 50 million people to marvel at our progress. And his most famous move was the creation of a new flag, replacing the old British Union Jack and Red Ensign with a red maple leaf, now the symbol of Canada around the world.

Despite all this, he and his government took a lot of criticism during their reign and always barely clung to power. He allowed American nuclear weapons into Canada (many thought he wasn't nearly tough enough with the U.S.), took no strong position on the Vietnam War, was constantly bested in the House by the dramatic Diefenbaker (unlike the Chief, he appeared to shrink on TV), often seemed disorganized, and was not nearly as charismatic as he had been in the 1950s. As Quebec demanded more rights and separatists' terrorist bombs exploded in the province, he barely responded. Some felt he never took a stand on anything. "Nailing Pearson down was like stabbing a sponge," said someone. The man who made many decisions earlier in his career with his heart seemed to make few at the top. Not many were impressed with his wisdom. At a quiet media gathering when he left office in 1968, he said simply, "C'est la vie."

But Pearson had become almost as good at fooling people as Mackenzie King, and learned to manage his country almost as well too. He was one of those quiet-on-the-outside, unusual Canadians. His career, including his time as Prime Minister, had actually been dynamic. He turned Canada into the international peacekeeper it was for the last half of the 20th century and made major changes in government.

In retirement he helped the World Bank figure out how aid should be given to Third World countries, lectured at Carleton University, and wrote his memoirs. He had many opportunities to cheer for his beloved Toronto Maple Leafs. But cancer hit him in 1970, and after a gruelling book tour two years later, he faded fast and died. His coffin was placed in the Parliament Buildings, draped with the maple leaf. The nation's largest airport, in Toronto, would be named for him, near the town, now swallowed up by the great city, where long ago he had sat in his father's church and learned right from wrong.

Though few noticed, he had set up the future. During his last days in power, sitting there in his cabinet, waiting, were three young men he had recruited. Their names were Pierre Trudeau, John Turner, and Jean Chrétien. Outside, high above the Peace Tower, flew an internationally recognized symbol of a vastly changed nation.

15th Prime Minister

Cool!

PIERRE ELLIOTT TRUDEAU

Born Montreal 1919, died Montreal 2000, Liberal. PM: 1968–1979; 1980–1984

During Canada's rocking 100th birthday, as a suddenly fascinating country swelled with pride and Quebec threatened to blow it up, a new sort of man leapt onto the stage. Pierre Elliott Trudeau danced with gorgeous movie stars, married a flower child and lost her to The Rolling Stones, pirouetted behind the Queen's back, and drove a way-cool silver Mercedes. He was an international star, our coolest ever, and totally changed us. He believed in Canada with his soul and fought for unity as surely as he paddled his canoe in the northern wilds. When he took power he was 22 years younger than Pearson and 24 years younger than Diefenbaker. And boy, did it show.

The Swinger

His father, Charlie, came from nine generations of poor Québécois farmers, but did much better. Educated as a lawyer, Charlie set up a business to make a mark in the English-run world of Montreal. Grace Elliott, the daughter of a successful downtown saloon owner, married him in 1915. Her Quebec heritage went way back to the days of Scottish Loyalists leaving the United States during its revolution, to stay British.

Quiet, tea-sipping, English-speaking Grace and loud, dynamic, French-speaking Charlie were living in a modest downtown Montreal home when Joseph Philippe Pierre Yves Elliott Trudeau was born on October 18, 1919, the second of three children. There was often tension in that home. Charlie was hard working and hard drinking; his business was a string of gas stations and the Automobile Owners Association. But as it grew in the 1920s, he was often in debt. Brains and toughness got him through. He chewed out his mechanics, punched out the lazy ones, and fixed cars himself. In 1932 he sold everything for $1.4 million. The Trudeaus were suddenly rich. And over the next few years, as Charlie invested in amusement parks, apartments, and the Montreal Royals pro baseball team, his fortune grew.

At home, young Pierre started shy and a bit frail. He would always need to push himself to be friendly in public. His father knocked some of the shyness and all the frailness out of him before he reached his teenage years, teaching him to box and toughening him up. Pierre would defend the honour of his neighbourhood against any French Canadian, Irish Catholic, or Jew who lived there. This love of competition would stay with him.

The growth of his brilliant, fighting mind began at Academie Querbes, a respected bilingual school where he studied in English for three years and then switched to French. At age 12 he went to Collège Brébeuf, a Jesuit Catholic school that deeply affected his life. There he was taught to strive for excellence, value reason, discipline himself, and overcome emotion. "Let us have cold intelligence," he would later say.

Then, in April 1935, disaster struck. His father, returning from a trip to the Royals' training camp in Florida, caught pneumonia and died. It shocked 15-year-old Pierre. He lost his father at a critical time in his life, and cried bitterly at the funeral. The family withdrew into their home.

At school Trudeau became a harder guy. He wanted to take on every challenge, determined to become the brightest and toughest student, desperate to be unique. He didn't care if others thought he was arrogant. His belief in his own willpower, taught by the Jesuits, grew. On the ice and in the fields, he did anything to win. Teachers threw him out of classes for disobedience. Though he sometimes rode to school in the luxury of a limousine, inside he was churning.

When he graduated from Brébeuf in 1940, he entered law school at the University of Montreal and found it boring. A year working at a law firm wasn't any better. Politics came into his life. His father had held boozy pro-Quebec-Conservative meetings in his basement, but Pierre was determined to be a rebel. The Second World War raging, he campaigned for Montreal mayor Jean Drapeau in his fight against forced military service, and in his many spare hours rode with a motorcycle gang wearing a German war helmet.

His life changed over the next few years. From 1944 through 1948, nearing the age of 30, he studied at three of the world's best universities: Harvard in the United States, the Sorbonne in Paris, and the London School of Economics. "Pierre Trudeau, Citizen of the World" read the sign on his Harvard door, and he roared through France on his motorcycle to meet the famous artist Georges Braque. He also matured: his politics were going to be Liberal, favouring the sort of nation Macdonald created at Confederation.

In 1948 he went off to explore the world. Throughout his life, even after he became Prime Minister, he took daring trips, anxious to learn about other cultures. As a kid he was taken to Germany as Hitler rose to power, and now he went to Israel, India, Vietnam, and even China. The trip became legendary. He travelled to places that foreigners stayed away from. He took chances. He wore a turban, grew a beard, was thrown in jail as a spy, defended himself against villains by waving a dagger and acting crazy, and was even attacked by pirates. When he arrived in China, the Communist rebels were invading the cities. Terror reigned. People were being executed in the streets. Many years later, he tried to take a peek at forbidden Cuba by paddling across the unpredictable waters of the Straits of Florida from the American mainland. Authorities arrested the future Prime Minister.

Back in Montreal in 1949, he made headlines by helping two friends who would become central characters in his life: *Le Devoir* writer Gérard Pelletier and union leader Jean Marchand. They encouraged him to attend a union strike demonstration in Asbestos, Quebec. There, instead of just speaking to workers about their rights, he unleashed a dramatic speech about *human* rights and the abuse of workers by big companies.

Soon he was writing for *Le Devoir*, and more importantly, for *Cité Libre*, a small, not particularly popular, rebellious paper. In it, he attacked the provincial government of Maurice Duplessis, which was in the midst of its long domination of Quebec. Duplessis wanted the province to be a sort of nation within Canada, and used the powerful Catholic Church to help him. He controlled everything; opposing his government was useless. Trudeau was blacklisted and barred from teaching at university.

Pierre didn't care. He wrote many loud articles, did legal work for unions and government enemies, and pushed the idea that Quebec was better off in Canada. He roared around in sports cars and managed the family fortune. A sensation with the opposite sex, he dated young women, even teenagers, when well into his 30s. Trudeau was a brilliant, rich, international adventurer. He wore leather and was always cool, though sometimes scary when he confronted others in arguments.

When Duplessis finally fell and the Liberals took control in 1960, Trudeau, known nationally now as a political commentator, became a professor at the University of Montreal. He no longer seemed so rebellious. The Liberals opened up government to everyone so that no one was blacklisted any more, and pressed for more Quebec rights, beginning the "Quiet Revolution." It became cool to be Québécois. A new generation turned against Canada.

Trudeau, Pelletier, and Marchand kept their pro-Canada stance, and in 1965 decided to do something about it. They joined Lester Pearson's national Liberal party and ran for office, shocking many friends. Trudeau, still wanting to play the rebel (standing on his head at parties for attention), took a lot of convincing. He was more interested in the young New Democratic Party, but their policy of a "two nation" Canada angered him. Anxious to put his ideas into action, he overcame his dislike of Pearson and "trained donkey" Liberals, and joined the party of Laurier. The Liberals disliked his nasty criticisms and style, but Marchand convinced them to take him. Ottawa was about to undergo a serious change.

Trudeaumania

He won in a safe downtown Montreal riding and was taken into Pearson's office as the PM's parliamentary secretary. He impressed everyone with his cool judgment and brains, even though he still dressed weirdly for a politician and went to Montreal on the weekends to dance in discos. By April 1967 he was Minister of Justice.

His appearance in the House of Commons in loud shirts and sandals outraged John Diefenbaker. Pearson, though, saw past the pose. At a Charlottetown conference, Trudeau made headlines by saying that Canada had given Quebec and the provinces all the power they needed. He wanted *some* changes: the French language made equal with English and every Canadian's rights protected.

But when Pearson resigned in December 1967, few saw Trudeau as his successor. There were many established candidates. When Marchand withdrew, Pearson leaned towards supporting Pierre. As Justice Minister, he had modernized Canada's laws on divorce, abortion, and homosexuality. "The state has no place in the bedrooms of the nation," he smiled. He also told Canadians he wanted to bring the BNA Act home from Great Britain and make it our own. Pearson took him to the federal–provincial conference, where Quebec Premier Daniel Johnson was poised to attack. English Canada braced itself. But when Johnson fired, Trudeau responded, on national TV. Here was a flashy fighter like no one had seen before. He stood up for Canada.

As separatist bombs exploded in the streets of Quebec, Pierre Elliott Trudeau became the man of the hour. The swinging success of Canada's 100th birthday celebrations helped his image too. "If Expo would have been a person," said someone, "that person would have been Trudeau." Expo 67 showed off Canada as modern, sexy, and exciting. So was P.E.T. He swept to the leadership of the Liberals, all of Canada ready for this hip guy who "didn't look like a Canadian" and wanted to make us into something new.

"Trudeaumania" seized the 1968 national election. In the words of the 1960s, it was a "love-in" for Pierre. Diefenbaker's effect had been like an evangelist's, but there was nothing churchy about Trudeau. He did flips off diving boards for photographers, wore a rose in his colourful lapels, ran like a rock star from adoring crowds, and made women swoon ("My goodness, Pierre is like a Beatle!" cried his sister). He said he wanted a "Just Society," fair and bilingual. Images of the coolest place on earth danced in Canadians' heads. In Toronto, 60,000 fans jammed the streets to scream for him. At the St. Jean Baptiste parade in Montreal, separatists threw rocks at the grandstand where he and Premier Johnson sat. As Johnson cowered and ran for cover, Trudeau pushed back his RCMP guards and stood his ground. His bravery, seen by TV viewers across Canada, made him an even greater star. On June 25, 1968, he became Prime Minister.

"Just Watch Me"

One of his first acts as PM was to pass the "Official Languages Act," making Canada bilingual. He also provided more money for the unemployed, accepted Communist China, created modern ministries, and held public meetings to hear what Canadians wanted him to do. He put together youth organizations to get the new generation involved. The government wanted to be closer to the people.

But many of these things didn't work, at least not how he had hoped. He increased the size and power of government. The economy began to look worse. And while Canadians liked to hear about him giving them more rights, and loved to see him dating movie star Barbra Streisand, hosting rock-music idols John Lennon and Yoko Ono, and marrying the beautiful 22-year-old Maggie Sinclair (two of their three boys were born on Christmas Day), they also began to see his icy arrogance. He swore at opponents in Parliament (claiming he just said "fuddle duddle"). A "supergroup" surrounded him, advising him like a king. His shrug became famous. Then, in October 1970, war came to Quebec.

It was called the "October Crisis" and involved the Quebec separatist movement, which grew every year of Trudeau's early reign. In seven years, 200 bombs were exploded in Quebec, many by the FLQ (Front de Libération du Québec). In 1970, FLQ terrorists kidnapped British diplomat James Cross and Quebec Labour Minister Pierre Laporte. The nation was stunned. Then Laporte was found strangled in the trunk of a car. Trudeau's response was almost as shocking. He called in the army, then used the War Measures Act, last enforced in World War II. It gave the police the right to arrest anyone whenever they wanted and by any means. Many Québécois were hunted down and thrown in jail. When Trudeau was confronted by a CBC reporter, he snapped that those who objected were "bleeding hearts [and] . . . weak-kneed." Asked how much further he would go, he stuck out his chin and said, "Just watch me."

Eventually the crisis died down: the kidnappers were caught and some were allowed to leave the country. The nation, upset as it was by the sight of its army in control of major cities, mostly supported Trudeau. To this day, the use of the War Measures Act, like the Louis Riel conflicts, is hotly debated.

Nobody said it was going to be dull under Pierre Trudeau.

Power, Man

He barely beat the boring Conservatives in the 1972 election. So, he became a sly politician and Canadian compromiser. He was less arrogant, got the NDP to help him, and did better in the 1974 election. But his troubles didn't end. The economy went into a nosedive. Because of "inflation" (a constant rising in the cost of living), he froze prices and some people's wages—which the Conservatives had earlier suggested and he'd vowed never to do. His marriage broke up and his wife partied with rock stars and revealed embarrassing details about her life with him. And in 1976 René Lévesque and his separatist Parti Québécois came to power, frightening the nation and beginning many Trudeau–Lévesque battles, Pierre's hands on his belt as he argued, a gunslinger PM.

When the 1979 election came he was beaten, for the first and only time, by Joe Clark, the youngest Prime Minister in history. But Clark was *too* young, and soon the Liberals defeated him on a vote in the House of Commons and forced another election.

Trudeau had already decided to retire. He'd grown a beard and gone to Asia, where he prayed and discussed life with monks. But he shaved off the beard and made another run at the Prime Minister's throne.

He won that 1980 contest and began an eventful final stretch that brought his reign to an amazing 15 years. A gunslinger once more, he stood up for Canada and dramatically defeated Lévesque and the Parti Québécois in a famous referendum vote that threatened to separate Quebec from Confederation. When attacked for his non-French middle name he electrified a Montreal crowd, proclaiming that the Elliotts had been in Canada for more than 200 years, "Elliott was my mother's name!" he shouted. "My name is a Quebec name! But my name is a Canadian name also!"

As promised, he brought the old BNA (British North America) Act home, an historic move that made it a truly

Canadian Constitution, and added a Charter of Rights and Freedoms for all citizens. He made Jeanne Sauvé the first woman Speaker of the House and then Governor General. And just before he left, he toured the world for peace, asking rich nations to help the poor ones.

As always with Trudeau, there were many difficulties too. The economy continued to have problems, he'd greatly increased the government debt, and his National Energy Program kept the price of Alberta's oil low. The program increased western Canada's dislike of the national government, and of him. They felt that central Canada and this Ottawa snob didn't understand them, and wouldn't even try. One day, in British Columbia, he gave "the finger" to a group of protestors. There was still never a dull moment with the dashing Pierre.

And then early in 1984, while walking through a beautiful Ottawa snowfall, contemplating life as usual, he decided to quit.

Dramatic to the End

He went back to Montreal, finished raising his three boys in a strange-looking house, danced in discos with beautiful women, worked for a law firm, and sometimes spoke out. Most dramatically, he was heard from in 1990, when the Meech Lake Accord of Conservative Prime Minister Mulroney tried to adjust the Constitution by giving more say to the provinces. He fought it and won, powerful even when out of power.

He continued his travels, wrote his memoirs, and seemed ageless, paddling canoes for film crews in his buckskin coat in the Canadian wilderness. His legendary mind, so amazing that he once recalled, word for word, a long page of information he hadn't seen for six months, was still extraordinary.

But in 1998 a tragedy hit him that even his courage couldn't handle. His youngest son, Michel, was killed while skiing in British Columbia. An avalanche swept him away and buried him forever, deep in a beautiful Canadian lake, like many his father loved. Pierre was staggered as never before.

In the year 2000 he left life as dramatically as he lived. Though he was 80, his death stunned the nation. He had always seemed young. Suddenly, many forgave him everything. They remembered the exciting man who had represented youth and the future, the one who stood up for Canada.

In the House of Commons, Joe Clark delivered the best tribute. He said he thought Trudeau had been wrong about many things, but that, like Canada's first legendary leader, he had courage and vision. Had Trudeau been faced, said Clark, with Macdonald's impossible task of uniting the nation long ago, he "would have built the great railway."

The funeral, watched by millions, entranced the nation. People cried in the streets and memories came flooding forward. Throngs filled Montreal. Prime Ministers, princes, and movie stars came; former U.S. President Jimmy Carter and Cuban legend Fidel Castro shook hands in international friendship. Pierre's former wife Maggie, looking older and regretful, stood there in black. Their Christmas baby, Justin, now a handsome young man, spoke through tears of a united Canada. Then he kissed the coffin, said "Je t'aime, papa," and put a dashing red rose on top.

Often criticized, he may or may not have been as great as Macdonald, Laurier, or King. But to many, he was our most intriguing PM. He was a puzzle: warm on stage and cool in private; causing passion but believing in reason; a swinger who was old-fashioned; a messenger of love who was a violent debater; a loathed man, deeply treasured.

Pierre Elliott Trudeau came along at a perfect time. He gave the nation a sparkling image of itself, a sign of its exciting adulthood; and he stood up for a united Canada like a hero. When he died, many dearly missed the cool knight with the red rose, despite his faults. They didn't want boring, less daring leaders. They needed him. They wanted *him* to come back.

16th Prime Minister

The High River Kid

JOE CLARK

Born High River,
Alberta 1939,
Progressive Conservative.
PM: 1979–1980

His start was amazing, a rise unlike any other: chief of his party at age 36 and Prime Minister at 39, the youngest in history. Then he was knocked from his throne in a flash, ridiculed as immature and awkward, with even his smart young wife considered a weakness. But long after his two great opponents (the immortal Trudeau, whom he alone defeated, and Brian Mulroney, who unseated him) were gone, Joe Clark remained in public life. He didn't have Trudeau's magic or Mulroney's smoothness, but there was something in him that Canadians admired: his failures were honest ones, and his rise was incredible. It all started long ago in a little Alberta town.

The Talker

High River would fit nicely onto a Canadian postcard. It's just south of Calgary, historic and western, next to a river at the feet of the majestic Rocky Mountains. Charles Clark arrived there from Ontario in 1905, the year Alberta began. He rode through ranch land into town, found a one-storey brick building, and started up *The High River Times*. He and his family were down-to-earth folk. They loved this Wild West place: cattle roamed near the saloons and wagonloads of immigrants poured in.

Charles II followed in his father's footsteps. Born in 1910, he was schooled at home as a writer and at the University of Alberta in Edmonton as a thinker, then came back and married schoolteacher Grace Welch. They had two sons. The first, Charles Joseph, was born on June 5, 1939. He could have been Charles III, heir to the family newspaper. But he never would be. He was plain Joe, even when he was Prime Minister of Canada.

Always unusual, he wore a tie to school, wasn't good at sports, and didn't hunt or fish or rope calves at the rodeo.

Somehow he got himself elected president of the student council. In class, he did well but was no genius, excelling in politics, history, and writing and struggling in French. When students were given five minutes to speak, most couldn't. Joe ran over time. On dates, he just about talked girls' ears off.

In Grade 11, Joe won a public speaking contest and a trip to Ottawa. There he positioned himself outside famous John Diefenbaker's door for hours, waiting until he met him. Later in the House he saw the nasty Trans-Canada pipeline debate that triggered the fall of Louis St. Laurent. He returned home disgusted and told his father that Canada didn't have real democracy. He vowed to change things.

The kind of Canada he wanted was one he would later call "a community of communities," where places like High River were important, just like Toronto or Montreal.

In those days Alberta was governed by the Social Credit party, begun by a religious evangelist named "Bible Bill" Aberhart, who was more conservative than the Conservatives. Aberhart's successor was another preacher, named Ernest Manning, whose son Preston would start a party called Reform, much like the Social Credit. Joe would spend his life fighting the Social Credit and Reform on one side and the Liberals on the other. His views lay in between, where he felt reason reigned.

During the 1957 election Diefenbaker steamed into High River. Anxious all day, Joe raced home to dump his books and sprinted to the public meeting. He loved the Chief's appeal to the "little guy" and his dynamic speaking.

At 18 Joe went to Edmonton to the University of Alberta. He got his arts degree in three years, but failed French. He skipped classes, his mind on politics, and spent a lot of time at his typewriter. In summers he helped the Alberta Conservatives and wrote for the *Edmonton Journal.* As boss of the student paper, he said "At the command of a college editor are several instruments by which hell can be raised . . . I hope to use some of them."

Students lived in rooms the size of broom closets. The Social Credit wouldn't help fund bigger ones. So, Clark organized a march on the Legislature and confronted the Treasurer about it. Then he went back to his closet and plotted the government's defeat. Soon he was driving the provincial Conservative leader around and writing his speeches.

But he was still gangly, awkward, brown-haired Joe. His rooms were mountains of mess, filled with unopened letters tossed in a pile. Popcorn disappeared by the boxload and Coke by the gallons. When he finally graduated, he didn't know what to do with his life and drifted to England, and then France, where he tried to learn French from a family who barely talked to him. Upset by his progress in everything, he worried that he should be home running the family paper.

Back in Canada, he took a job writing speeches and doing publicity in Diefenbaker's Ottawa office, then tried the Dalhousie Law School in Halifax but found it boring and the students snobby. ("I wanted to become a lawyer," he said, "until I met one.") Broke, he drove a school bus across Canada for a fee, and went back to law, at the University of British Columbia.

But in Vancouver, politics again cut into his school time. He won the presidency of the national Progressive Conservative Student Federation and entered the fight over Diefenbaker's dying leadership. At the 1964 convention, leading undecided students, he introduced the Chief with a careful, supportive speech. The legend was charmed and rated the introduction by "the brilliant Joe Clark" among the greatest in his career.

But Joe barely attended classes at UBC, and flunked out. He returned to Alberta to study politics again and teach, and to get behind Peter Lougheed, the young Calgary businessman who wanted to be Premier. Lougheed was astounded by the political smarts of this 26-year-old kid, who helped the Conservatives build and then gain six seats from the 35-year-old Social Credit government. Anxious to do more, Joe ran in Calgary South in 1967. The riding was a government stronghold and held by none other than the Speaker of the Legislature. Still, the young student-teacher took him on. After running his scrawny frame into the ground, Joe was in bed when voting began. But he nearly won.

That same year he impressed new Conservative boss Robert Stanfield at the party's national convention in Ottawa and was hired to work in the leader's office for a few weeks. But Joe became invaluable and stayed much longer, writing Stanfield's speeches. He had reached the Centre Block of the Parliament

Buildings and was soaring. Only Trudeau stood between his boss and power.

Clark remained odd. Stanfield relied on him, but thought him "highly strung and nervous." He frustrated others by vanishing, almost in mid-sentence, perhaps off to catch the latest blockbuster movie. Still trying to learn French (and staying up late at night reading French novels), strange foreign sentences came out of his mouth. Determined to improve in other ways, he enrolled in kids' swimming classes at the local YMCA.

Unlike many powerful men of his time, he respected the opinions and brains of the young women he dated. He'd gone out with Catrina Gibson from Alberta for several years after he'd knocked on her door while campaigning during an election . . . and she appeared in nothing but a towel. Catrina became the top law student at Queen's University and went on to more studies in Toronto. In 1969, after spending time together in cottage country near Peterborough, they headed back separately to their homes. But she never reached Toronto . . . a car crash took her life.

He was devastated, and the next year fled overseas.

Clark stayed with a journalist friend in London. He slowed down, going to movies and rock concerts with different dates and watching British politics. He interviewed the British Arts Minister for the CBC. He went to Europe and hung out in cafés and tried to learn French, again. But mostly he reflected on life, writing thoughtful letters to friends. Then he readied himself for a huge charge forward.

A Rapid Rise

His first move was remarkable. He went to Alberta and entered the election in the giant riding of Rocky Mountain where he had no chance of winning. But he'd made up his mind. Life could end any minute. He wanted to seize things now.

A poll said that 85 percent of voters didn't have the slightest idea who he was. So he got into his car and travelled, knocking on every door he found. He learned to be a better speaker and to make fun of himself. "Quand je parle français," he said to French country folk, "les Anglais comprennent toujours, mais les français ne comprennent pas." He joked that he once mangled the language so badly that he asked a French crowd to "forgive me for my fishes." Right before the 1972 election he worked a 17-hour day and defeated his Liberal opponent, an assistant to rising young star Jean Chrétien, by 3,000 votes.

At the tender age of 33, Clark was in Parliament. But his confidence grew quickly. He had the boldness of youth. No one scared him—no inflated reputation, whether Trudeau's or a famous cabinet minister's. He went on the attack. His arguments were clear, his self-written speeches perfect, and his wit stinging. In party meetings he also spoke up. Some found him too aggressive for his age. Veterans worried as he chopped up Liberal legends without thinking twice. But such battles with "sacred cows" made most Conservatives proud. One said he was "the best heckler by far on our side of the House."

Late in 1972 an attractive, dark-haired, 20-year-old woman came to work for him. Maureen McTeer had grown up in a political family. She was a hockey player, scholar, and strong-minded feminist. Joe was impressed. On June 30, 1973, they were married.

The next year he won again in Rocky Mountain, by an amazing 9,812 votes. His star rose higher after Stanfield resigned as leader and Lougheed (now Premier of Alberta) refused to be the Western guy to replace him. Respected people pressured Joe to try. It seemed incredible that he was even considered, but he moved forward like a veteran: he made sure he had solid support, at last perfected his French, and told everyone he wasn't in it for future votes—he wanted to win.

It was one of the most stunning political leadership conventions in Canadian history. He had shaken the hand of nearly every Conservative in the nation, and had careful ideas. He was everyone's second choice. But when front-runners slipped, votes came to him, the party took a chance, and he won. He had rarely been in a limousine, but one picked him up afterwards—he missed the back seat and fell on the floor.

"I distrust words like vision and grand design," he said in his victory speech. Instead, he believed in his "community of communities," in consulting the people, and in building agreements within the party and the country. Canada had had enough of Trudeau's grand designs. Times were bad and there was trouble with Quebec. Clark was younger than Trudeau, just as aggressive, and (finally!) spoke French.

He spent three years as Leader of the Opposition, continuing his strong performance in the House and solidly re-organizing his party. But his image outside Ottawa began to crumble. On an international tour, first he lost his luggage and later stepped into a bayonet while inspecting troops. He was criticized for his awkward walk, wooden speeches while on tours, and nervous laugh. Maureen McTeer kept her last name, somehow proving to some that he wasn't a manly leader. "Mo and Jo" lived at the official Opposition Leader's residence on a shoestring, driving a second-hand car, buying used clothes, and keeping the heat low to save money. The press took to calling him "Joe Who?" And cartoonists drew him wearing mittens tied to his coat. He didn't have much charisma and didn't care. He wanted to be himself.

And yet, when Trudeau called an election for May 22, 1979, it looked like the Conservatives could win. The voters wanted the old Quebec wizard out even more than they wanted the young, stumbling Joe in. And so, he became the youngest Prime Minister in history, more than six years Arthur Meighen's junior.

Joe Honest

It would not be a great reign. Clark had made too many promises he couldn't keep. One was almost ridiculous. He said he would move the Canadian Embassy in Israel to Jerusalem. That angered Arabs who claimed the city as their ancestral home, and brother nations threatened to not just stop selling oil to Canada, but to stop trading altogether. He had also promised tax cuts. Then he looked at the big government debt Trudeau had created and realized he couldn't do that either. He hesitated. Four months passed without Parliament even happening.

The election results had been close—the new government had not won a majority of seats. If the NDP voted with the Liberals in the House, the Conservatives would be defeated. But Clark decided, at a big cabinet meeting in the beautiful Alberta Rockies, that he had to run things as if he couldn't be beaten. He changed policies on several things, including the embassy move and taxes. So the party went to Parliament in October and tried to actually increase taxes, including taxing gasoline. He told Canadians that the government had to stop spending and get rid of its debt. He also offered help to Alberta's oil industry.

In November, Trudeau quit. It seemed like a good sign. The Liberals wouldn't dare defeat the government without a leader. But they did. Joe's short reign collapsed.

The February 1980 election ended before it started. Clark, now a "wimp" to the public, couldn't win. Voters didn't want his tough ideas. The Liberals convinced Trudeau to give up his retirement idea. He sailed back into power.

Clark was Opposition Leader for three more years. Trudeau's Liberals used his policies (which they'd criticized), including the tax on gas. Alberta felt left out and bitter.

The way he left leadership was unique. Some said it was wimpy, but others argued that it showed his honesty. Upset at criticism from his party, he asked for a vote of confidence. They backed him at 66.9 percent. He said it wasn't enough. He needed more support to be a true leader in a democracy, so a convention was called for June 11. Slick Brian Mulroney, who had been angry when he lost to Clark in 1976 but said he supported him, jumped in. He offered to run Canada like his booming businesses, and knocked Joe Clark right out of the leader's chair.

His loyal workers were devastated. "Nothing, other than death, will ever hurt me again in that way," said Maureen. Joe stood in the Château Laurier hotel for nearly half an hour afterwards, hugging teary friends, but never breaking down.

His short term in office left more behind than is often noted. He drafted the Freedom of Information Act. His tough money ideas were the sort that governments used for the next two decades, trying to reduce debt. He put the first Black Canadian (Lincoln Alexander) in cabinet. And during his term Canadian diplomats saved Americans from possible death and certain imprisonment in Iran in a daring "caper" praised around the world.

His class showed throughout the following years. Holding no public bitterness towards Mulroney, he accepted the powerful job of External Affairs Minister and excelled at it. In 1991, Mulroney asked him to try the scary job of rebuilding

Canada's Constitution. He came up with the Charlottetown Accord, and for the first time in history all the provinces, the federal government, and native people agreed. More rights for the provinces and a form of native self-government were included. It was defeated in a national referendum (offered against Clark's advice), hurt by Mulroney saying that voting against it would be like treason.

The Comeback

In 1993 Clark retired. Soon he was a visiting professor at a California university, a special United Nations representative, and managing highly successful businesses. His family was freed from politics and travelled a great deal, often to the Clarks' beloved Paris.

But when the Progressive Conservatives were destroyed at the polls after Mulroney's reign, he knew where his duty lay. So, in 1998, he came back. At his press conference he claimed that he wasn't too old (he'd once been too young): "I prefer to call it experience," he cracked. "At my age, I am well beyond the help of image makers." In November he became national party leader again. Things were rocky at first. Members were defecting to the Canadian Conservative Alliance (Social Credit and Reform in disguise). The legendary party was under pressure to join in a partnership. It was said, as the November 11, 2000 election neared, that the Conservatives would be wiped out and that Clark, running in another of those "impossible" ridings, in Calgary Centre, would be crushed.

He won. The party held on to 12 seats and party status. Joe Clark returned to his post in the House of Commons.

By the year 2001 he was arguably the most trusted party leader in Canada. His failures were seen as the result of his decency and honesty, often said to be lacking in politicians. CBC commentator Rex Murphy said: "Mr. Clark is virtually alone in Canadian politics in having a long and tumultuous career and, having at the end of it, the respect and affection of very many Canadians. He deserves both."

Murphy was wrong about one thing. The dramatic career of the awkward kid from High River, now a jowl-shaking statesman, wasn't yet entirely "at an end."

17th Prime Minister
Blue-Eyed Handsome Man
JOHN TURNER

In the summer of 1958 a sensation shook the Dominion. Beautiful Princess Margaret, sister of the Queen, appeared to have fallen in love with a Canadian. Twenty-nine-year-old John Napier Turner was as handsome as a prince: a tall, athletic, intelligent, swinging bachelor, with a rock jaw and incredible blue eyes. The Princess had danced with him all night in Vancouver, waving off guests lined up to partner her. Then she flew across the country to be with him in

Born England 1929, Liberal.
PM: June–September 1984

Ottawa. But that fairy tale would end. And so would John Turner's. For much of his life people predicted he would become Prime Minister. He had the brains, the looks, the friendly style, the drive. No Canadian ever seemed more destined. But somewhere on the way to the ball it all fell apart, and a fascinating, fated life spent just an instant on the throne.

The Eligible Man

He was actually born in the land of royalty, on June 7, 1929, in the London suburbs, the son of a shadowy figure named Leonard Turner. Leonard died in 1931, likely of malaria, and then became a mystery, even to young John and his sister Brenda. He was said by some to have been a Far East adventurer, by others a journalist or gun maker. John's mother never explained. She was a towering figure in his life, another of those powerful Prime Minister moms. But Phyllis Gregory was bigger than the rest: she could have been PM herself.

She grew up in Rossland, B.C., a gold rush town in the Rockies with saloons and adventure. Her father, Jim Gregory, was a hard-nosed miner. Phyllis was a brain from the start. At 17, after many first-places in school, she headed to the University of British Columbia in Vancouver and thrived. She studied economics and politics, unusual for a woman in the 1920s, won an award that sent her to a big college in the

United States, then enrolled at the famous London School of Economics in England. There, life changed.

She was a gorgeous, dark-haired woman, energetic and attracted to unusual men. Such was Leonard Turner. She was just 29 when he died, poor and with two small children. She loaded them up and came home. The train ride from Montreal to B.C. became John's first memory of Canada. The magnificent wilderness, open prairies, and towering mountains captivated him. He never lost his love of the Canadian outdoors.

Phyllis and the kids didn't stay long in Rossland. In 1934, she got a job at the Tariff Board in Ottawa. The family started poor, the children in cupboard-like bedrooms in an apartment, but after a quick rise through the civil service (she became one of its great economists), they moved into a house. Though she was never paid as much as men (which angered John), the closely knit family got to know the stars of the day. Not only did Prime Minister Bennett fall in love with Phyllis and send her roses (word was, he also proposed), but Mackenzie King became a friend too. They all discussed politics in the small Turner home. Young John was invited to the Governor General's parties.

In school he was as dynamic as his mother, leading in marks and sports. Early in his school days, he was named best all-round student. He was junior debating champ, left wing on the hockey team, and ran the 100-yard dash in 11 seconds at age 12. In teenage years, he kept winning, scoring a 92-percent average, 10 marks higher than anyone else.

Despite his accomplishments he was popular with the other students, mostly because he worked hard at being a good guy and making friends. And he liked to kid around. As a church altar boy, he enjoyed twirling the incense as it hung down on small chains, once sending pieces of charcoal flying past the pews. One day he leaned too far over an open grave while sprinkling holy water, and fell in!

In 1945 Phyllis married millionaire Frank Ross and moved into his beautiful oceanfront mansion in Vancouver. John, just 16, enrolled at the University of British Columbia. He scored a couple of perfect 100s his first year, wrote about sports for the student newspaper, and became the greatest runner in Canada. For two straight years he won the national championships, acing the 100-yard dash in a world-ranked 9.7 seconds. He seemed a cinch for the 1948 Olympic team, but while driving home with a girlfriend during a fog, a train struck his car and dragged it 100 metres. His knee was smashed, ending his Olympic dreams. But he was still a "big man on campus." The most beautiful girls wanted to date him, he partied, and won a Rhodes Scholarship as the best school-and-sports student in B.C. His prize was entrance into Oxford University in England, a world-class place.

He arrived in 1949 and left in 1952. For the first time in his life he didn't come first in everything. There were students there who could keep up with him, like two future Australian

Prime Ministers and great British scholars. In athletics he met Roger Bannister (who would become immortal by breaking the world record for running the mile in less than four minutes) and racked up many more friends.

Turner studied law at Oxford, then spent a year at the University of Paris, mastering French, making more friends, and dating more gorgeous women.

On his way home in 1953 he fell for Montreal. He liked its fast pace and French style, and spent 11 years practising law there, working for a large firm. He was an excellent lawyer, representing big companies as well as the Montreal Canadiens and Alouettes. Of course, he hit the parties, but also did charity work for disabled kids. He loved to laugh and had friends everywhere: in business, politics, French and English Canada, and Europe. At a party on a boat, he fell into a big kettle while dancing with Mayor Jean Drapeau's wife. "Drapeau wasn't too pleased about that," he cracked. Then he fell asleep on board and woke up at the docks in Quebec City.

It was about that time that he met Princess Margaret. His stepfather and mother, by then Lieutenant Governor and "first lady" of British Columbia, arranged it (his mom later became UBC chancellor, the first woman to lead a university in the British Commonwealth). John and the Princess stayed friends for many decades, and the Queen watched carefully.

Sprinting to Fame

All of this was leading in one direction: politics. For years he had spent holidays at his stepfather's magnificent New Brunswick farm, where the famous Liberal cabinet minister C.D. Howe came to chat. In young Turner he saw the brains, looks, and charm of a future leader. Howe invited him to speak at Liberal meetings.

In 1962 the party pressured him to run. Before long he won a Montreal riding with a dazzling campaign that featured beautiful girls in convertibles, a big balloon above the streets, and a huge public party for Liberal leader Lester B. Pearson. The newspapers took notice. Handsome, bilingual, 33-year-old John Turner was a new kind of politician, drawing comparisons to young American President John F. Kennedy.

During the campaign he fell in love with one of his supporters: smart, attractive 25-year-old Geills Kilgour, daughter of a rich Winnipeg insurance company owner. She was a graduate of Harvard University Business School and specialized in computers. Geills plugged John's career into this new technology and helped him stay ahead of the crowd. In 1963 they were married.

It didn't take him long to get going in his old Ottawa stomping grounds. His first year wasn't too spectacular, but after being re-elected the next year by a bigger margin and becoming a part of Pearson's new government, he became a force. So bold was he that at 34 he expected a cabinet post and was grumpy when he didn't get it.

He became known as a leader of the "young Turks," new Liberals who demanded that the old ones not only listen to their ideas, but sometimes let them lead. They wanted Parliament and government to run smoother and faster.

It wasn't just his ideas that marked him as a "new man," but also his attitude towards the enemy. As an athlete, he respected his opponents. He made many Conservative friends and often mingled with them in Parliament. One of them, strangely, was former Prime Minister John Diefenbaker, the greatest of all Liberal enemies. Turner liked his skill and theatrical style, and a few fateful meetings bonded them.

In 1963 John and Geills found themselves on holiday on a little island in the Caribbean Sea near John and Olive Diefenbaker. Soon they were having a wonderful time together, and young John often sat on the beach listening to old John's stories and advice. Two years later, on another island, Turner noticed someone drowning. He leapt into the ocean, swam out, and towed the man back to shore. He was about to revive him, mouth-to-mouth, when the man sat up. It was Diefenbaker. Turner had saved his life!

Back in Montreal he won again in 1965 and got into the cabinet. In his new role he asked for government money to get Canada into the tech age. He also spoke out on national issues, among them the growing unrest in Quebec. "We are Quebeckers too," he said of the province's English residents in a noted speech. "Our future is here." He wanted his party to bring in a new age: "A Liberal," he said, "is a reformer."

A star was rising. "Wiry, tough, able and admirably bilingual," wrote the *Financial Post*, "John Turner is often tipped as
a possible Prime Minister. . . ." It seemed to be destiny. As far
back as university, fellow students had predicted it for their
handsome buddy, amazed at his brains, charm, and ability to
make so many friends.

But by the time Pearson put the job up for grabs there were
many contenders. Jean Chrétien wasn't ready yet, but Pierre
Trudeau and others were. In a dramatic convention in 1968,
Turner put on a snappy performance, showing Canadians that
despite his youth (age 39), he was ready to lead. He came third
to Trudeau.

He and Pierre never got along. He was loud and friendly,
Trudeau secretive. Polls named Turner the second most powerful politician in Canada. That made him a threat. As Justice
Minister he modernized laws, and okayed the use of troops in
Quebec during the 1970 October Crisis. But Trudeau dominated his department. In 1972 Turner was made Finance
Minister, a big job but one that could hurt a politician's reputation during such difficult economic times as the country was
then experiencing. The differences between the two men came
forward. Turner tended to back businesses while Trudeau liked
the government in control. In 1975, they had their confrontation. Turner went to see the PM to threaten to resign. He
expected Trudeau to try to stop him. Instead, the resignation
was accepted.

The Return

Turner stormed out of the meeting and back into private life, this time into a huge law firm in big-business Toronto. Soon he was making loads of money, living in luxury, and Geills and the kids were very happy.

But politics wouldn't let go. He was a legend to many, the man who could be Prime Minister by just saying that he wanted it. For almost 10 years he was featured in magazines and on TV as the leader in waiting, an awesome presence in the business world. When Trudeau left in 1984, he couldn't resist. The magic was about to return. The nation waited to be dazzled by the dazzling John Turner.

They would wait forever. Though he beat Chrétien for the leadership that year and was automatically made Prime Minister as Trudeau's successor, it was obvious something was wrong. He had been away too long. His knowledge of the issues was rusty. He was older, and his breathtaking ability to memorize facts seemed gone. At times he even appeared nervous and took to the annoying habit of loudly clearing his throat. Above all, he didn't seem to have solid opinions or passions. The young lion with the new ideas now looked like a mere supporter of his big-business buddies.

Then he made the terrible error of calling an election almost immediately. He asked for votes without having shown the people any ability to rule. Worse, he had just agreed to appoint a group of Liberals (at Trudeau's request) to rich government jobs. It looked bad.

During the campaign he bumbled, and didn't seem different enough from his opponent, Conservative Brian Mulroney, another business guy. Then he patted a Liberal woman on the bum on television, drawing nationwide criticism. And in the TV debate Mulroney destroyed him with a vicious attack, demanding that Turner apologize for his government appointments. "I had no option," Turner said weakly. That was it. Mulroney crushed him, winning 211 seats, the largest number in history, leaving the Liberals with a paltry 40.

He wasn't much better as Opposition Leader. Even when he stuck to his beliefs he had problems. When he supported Mulroney's Meech Lake agreement that recognized Quebec as a "distinct society" within Canada, many Liberals, especially the retired Trudeau, were shocked that he took such an un-Trudeau-like position. Turner, a Montrealer at heart, believed it was what Quebec needed.

Eventually there were calls for his resignation. And by the time the 1988 election rolled around, Mulroney was expected to clobber him again. The issue was free trade with the Americans, supported by the Conservatives who had opposed it since Macdonald's day, and opposed by the Liberals who had favoured it as recently as Pearson's reign. The politicians readied themselves for another TV debate. This time there was a surprise.

Suddenly, it seemed as though the fire was back in Turner's piercing blue eyes. He turned on Mulroney when free trade came up and attacked with passion. "I happen to believe you sold us out as a country," he growled. "We built a country . . . deliberately resist[ing] the continental pressures of the United States. For 120 years we've done it. With one signature of a pen you've reversed that."

It wasn't enough to save the Liberals or John Turner. But it saved his reputation. The party lost, but more than doubled their seats, and returned to respectability. It was the first crack in Mulroney's armour—not much would go well for him after that. Turner had recaptured his fire for Canada, if only for a brief moment.

In 1990 he quit and left the job to Chrétien. He returned to Toronto to another big law firm, and his family's happiness. All his life he enjoyed the outdoors. He spent more time canoeing and exploring—he would always be more passionate about Canadian rivers, forests, and wildlife than politics.

But he must have wondered how all that potential had vanished, how the most perfect and exciting man for the job of Prime Minister in history had not been able to carry the puck when it was passed to him. In 1968, handsome, royally charming, and full of young energy and ideas, he had told the Liberal convention, "I'm not here for the next time. I'm not bidding now for your consideration at some vague convention in 1984 when I've mellowed a bit." He had been perfectly incorrect. That "vague convention in 1984" actually happened. And when he won it, he had mellowed indeed.

18th Prime Minister

Mr. Smooth

BRIAN MULRONEY

*Born Baie Comeau, Quebec
1939, Progressive Conservative.
PM: 1984–1993*

M eeting "Bones" Mulroney as a teenager was a bit of a shock. He was a short, scrawny kid, but had a big Dudley Do-Right chin and a deep voice. It made him unforgettable. Many years later, he changed Canada, appearing upon the national scene like a charm from Quebec: tough, pro-American, speaking in street French and business English. By election counts, he was the most loved Prime Minister ever, but by public opinion, he may have been the most hated. He was unforgettable.

Son of a Mill Worker

Baie Comeau, on the north shore of the St. Lawrence River, many hours northeast of Quebec City, formed Brian Mulroney as much as any hometown ever formed a Prime Minister. In a mostly French Catholic and slightly English Protestant town, his family was neither. They were Irish Catholic: English by language, French by religion.

Ben Mulroney married a lass named Mary O'Shea from the Quebec City area, as Irish-Canadian as he. They came to Baie Comeau before it even existed, when it was just a dream of rich American businessman Colonel Robert McCormick. The Colonel needed a place to make paper for his *Chicago Tribune*. So, with the help of Ben and others, one of the world's largest paper mills soon belched smoke near neat rows of new houses winding along the beautiful St. Lawrence River. The Mulroneys, with Ben's position at the mill locked into a lower level (because he was Irish Catholic), lived at the bottom of the hill, far below the rich guys in the big houses at the top.

Martin Brian Mulroney was the first boy of six children, born on March 20, 1939. Right away, he set about to move up to the top of the hill. Though his parents were quiet folks, he burst into the world loud and ambitious. On the streets he got along with everyone: French, English, Catholic, Protestant. While others stuck to their own, he was a bridge between them all—popular, solving problems, a smoothie. He could talk like no one else.

He played a little hockey, but was always a runt. Mostly he loved to read, particularly stories about how people became great. A hard worker like his father, he was determined to succeed at everything he tried. He even gained a reputation as a singer, and whenever the Colonel visited, young Brian was called on to perform: an old Irish song or something in French. A crisp American $50 bill was dangled as a reward.

When he won the Rotary Club's public speaking contest at age 10, he was so dramatic that a family friend remarked, "That boy is going to make a [darn] good bishop someday." After he sang for another celebrity at a local theatre, he was asked what he wanted to be. "Prime Minster of Canada," he said clearly into the microphone.

School was very important to the Mulroney family. "Listen, Brian," Ben told his son, "the only way out of a mill town is through a university door." He started out in the local French school and then studied with the town's few English-speaking Catholics. But at age 14, still just a little guy, he was sent away to New Brunswick to a better, more costly place. There, under the strict discipline of priests, he had to grow up before his time.

Two years later, just 16, he graduated and went to St. Francis Xavier University in Antigonish, Nova Scotia. Mulroney later said that if he hadn't, "I'd be back home in Baie Comeau, driving a truck." (He actually did drive one, but only for summer jobs.) Called "Bones" for being so skinny, he stepped forward at St. F of X and began the political career that would carry him all the way to the leadership of Canada.

He had started out studying economics but soon changed to political science, and zeroed in on the Progressive Conservatives as his party. The Liberals had dominated Nova Scotia and the nation for many years, so Mulroney opposed them to make his mark.

At age 17 he campaigned for Robert Stanfield as he became provincial Premier. "Even in those days, Brian was thinking big," said a friend. So big that in 1956 he was a delegate to the national PC leadership convention in Ottawa. There he got behind John Diefenbaker and impressed party members with his energy. He organized support and put up tons of posters in the freezing cold. No matter what job he was given, he'd soon ask for another. By the time the convention ended he was Vice-Chairman of Youth for Diefenbaker and his new friend, the Chief, was party leader, soon to be Prime Minister.

In Brian's remaining years at St. F of X, he won three straight public speaking contests, became vice-president of the National Student Conservatives, built up a group of friends (later called the "Mulroney Mafia"), and did well in class. He often spoke on the phone with the Prime Minister, though few fellow students believed it.

He grew, miraculously, to six-foot-one. His big voice now fit his tall, handsome frame. He began dating more and fell in love with a beautiful, dark-haired Newfoundland girl. Wanting to be near her, he went to Dalhousie Law School in Halifax instead of Laval University in Quebec City, as he had planned. But she left him and he failed at school. It didn't help that he spent most of his time in politics.

In 1960 he finally headed for Laval. He wanted to refresh his French, get his law degree, open a Baie Comeau firm, and launch a political career. But Laval would be much more to him than he ever imagined. It was a thrilling time to be there: Jean Lesage became Premier and the "Quiet Revolution" began as Quebeckers declared themselves "masters in our own house." Mulroney got into the thick of things. He was unusual: a pro-Quebec, English Conservative, able to speak French like a guy on the street.

Four years later, in 1964, he graduated with a law degree and average marks. It was what he did away from classes that made him exceptional. He had expanded his network of friends, many of whom would become influential in the nation's future (including Lucien Bouchard, who became a separatist Quebec Premier). In 1961 he had helped organize the sensational "Congrès des Affairs Canadiennes" conference, which questioned the very idea of Canada. Powerful politicians came, loud debates made national headlines, and Quebec separatism was brought out into the open. Mulroney was interviewed for *Maclean's* magazine as a "Young Canadian" set to influence the nation. He brought Prime Minister Diefenbaker right into his class one day to shut up students who doubted their phone conversations, and got Premier Lesage onto his local TV show. It was a wild, high-flying Quebec City life for the deep-voiced charmer, filled with parties, beautiful women, and big-league politics. But it would grow even more exciting.

His plans for a hometown law career changed when he was given a chance to join the biggest law firm in what was then Canada's biggest city. He aced his Montreal interview.

A dynamic speaker, desk jobs bored him. But he was good at working with people, bringing opponents together, and finding solutions to problems. The job of cleaning up difficulties between unions and companies in Montreal's huge shipping industry was given to him and he excelled. Everyone on both sides was impressed, strikes were fewer, and business was better. It added to his list of friends.

In politics, he broke with Dief, disappointed in his old-fashioned Quebec views, and wisely supported Robert Stanfield when he won the leadership in 1967. Mulroney's position in the party grew. His goal was to help steal Quebec back from the Liberals.

In Montreal, living the life of a swinging bachelor, he gained more attention by solving the eight-month-long strike at *La Presse* newspaper. He locked opponents in a hotel room for a week and forced a settlement. They were amazed at his ability to be smooth and sweet, then suddenly tough and demanding as a deal neared. In early 1973 he was made a partner in his firm. His fame and bank account grew, but his bachelor life ended. A chance meeting by the pool of a swanky tennis club saw to that.

Mila Pivnicki wasn't quite 19 years old when Mulroney spotted her, looking dazzling in a bikini in the summer of

1972. It was love at first sight. And when he invited her for a drink he learned that she was intelligent and charming, even more charming than he was. Born in Yugoslavia to a wealthy psychiatrist, she was studying engineering at university. By Christmas they were engaged, and in May 1973 they married. They would have three children and become a potent political team. Mila Mulroney was beautiful, friendly, and outgoing. She helped him greatly throughout his political career.

That career was rising in the '70s, though he still hadn't run for Parliament. He didn't need to—he was often in the spotlight. The loudest member of a group investigating Quebec's huge construction industry, he had revealed that the workers' union was corrupt and violent and that the Quebec government was part of the problem. It was sensational news. Fearless, he had public fights with powerful men in both languages, and seemed to be single-handedly cleaning up the worst industry in Quebec.

In 1974 Brian and Mila bought a beautiful home in the rich Westmount area of Montreal, and later an even bigger one at the top of the hill. Then he took aim at the job he'd been preparing for all his life.

Learning Lessons

In November 1975 Mulroney announced that he wanted the leadership of the Progressive Conservative party. The winner would face Pierre Elliott Trudeau for the Prime Minister's job. His charm, strong speaking style, and passion for a united Canada and strong Quebec jump-started his run and pushed him towards the front of the race. He also had many friends in the high offices of Canadian corporations. But that soon caused an image problem. Though he was the son of a lowly electrician and had succeeded in life through hard work, his fancy suits, jet, and big-money buddies made him look like a slick business guy. As an unelected upstart, he also got little support from elected members. Old Dief proclaimed that the next leader should have experience in Parliament. After voting began, Mulroney was stuck in second place, sandwiched between another Quebec candidate and Joe Clark (36 years old, just like him). Unable to choose between the two, the party went for Joe.

Though still young, Mulroney's expectations were high and he was crushed by the loss. For three years he fell into a sort of depression and began drinking heavily. He felt bitter about Clark, attacked him in private, and told friends he was through with politics. His health was poor and his marriage teetered on the brink of collapse.

Surprisingly, during this period he thrived in business. An American corporation called The Iron Ore Company of Canada hired him to run their failing mining industry in Quebec and Labrador. He moved them from huge losses and constant strikes to a $100-million profit and peace, and still increased workers' wages and pensions.

He was soon rich, flying around the world swinging deals and acquiring more friends in high places. Even when the company had to close down the town of Schefferville, Quebec, in 1983 he came out smelling like a rose. He did it in a public way in front of workers, media, and politicians, showing why the step had to be taken and offering miners lots of money for losing their jobs. *Canadian Business* magazine asked: "Could . . . Brian Mulroney run the country like he runs Iron Ore Co.? The country should be so lucky."

Such triumphs pushed him back into the political arena. He quit drinking, Clark ran into leadership problems, and a huge network of Mulroney friends went on alert. Though Brian publicly supported Clark, many felt that the Conservative army he raised in Quebec was really for himself. That was clear at the 1983 leadership convention.

Mulroney was now a very smart political guy, and this time he smoothly corrected the errors he had made during his first campaign. He got rid of his jet, spent most of his time in a rusty station wagon, and promised he'd run for Parliament whether he won or not. He and Mila quietly travelled the country meeting every Conservative with a vote.

It paid off. He defeated Clark and took over the leadership. Entering Parliament, he didn't miss a beat. The crafty Trudeau set a trap or two for him, but Mr. Smooth never got caught. The old question of French-language rights in Manitoba came up and he stepped forward strongly, supporting bilingualism. His party was impressed, and after Trudeau retired and new Liberal leader John Turner called an election, they were ready.

Brian Mulroney conquered Canada in 1984. He didn't generate the Diefenbaker excitement of the massive 1958 win or the Trudeaumania of 1968. But his thunderous victory outdid both, the greatest in history (for seats won, 211). What Canadians saw was a handsome, aggressive, bilingual man with a beautiful wife, who told them many times that he had risen from almost nothing. "It is a great country," he said, "where the son of an electrician can seek the highest office in the land." Times had been tough during the Trudeau years, and here was a man who oozed success, a winning business-man and problem solver. In person, he had amazing charisma. During the TV debate, he lit into Turner, fascinating Canadians with his fighting style.

Brash Leader

He would be aggressive in power too, with a bold agenda to reduce spending, make better U.S. trade deals, and fix the Constitution so that Quebec was part of it. He told the world that Canada was "open for business." He wanted it to modernize and grow.

His coziness with the Americans was shown at a fancy meeting he threw in Quebec City with movie star U.S. President Ronald Reagan. Mulroney actually burst into an old

Irish song while publicly holding hands with Mila and the Reagans. It was as if he were back in Baie Comeau, performing for Colonel McCormack.

His biggest effort, one that will live in history, was his attempt to get Quebec into the Constitution through his Meech Lake Accord. Trudeau had brought our Constitution home from England and made it fully Canadian, but without Quebec's approval. Quebeckers wanted more powers to protect their language and culture. Mulroney called the Premiers together to hammer out an agreement. He brashly spoke of "rolling the dice," and shut them indoors to argue. But Premier Clyde Wells of Newfoundland, a Liberal and old Trudeau supporter, was concerned about increasing provincial powers and calling Quebec "a distinct society." So, he and Manitoba native MP Elijah Harper helped kill it in their provincial legislatures.

Mulroney also wanted an agreement to greatly increase trade between Canada and the United States, the old "Reciprocity" that had long been a Liberal idea. Now it was called "free trade." He used it as the big issue in the 1988 election.

It would be one of the loudest in history. There was stinging opposition to free trade. Many felt that Canada would be swamped by the United States—that they would drain our resources and hurt our national purpose and identity. There were violent demonstrations. And in the leaders' clash on TV, the previously weak John Turner turned on Mulroney and used patriotism to score points. But come election day

Mulroney won with another big majority. His popularity, however, would decrease drastically during the next few years.

He would do a few popular things, like make a deal with the Inuit people to create the new territory of Nunavut. But the Free Trade Agreement, Canada's part in an American-led war in Iraq in 1991, and especially the Goods and Services Tax (or GST, which added a tax to nearly everything Canadians bought) were controversial.

Mulroney tried to solve things in 1992 by asking the respected Clark to involve all the provinces and native people in a search for another constitutional agreement. It tried to reach out to everyone, but Canadians voted against the Charlottetown Accord.

By the time he left office in 1993 some said he was the least popular Prime Minister in history, which was strange, since he had twice had such massive election wins. But the charming man had become, in the eyes of many, a smooth-talking salesman who had sold out Canadian interests to the Americans, taxed us to death, and tried to force the nation into an agreement and failed. He was seen as shady and untrustworthy. "Lyin' Brian" some called him. After he left, the Conservatives were beaten in the 1993 election more decisively than any major party in history. They fell, incredibly, to a mere two seats.

By then the Mulroneys were back in their rich neighbourhood in Montreal and Brian had returned to business with great success, managing many large companies and giving deeply valued advice to powerful people. In recent years there were claims that he was guilty of corruption while in power, and received improper payments in an airline deal. He strongly denied everything, and sued the RCMP and the government and won, not only gaining money but a full public apology.

One of the curious things about his reign is what happened after he left. He was hated for his big policies, and the Liberal party vowed to take them apart. Once in power, though, they quietly kept them. They promised to get rid of the GST, but found the country needed the money and backed off. They were against free trade, but continued it without a squeak of opposition. Prime Minister Chrétien himself opposed the Meech Lake Accord, but when faced with Quebec's massive opposition and a separatist vote, changed his mind.

Mulroney always claimed that he did what he did because the country needed it done, not because it was popular. To him, the Liberals' use of his plans proved him right. History, of course, will judge these things, as it has judged Prime Ministers before.

But one thing is for sure: the little boy from Baie Comeau who lived at the bottom of the hill certainly made it to the top.

19th Prime Minister

Unusual Woman

KIM CAMPBELL

After 126 long years, Canada finally got its first female Prime Minister. She hoped to be a new sort of politician. But she was like other leaders too: talented, ambitious, unusual, with a dramatic past. She rose from a tough childhood and personal battles to get to the top. This guitar-playing former carnival queen and class brain would be like a shooting star in our history, shining brightly for an instant and then burning out. But she boldly paved the way for women of the future.

Born Port Alberni, British Columbia 1947, Progressive Conservative. PM: June–November 1993

Becoming Kim

Her parents were unusual too. Like her, they seemed to be desperately searching for something. They met in the paper mill town of Port Alberni, B.C., on beautiful Vancouver Island just as the Second World War was changing lives. Phyllis Cook was an attractive, red-haired girl with smarts. Her father had been a dentist who liked to play guitar and sing for his children. When she was 12 he changed her name to Lissa because kids were calling her Phil. Two years later he broke her heart, dying while climbing a hill for exercise. At 18, anxious to get away, she joined the Canadian navy. As she went east, the memory of a young man in the Coast Artillery stayed with her.

George Campbell was smitten with Lissa Cook the moment he saw her. Lucky for him, he too was sent east. There hadn't been much luck in his life until then. Abandoned by his parents, left alone in his teens, he somehow got his education and joined the war effort. Stationed in Nova Scotia, he found Lissa at work tracking "wolf packs" of Nazi submarines by radar. They were married in 1944, and their first daughter was born the following May. On March 10, 1947, a second girl arrived, Avril Phaedra Douglas Campbell.

At first the family got by without trouble. They lived in the Vancouver area while George got his law degree at the University of British Columbia. But as Lissa worked at low-paying jobs to support her husband, she dreamed of bigger things.

Avril would be a confident kid: a tomboy when she was small, musically talented as she got older, and always popular at school. Music filled the family home. Avril even performed on TV, and left her parents' church for one with a rocking band.

George, now a downtown lawyer, was often away and far from a model husband. And in 1958 Lissa met a rich real estate agent who wanted to sail and see the world. The following year she fled to England with him, then to the exotic Mediterranean Sea, working on cruise ships, doing the things she'd always dreamed of. Avril, just 12 years old, was sent away to a Catholic school in Victoria, where one month later she received a letter from her mother with an explanation. It was heartbreaking. Though they exchanged more letters, it would be 10 years before they met again. But Avril was tough. She worked hard at school, impressed teachers with her amazing brains (her "IQ tests were beyond perfect scores") and friendliness, and became Carnival Queen. She made up her mind to start over again and even changed her name. She was now "Kim" Campbell.

New Lives

When she returned to public school in Vancouver she really took off. Again at the top of her classes, she dated the best-looking guys and was fun at parties, where she'd play guitar and sing. Her father was now married to a woman barely out of her teens, and at home Kim and her sister did nearly anything they wanted. She was mature beyond her years, and a leader: the first female president of the student council in the 42-year history of her high school, a contestant on the TV quiz show *Reach for the Top,* and school valedictorian. She told a friend that she wanted to be Prime Minister of Canada.

In 1964 she became the first woman president of a freshman class at the University of British Columbia. When a male student made stupid comments in the student newspaper, she lashed back. "What's all this garbage about women trying to dominate the world?" she wrote. "Women ought to and women do. . . . Now is the time to stop letting men take credit for what we are accomplishing. Rise, women, let's tidy up the world."

The next year she fell for a man 22 years older than she. He was fat and had funny-looking hair. But he had something that always impressed Kim Campbell—brains. "Tuzzie" Divinsky was a brilliant mathematics professor, a master chess player, and a clever talker. He was also very Conservative. His influence on her as she served on UBC student council was obvious—she wasn't part of campus rebellions in those wild 1960s.

Graduating with a BA in 1969, she and Tuzzie went to England in the early '70s, where she studied at the famous London School of Economics. They married and she developed stronger political views, but never graduated and returned home. Her bubbly personality had faded. She dressed and acted older, and seemed kind of snobby. A housewife for a couple of years, she struggled with being married to a much older man, one who was gruff and set in his ways. She wanted to have a child but couldn't, and was upset when UBC refused to hire her as a full professor. She felt it was because she was a woman.

When she did teach, specializing in politics at Vancouver Community College, her students loved her, finding her helpful and smart. Meanwhile, Tuzzie was elected to Vancouver's School Board in 1974.

But Kim remained unhappy. So, at age 32, she did something about it. First, she went to law school, unconcerned about being older than other students. From that moment onward, her career zoomed.

When Tuzzie left the School Board to win a seat on Vancouver City Council, she got herself elected into his place. For the next three years, as she completed her law degree and grew to local fame, she seemed like two people. At school she was warm and popular, performing in musicals and helping others. But on the School Board she was "an attack dog," adopting the tough Conservative views of the B.C. Social Credit government. She wanted to cut education costs and was hard on unions. The city got to know this blonde dynamo, as she boldly rose to Chairman. Some despised her; others were impressed. One of her fans was B.C. Premier Bill Bennett.

By the time Bennett asked her to run for a Social Credit seat in 1984, many things had changed in her life. She had left

her husband, got her law degree, and was quitting the School
Board. Bennett's offer came at the right time. But the election,
fought in a strong downtown NDP riding, was a disaster. She
seemed uncaring, was often egged into losing her temper, and
made dumb comments, once telling the city's poor that she
knew about disappointment in life because "when I was a
teenager I wanted to be a concert cellist." She gained a reputation for thinking she was a lot smarter than others, and
came third.

She joined a law firm, but was rarely given the chance to
take on big cases and became bored. So, when the Premier
asked her to be his executive director in 1985, she jumped at
it. He saw a courageous, strong-willed woman of the future
who could connect him to the public. Kim was finally in a
position of power, one that challenged her abilities.

About that time she met a smart 46-year-old lawyer named
Howard Eddy. A divorced father who worked for the govern-
ment on native land claims, he looked like Abraham Lincoln
. . . with a yacht. Together, they sailed Georgia Strait between
Vancouver Island and the city, playing guitars and having fun.
They soon married.

Go Girl

Kim had power, but she wanted more. So, just 39 years old
and never elected to the legislature, she decided to go after the

Premier's job when he quit in 1986. Friends warned her that she'd get thumped. They were right. She raised hardly any money, and at the convention made Rice Krispies squares in a K shape while others had high-powered parties. But, even though she finished last, she made an impression. She presented herself as a change in leadership. And, despite moments when her snobbery surfaced, she became more confident and charming with voters, unafraid to make fun of herself. Her speech was among the best. She said she'd give more money to education and rise above differences between people. Then she delivered her first famous line: a real whammy. Obviously referring to smooth-talking Bill Vander Zalm, who would become Premier but resign in disgrace, she said, "Charisma without substance is a dangerous thing."

Later that year she ran again in Vancouver. By now she was maturing, learning to compromise, and became one of only nine women elected to the Legislature. Vander Zalm didn't put her in the cabinet, but she made herself known, giving 128 speeches in her first year. Some of her old-fashioned colleagues claimed that she displayed "mainly male attributes," whatever that meant. In 1988, when the Premier tried to stop B.C. women from having legal abortions, she loudly disagreed with him. It embarrassed him and made him change his tune. His downfall was coming.

Kim was being noticed all the way to Ottawa, and soon the federal Conservatives convinced her to run for them in Vancouver. It would be a tough fight, but she was up to it this time. She still lost her temper at times, but her brains and maturing skills showed.

Brian Mulroney could hardly wait to get the bright young star into his cabinet. He needed members from B.C. and wanted women in power. He admired her toughness and her French (she claimed to also speak Russian and German). In 1989 he named her Minister of Indian Affairs. Mistaking the time for her official appointment, she almost didn't show up. "Oh God, what a turkey!" she quipped.

But she was far from a turkey in cabinet. Some said she was so ambitious that she compromised too much, but others were impressed. She learned quickly and defended herself expertly in the House. "She soaks up information like a sponge," said a colleague. Her new ability to compromise would play a key role in her future.

In 1990 Mulroney made her the first female Minister of Justice, and three years later a groundbreaking Minister of Defence ("Holy Cow, Prime Minister!" she said.) She brought in a law that restricted guns and pushed through another on sexual assault that women praised. Slowly she was seen as a potential national leader, a "feminist" but acceptable to most everyone. There were errors too, like when she changed her mind about buying army helicopters. But she was tough, smart, and capable, a woman who might finally ascend to Canada's throne. A rather famous photograph helped her immensely.

In it, Kim appeared to be naked . . . barely covered by her lawyer's gown that she held in front of her on a hanger. It caused a sensation. The "Madonna of Canadian politics" became famous everywhere.

But privately, she suffered from the failure of her second marriage. Eddy had walked out on her in 1991, fed up with this new life that buried her in work and kept her away from home. She was hurt and vowed to remain single while in politics.

Mulroney resigned in February 1993. Kim was considered the front-runner for leader, and many in power knew that the PM favoured her. She, of course, was ready. She wanted the job and built a strong team, supported by some Conservative heavyweights. She said she hoped to be a new kind of politician, one who involved everyone. "In a democracy, government isn't something that a small group of people do," she insisted.

But on the campaign trail she often stumbled; saying, for example, that people who disagreed with her economic policy were "enemies." Mulroney began to wonder if she could win the next election. By the time the convention began it was rumoured that he had moved his support to 34-year-old Québécois Jean Charest, a brilliant young veteran. Campbell's lead shrunk. But she hung on. At 46, she became the first female Prime Minister of Canada. It was an historic moment, and many women in the crowd cried.

Campbell, of course, didn't take much time to dwell on it. She started working hard and her popularity rose. First she formed a smaller cabinet than previous ones, then called the Premiers together for a Vancouver conference, and flew to

Tokyo for the G-7 Summit of international leaders. There she stated strong Canadian positions to American President Bill Clinton and pleased Russian leader Boris Yeltsin by speaking Russian.

Back home, she visited the Art Gallery of Ontario in Toronto for the premiere of a film about the twist (a dance craze in the '60s) and was caught on camera doing a snazzy version of it at a reception. Large crowds began to greet her, intrigued by her style.

But she would never sit in the House of Commons as Prime Minister. She called an election, and from that moment until the big day on October 22, her popularity plunged. There were many reasons. She made mistakes. Her belief in a "new kind of politics" turned ridiculous—she was *so honest* that she suggested there were few things she could do to help Canadians. She said that little could be done about unemployment, and that, incredibly, an election was not a time to discuss "serious issues." Her snobbery surfaced and she got into fights with the media, once snapping that they needed hearing aids. She was also saddled with Mulroney's huge unpopularity and his election team. They were out of synch with her. She felt that this nearly all-male team misunderstood her.

Then a Conservative advertisement used a photograph of opponent Jean Chrétien that emphasized his crooked mouth, a result of a childhood problem. She publicly apologized. It all made her party look like unkind fools.

Mending a Broken Heart

The party was absolutely crushed in the election. The glorious Conservative force of Sir John A. Macdonald was reduced to a mere two seats, and Campbell was defeated in her own riding. The party came fifth, behind the Reform and the Bloc Québécois, two groups whose strong regional support threatened to divide the country.

She spoke bravely that night, but her heart was broken. Her grand try was dead. An experiment for women had suffered a setback. And her party had been creamed.

But Kim Campbell, of course, landed right on her feet. She resigned the leadership and began a new life. First she was a lecturer at classy Harvard University in the United States. Then she was appointed Canadian Consul General to Los Angeles, a wonderful job that had her working with Canadian Hollywood stars. She travelled worldwide, making appearances and lecturing on international relations, and headed the Council of Women World Leaders. Free from politics, she had a whale of a time and her style resurfaced. She appeared on the hit American TV show *Politically Incorrect* with comedian Bill Maher and charmed him and his audience. Still interested in music, she fell in love with a composer 21 years younger than she. Songs from a musical they wrote together were performed and praised.

"It doesn't matter what you're doing," she said with a laugh about her musical, "you get people who love it and people who hate it." The same thing could have been said about her life as a politician. But that world seems far behind now. She has become happier, more relaxed, and far from snobby about anything, as if she has grown into her brains. Kim Campbell, Canada's first female Prime Minister, has picked herself up from her defeat, as she's done so many times in her amazing life. This woman never really needed politics to be extraordinary. She will always be a trailblazer for Canadian girls.

Keeper of the Key

JEAN CHRÉTIEN

And so we come to our 20th Prime Minister. Well, Sir John A. Macdonald, he isn't, eh? Nor is he Laurier, King, or Trudeau. But look closer and you'll see the trademarks of a great Canadian leader. First of all, he is unusual. When he was a little guy, he was half a head shorter than his friends, had big floppy ears, and a partially paralyzed face. As a teenager he got into brawls, was kicked out of school, and didn't pronounce his words very well. He even had trouble

Born Shawinigan, Quebec 1934, Liberal. PM: 1993–

reading. But Jean Chrétien had a spirit unlike anyone else, and proved his many critics wrong. He rose to be the youngest cabinet minister in the 20th century and won three straight elections as Prime Minister. Like Canada, he is much more than he seems.

Rebel Without a Cause

He was born on the same day as Sir John A., January 11, in 1934, just outside Shawinigan, Quebec. A huge pulp and paper mill cast a smoky shadow over everything. His father, Wellie, was a machinist in the mill, but that wasn't all he did. He had two other jobs and barely stopped to think. When he did, he insisted on two things: that his children be good and that they be educated. A man of few words, Wellie ruled with an iron fist, holding his hand straight up in the air to send his children running upstairs to their bedrooms if they upset his evening reading. At night he studied English at school. "Instead of fighting it, you learn," he insisted. "Learn, learn, learn. Then you become somebody."

Wellie's wife, Marie Boisvert, agreed. She had been making independent decisions since age 17, when the rest of her family left for Alberta to seek their fortune in English Canada.

In the hands of two ambitious parents like these, the Chrétien kids had drive. They would need it. Of the 19 children Marie gave birth to, just nine lived. Jean was the second last, filling the role of the "little guy," even to his younger brother. There had been a Jean before him, who had died on the kitchen table at age two. That one was called Gros Jean for his great size, but this one, this future Prime Minister, scrawny and short with huge ears, deep-set eyes, and a forehead the length of a hockey rink, was Ti-Jean (Little Jean).

Almost from birth he had great energy, though at first he used it in the worst possible way. When he started school at five, he was a pest. He made noises, talked back to the nuns, and once ducked a punch from a teacher that landed on another kid's face. On the streets he wasn't much better. He was a leader in brawls and a runty boss at other things— captain of the hockey team, violent baseball player, and organizer of mischief. When he wasn't good enough to dominate in hockey, he became the coach, in charge of older kids at age 12, barely able to see over the boards, his star an illegal, overage "ringer" he had imported to win. And win he did. That was his obsession. That, and talking. He would yak and yak, bragging and scheming and plotting, until everyone wanted to shut him up. "He's different from the rest," said his father.

Never were truer words spoken. But the whole Chrétien family was different. Though the 11 of them lived in a little three-bedroom brick house, they had an air of superiority. The oldest boy, Maurice, 22 years Jean's senior, became a doctor and a big name in Shawinigan. Madame Chrétien didn't dare shell peas on the front porch like others, and refused to rush downtown with her husband's pay cheque the minute it arrived—she waited a respectable two days, dressed well, and then proceeded with dignity.

But her Ti-Jean seemed cursed. Two friends once picked up the little guy and pitched him into a river: his head smacked a rock, blood filled the water, and he barely survived. Then it was discovered that he was deaf in his right ear. And when he was 12, he went for a long walk in a frigid February night to get to his sister's wedding and froze the left side of his face so severely that it never recovered. There was nerve damage (Bell's palsy—facial muscle paralysis) that left him with a drooping mouth. Other kids called him "crooked mouth," and risked getting their teeth punched in for it.

He would be hyperactive all his life, but it was raging when he was a child. He was sent to a Catholic private school at nearby Joliette, run by priests. There he struggled with discipline, again loud and rebellious. "Chrétien, take the door!" screamed one teacher at him, fed up with his antics. "Yes, Father," he cracked, "and where would you like me to put it?" Matters weren't helped by younger brother Michel being a model student. Jean's fear that he wasn't as good as others grew. Once, he pretended he had stomach pains so he'd be sent home: he'd learned how to fake an appendix attack. But his father put him in the hospital and soon his perfectly good appendix was surgically removed!

The Chrétiens tried another school, this one in Trois-Rivières. On the first day, he got into an argument and slugged

a big, blond kid, dropping him to the ground. Later a menacing weightlifter challenged him. Pretending to have a bad
foot, Jean waited for his enemy to relax, and then drilled him.
He also became "the keeper of the key," having secretly gotten
his hands on a key that unlocked every door in the seminary.
He hid it in the folds of a fire hose in a hallway, and every
now and then he and the boys would sneak out and go into
town, have a great time in the local bars, and then sneak back.
Another time they broke into the priests' rooms and stole
their food.

Straightening Out

But at age 17, this "black sheep" with the tough-guy way and
slicked-back hair met his angel and life began to change. Her
name was Aline Chaine. She was the most beautiful girl in
Shawinigan, dark haired, dark eyed, and elegant. She appreci-
ated the quick mind and great ambition inside this fast-talking
rebel.

Others things were changing in his life too. A few years
before, feeling the pain of being a runt, he rushed over to his
doctor brother's office and demanded something to make him
grow. His brother gave him vitamin pills. Ti-Jean took them . . .
and began to shoot up! By his late teens he was six-foot-one.

Back at school, he missed Aline. Determined to be someone
she could be proud of, he tried to keep out of trouble. His

marks began to climb and he became more serious. He was still a "talking machine," but now used his words in class.

One of the things he trained his great energy on was politics. His father was a Liberal, and Jean followed in his footsteps. He began helping local candidates, and at times got up on stage to talk. Before long he was a crowd-pleasing warm-up act, capable of moving audiences to laughter with his wit and his down-home ideas. He even won the Shawinigan Junior Chamber of Commerce public speaking contest.

On his father's advice he eyed a law career, hoping it would be a path into the political arena, and in 1955 began studying at Laval University in Quebec City. Under Aline's influence, he was a hard-working student. He drank little and didn't smoke. But he kept talking and dove into a bigger political world. He was elected president of his class and re-elected every year he was there. When he came back to Shawinigan to work in the mills in the summers he appeared at Liberal rallies, leaping onto mill cafeteria tables to talk. "The kid had guts," remembered one worker. He spoke in street language directly to the other "little guys" and hardly knew any English.

By his third year in Quebec City he had built up a network of friends and had developed big ambitions. Could Ti-Jean actually be destined for some sort of greatness? But his strange looks, hot temper, and funny way of talking were against him. Another student later said, "His chances of becoming Prime Minister were about the same as me becoming pope." But he had energy that no one else could match. "I'll become number one," he told a friend. "I won't be there to finish second."

He married Aline in 1957, and two years later graduated from Laval. He came home, joined a law firm, and did very well. His goal was to help other little guys. He could fix problems for the rich too. He could get anyone out of any scrape.

At times his old self surfaced. One day, a discussion in a bar with another lawyer turned violent. Despite being 27 years old, and married with a child, Chrétien got into a brawl and decked his debating partner.

In 1963 he not only got the Liberal nomination but won the riding and, amazingly, entered Parliament at the age of 29. No one had given him a chance, but he talked his way into people's hearts, a rough but powerful speaker with a passion for Canada. He attacked opponents without hesitation, and knew how to organize rallies and fill them with his supporters. In Trois-Rivières with Lester Pearson, a friend held up a sign: "We're Voting for Jean Chrétien. Our Future Prime Minister." Pearson pointed to it and laughed.

Training

Pearson would be a bit of a roadblock. He wanted Quebec to be well represented in his cabinet, but with thinkers. To him, Chrétien wasn't one. Jean took criticisms and kept on working, talking, and solving problems. In his second year in Parliament, he made history by changing the name of Trans Canada Airlines to Air Canada. In the future, everything from Information Canada to Team Canada would be similarly named. He was proving himself to Pearson.

He began a quick climb. Pearson named him his assistant in 1965, and by 1967, at age 33, the youngest cabinet minister in the 20th century. He dreamed of more, of a bigger job, like becoming the first French-Canadian Minister of Finance.

At home he built a huge political organization and became as tough a politician as he had been a street fighter. Too tough, really. He controlled everything. He persuaded friends to run against him but never to speak in public, a dirty way to keep winning. He didn't need it. His straight-from-the-heart style was winning fans across Canada. In later years he would clean up his ways and loosen his stranglehold on his riding.

Another French Canadian entered the cabinet in 1967. A good-looking, deep-thinking rich man from Montreal named Pierre Trudeau. He looked down on Chrétien, and for a while they disliked each other. But as Trudeau closed in on Pearson's job at the 1968 leadership convention, Chrétien threw his support behind him.

Trudeau slowly learned to trust Chrétien's style, so different from his own. He came to see that the guy with the crooked mouth who mangled both languages ("You should hear his French," said Trudeau when someone complained about his English) also had a sharp mind, good judgment, a wonderful memory, and a way that appealed to people. Trudeau gave him a record-breaking nine more cabinet posts. "See Chrétien," he once remarked when someone had a problem, "he's the one who gets things done around here."

In 1977, Jean got his wish and became Minister of Finance. But the country was having money problems and he couldn't make a difference. Again, some doubted his brains.

Three years later he was made Minister of Justice and began two of the most important years of his career. First he fought Quebec separatists during the independence vote, Trudeau's main man, scrapping like the fighter he was. Many Québécois thought he was a puppet of English Canada and a lower-class guy. He was sneered at and belittled. But he was true to who he was, spoke in his own way, and moved sympathetic audiences with the depth of his love for his country.

The minute that battle was won, Trudeau sent him on a cross-country tour to help make a new Constitution for Canada. He used his talking skills to get all the provinces close to an agreement, and then, in heated Ottawa discussions, saved Trudeau's dreams with a last-minute deal. Only Quebec's separatist government didn't agree. In 1982, the "little guy" co-signed Canada's new Constitution with Pierre Trudeau and Queen Elizabeth.

He would be Trudeau's greatest cabinet minister. Chrétien once compared their success to a football game. "Trudeau give me da ball," he said, maybe playing up his working-class accent, "den everybody pile on me. But when dey get off, who still got the ball? Da little guy from Shawinigan!"

He was even tough while on vacation. In Hawaii, he insisted on surfing gigantic waves. The raging water picked him up and threw him towards shore, where he landed on his head and blacked out. A friend leaned over him anxiously. "Jeez," Chrétien suddenly said, coming to on the sand, "this is harder than politics."

He was such a frantic personality, driven to succeed at everything, that he found it difficult to sit still. Often he had to take long walks at night just to slow down so he could sleep.

By 1984, when Trudeau retired, Jean seemed ready for power, at 50 years old. But there was an unstated Liberal policy that the party alternate between French and English leaders, and the nomination, hotly contested by Chrétien, went to John Turner. Jean was bitterly disappointed. He became Turner's Deputy Prime Minister, but found it hard to be number two when he felt he deserved better. He won again in Shawinigan as Turner was crushed across Canada, stayed on for two boring years in Opposition, and then quit.

Number One

Then, wonder of wonders, the little guy became a millionaire, by working as a big-time lawyer and investing in a company that discovered gold. He also kept a close eye on Turner, some said too close. He was once heard to say that he'd like to "drive a stake through Turner's heart" politically. As Turner kept stumbling, many looked to Chrétien as the one they should have chosen the first time. He wrote a book about his life and it became a national bestseller. It seemed that Canadians, in the midst of the Mulroney years, yearned for the honest "little guy."

In 1990 Turner finally quit and Chrétien easily became party leader. But would he be like Turner? Had he lost his human touch during his days with the rich? The Conservatives called him "yesterday's man" and laughed at him. But laughing at Jean Chrétien was always a bad idea. He started slowly, but soon got rolling.

In the 1993 election he crushed his opposition. So much so that the Conservatives, who had criticized his crooked face in advertisements, were almost wiped out. He would rule without much opposition, and was re-elected PM in 1997 and 2000, both times winning big majorities, a record three times in a row, unmatched in Canadian history.

He has often been criticized for not doing much as leader. And it's true that, even though he opposed Mulroney's policies of free trade and the Meech Lake Accord, he later accepted them. But he has always been a practical man. "Don't try to label me," he once said. "Sometimes I side with the Left, sometimes with the Right." Whatever works. He is both a working-class guy and rich; a French guy and English; smart but ordinary. He reflects Canada.

Though he doesn't have a grand vision like Macdonald or Trudeau, he has a solid sense of values. And his human touch is unquestioned. He once visited his hometown paper mill at election time. When the men had to shower, Chrétien took off his suit and tie and got into the showers with them, still talking. That is Jean Chrétien. And that, in a politician, is unique. As one opponent put it, he's "spectacularly unspectacular."

During his reign things have certainly been done. In 1995 he fought the separatists in Quebec again. At first he wanted to stay away, but when the vote seemed terribly close, he went to Quebec and gave passionate speeches. Canada's debt has been erased under his and Finance Minister Paul Martin's control. Critics say he is acting unlike a Liberal by cutting government spending. But he isn't afraid to do what he thinks is necessary, and contents himself with being a Liberal in other areas. Like Mackenzie King, the Prime Minister he most resembles, he seems to be able to hold many positions at once.

When Memorial University in St. John's, Newfoundland, gave him an honorary doctorate, his brother Michel, now an important medical researcher, received one too. Jean wished their parents had been there. "In the case of Michel, it would come as no surprise," he said. "In my case, I'm telling you, they would have been amazed."

Despite criticisms, there are moments when it's clear that he is the true successor to the many great and unusual people who have led this great and unusual nation. Such a moment came after the September 11, 2001 horrific terrorist attacks on

Part Three: Our Prime Ministers   315

the United States, at the World Trade Center and the Pentagon. The Canadian government was under pressure to do everything the United States wanted: accept most of their ideas about terrorism, change our ways when admitting immigrants into our nation, and help attack any country even remotely connected to the terrorists. Chrétien supported the Americans. He expressed his deep sadness and willingness to have Canada unite with them as brothers in the cause of freedom. He stood with 100,000 Canadians on Parliament Hill and said so. Then he said so again in the House. But he knew that Canadians were not and have never been Americans, not in the time of Macdonald, Mackenzie King, or Jean Chrétien. He knew that in a crisis Canadians had to be Canadians. We had to stand up for what we believed in. And it was different from what they believed in.

He told Canadians not to lash out against Muslims (the terrorists had been Muslim). It was simply not Canadian. "This," he thundered, "is completely unacceptable."

And then he made a point to everyone in the world, both to the countries we strongly supported and those we fiercely opposed. He said he would change Canadian laws if they needed to be changed to suit the crisis. "But we will not give in to the temptation, in a rush to increase our security, to undermine the values that we cherish and which have made Canada a beacon of hope, freedom and tolerance to the world." Canada is "a nation founded on a belief in freedom, justice and tolerance."

Our country is unlike any other place. It was built that way. To be a Canadian, and certainly to be one of our Prime Ministers, is to be someone unusual in this world. Jean Chrétien, the once-hopeless kid from Shawinigan, is exactly that.

Not the End

And so we look back over centuries of Canada and its leaders, back to the many brave native chiefs, to French commanders at fortresses in Quebec, to the rebels who wanted democratic "responsible" government, to those Fathers of Confederation who tried to build a nation called Canada with their minds. And of course we look back to each one of those unusual people who have been our Prime Ministers. Canada and its leaders have made many mistakes. Our native people, for example, have been abused and neglected in a nation that stands for reaching out to others. But the mission goes forward to do better, to live up to our original ideals. There have been many triumphs.

Canada is perhaps the only nation in the world created not out of desperation or passion, but by people sitting down and using their brains, and their spirits, to forge a country. It is a nation that thinks. The Fathers of Confederation took French and English, Catholic and Protestant, Maritimers and mainlanders and argued and reasoned until they came up with a plan. It was a great experiment. An unusual one. It is held together by the belief that it is right, and that everyone has a say. It is constantly changing and being challenged. Only leaders of unusual skill, unusual character, and unusual ambition ever stay its leaders for long. Only unusual heroes.

What will the future hold? Today there are men and women sitting in the government's cabinet and perhaps on the Opposition benches who may one day run this country. They confront one another every day in dramatic battles in the House of Commons, arguing, as the nation looks on and judges them. Our Prime Minister is there with them, not a king or a president sitting in a distant office, but a leader who must defend himself and his views before the whole country. Will the future bring more women to the throne? More Christians? Jews? Muslims? Will they all possess those unusual skills of compromise and tolerance that the others learned to use? Of course they will. They will be Canadians.

There have been many dramatic moments in the lives of our leaders. Think of the big-bearded W.H. Pope rowing out in that little fishing boat to find the awe-inspiring George Brown, Alexander Galt, and other giants on that steamer in the bay at Charlottetown. Think of Thomas D'Arcy McGee who came to Canada because he believed that here, unlike his native Ireland, people weren't persecuted for their beliefs. Think of the bravery he showed us, of his golden words for Canada . . . think of him being gunned down in an Ottawa street, a martyr to Canadian tolerance. Think of that magnificent rascal Sir John A. Macdonald, the genius who put us all together, riding through the Rocky Mountains on his nation-building Canadian Pacific Railway, the wind blowing back his grey hair, a smile on his face. Think of the legendary Laurier, who stood up to narrower thinkers, talking quietly at a railway station in Saskatoon with little John Diefenbaker, the son of a German immigrant. Think of Mackenzie King, the magician with the mind like a labyrinth who would do or say anything to hold the nation together—think of him in a dark room, asking even the spirits of the dead to help us go forward. And think of Pierre Trudeau, the gunslinger who defended his English name in Quebec, who twirled behind the Queen's back like a naughty boy, and deeply saddened the nation with his death.

And finally, think of the day Cartier died in 1873. Macdonald, the leading English Canadian, was the first man in Ottawa to hear the news of his great French-Canadian friend's death. He stood at the desk where they both usually sat in the House of Commons and tried to speak. But he couldn't. He fell back and reached out for his fallen ally, just like all our people, whatever their race, their religion, or their beliefs, are asked by the ghosts of our Fathers of Confederation and Prime Ministers to reach out to one another, like Canada asks the world to do in times of trouble, our nation the example. In tears, he reached for the empty desk, lowered his head, and gripped it in a hug.

Acknowledgements

There are many people to thank for their contributions to this book and books past: foremost at Penguin Books to Barbara Berson, senior editor and friend; also to Cynthia Good, who showed confidence in me at the very beginning; to Michael Schellenberg, who faced a massive manuscript undaunted; and to Karen Alliston who brought it all to a conclusion. In production and design: thanks to Tracy Bordian, Catherine Dorton, and Cathy MacLean. Thanks also goes to my agent, Pamela Paul; to Jackson Peacock for filling my head with a love for Canadian history; to Susan Peacock for giving me the soul to write about it; and finally, to Sophie, for her intelligent reading of every last thing I write, and for understanding, when billions wouldn't.

Index

Abbott, Sir John, 43, 70, 108, 120, 122, 134; brother Harry 95, 96; childhood 92–93; death 100; early careers 94–95; father 92, 94; life 91–100; Pacific scandal 97; Prime Minister 98–100; wife Mary Bethune 94

Air Canada (Trans-Canada Airlines), 310

Allan, Hugh, 46, 69–70, 97

Amherst, Nova Scotia, 127, 128, 136

Annexation manifesto, 26, 94

Archibald, Sir Adams George, 10–11

Arthabaska, Quebec, 141

Avro Arrow, 225

Baie Comeau, Quebec, 279, 280, 288, 290

Belleville, Ontario, 115, 117, 121, 124, 125

Benjamin, George, 115, 116, 117, 118

Bennett, (Viscount) Sir Richard Bedford 173, 174, 186, 188, 208, 233, 269; Bennett buggy 199; Calgary 194–197; death 201; Depression 198–201; early years 193–194; life 192–202; parents 193; Prime Minister 198–201

Berlin, Ontario (now Kitchener), 179

bilingualism, 238, 286; Official Languages Act, 248

Bill of Rights, 227

Blake, Edward, 71, 89, 143, 144, 188

Borden, Sir Robert Laird, 148, 149, 150, 169, 170, 185, 196; death 164; early years 153–154; lawyer 155; life 152–164; political start 155–159; Prime Minister 159–163; retirement 163; wife Laura Bond 155, 158, 160, 163; World War I 159–162

Bourassa, Henri, 145, 150

Bowell, Sir Mackenzie, 112, 126, 134, 145, 155; cabinet posts 119–120; early days 115–116; elected 118; fired 124; life 114–125; mellows 119–121; Orangeman 116–117; parents 115; Prime Minister 121–124; retirement 124–125; wife Harriet Moore 116

British North America Act (BNA), 18, 66, 246, 250

Brown, George, 6, 28, 45, 58, 64, 65, 82, 83, 84, 89, 126, 226, 318; life 30–39; childhood 31; Confederation 36–37; death 38; early politics 32–35; *Globe, The* 32; marries Anne Nelson 35; parents 31

Calgary, 146, 195, 196, 197, 255

Campbell, Kim (Avril), cabinet posts 298–299; defeat 301; early politics 295–297; early years 292–294; husband Tuzzie Divinsky 294, 295; husband Howard Eddy 296, 299; parents 292–293; life 291–302; Prime Minister 299–300; school board 295

Campbell, Sir Alexander, 11

Canadian Conservative Alliance (*see also* Reform party), 265

Canadian Pacific Railway (CPR), 98, 118, 168, 207, 252, 319; Abbott 95; Cartier 45; Macdonald 69; Mackenzie 86; Tupper 133; scandal 47, 97

Cartier, Jacques 41, 47

Cartier, Sir George-Étienne, 1, 13, 17, 21, 36, 51, 58, 84, 111, 139, 140, 141, 185, 319; boyhood 41; Confederation 44–45; duel 43; life 40–48; Macdonald 44, 64; Rebellion 25, 42–43; scandal and death 46–47, 97

Catholic (church), 7, 32, 135, 244, 279, 280, 306, 317; Bowell 116, 118, 121, 122; Laurier 139, 141, 146, 147, 148; Macdonald 67; rights 110; Thompson 103, 108, 109; ultramontanes 119

Charlottetown Accord, 265, 289

Charlottetown Conference, 6, 7, 10, 18, 318

Charter of Rights and Freedoms, 251

Château Clique, 42

Chrétien, Jean, 239, 260, 274, 277, 290, 300; cabinet posts 310–313; early years 304–308; lawyer 309; life 303–316; Maurice 305; Michel 306, 314; parents 304, 305; Prime Minister 313–316; Trudeau 310–312; wife Aline Chaine 307, 308, 309; Chrétien, Michel, 306, 314

Clark, Joe, 250, 252, 285, 286, 289; Charles Clark I 255; comeback 265–266; early days 255–259; life 254–266; loses leadership 264; MP 260–261; parents 255; PC leader 261–262; Prime Minister 262–263; wife Maureen McTeer 262, 264

Compton, Quebec, 204

Confederation, 10, 57, 71, 124, 243, 317, 319; Cartier 44; Galt 24, 28; idea of 4–6; Laurier 140; Macdonald 65; Mackenzie 84; McGee 17; Tilley 52; Tupper 56, 130, 131, 136

conscription, 160–161, 169–170, 174, 189, 209–211; riots 161

Conservatives, 17, 27, 84, 89, 96, 117, 124, 146, 157, 183, 208, 214, 223, 226, 249, 260, 286, 297; conscription 149; Diefenbaker-style 220; huge losses 201, 289, 313; King–Byng Affair 197; Pacific Scandal 69, 119; progressive ideas 158; Quebec gains 224; Social Credit 256

constitution, 251, 265, 287, 288, 311

Co-operative Commonwealth Federation (CCF), 174, 175, 200

Criminal Code, 107, 108

Depression, the Great, 186, 189, 198–201

Diefenbaker, John, 148, 176, 214, 229, 238, 241, 246, 256, 257, 258, 273, 281, 282, 283, 285, 319; Diefendollar 225; early politics 221; early years 217–219; last years 226–228; lawyer 218–219; life 216–228; parents 217; Prime Minister 22–226; wife Edna May Brower 218–219, 221, 222; wife Olive Freeman 222, 227

Dorion, Antoine Aimé, 34, 140

double shuffle, the, 28, 34

Duplessis, Maurice, 213, 244, 245

Eagle Pass, British Columbia, 75

England (Great Britain), ix, 2, 24, 87, 108, 111, 114, 117, 125, 136, 146, 163, 184, 188, 201, 214, 224, 246, 257, 293, 294; colonial attitude 5; World War I 169–172; World War II 189–190

English Canada (English Canadians), 3, 18, 120, 159, 178, 185, 203, 207, 208, 227, 246, 271, 304, 311, 312, 317; Confederation 4; Laurier 145, 147; Manitoba Schools Question 122; prejudice 118; Riel 106, 142, 144; World War I 149, 150; World War II 189, 210

Expo '67, 238

Fenians, 5, 19–20, 53, 131

Fisher, Charles, 10, 51

Free Trade Agreement (FTA), 276–277, 288–289

French Canada (French Canadians), 4, 6, 92, 106, 147, 158, 159, 203, 207, 208, 227, 237, 238, 241, 245, 271,

273, 310, 311, 312, 317; Manitoba Schools Question 122; Rep by Pop 33; Riel 87, 118, 119, 142, 144, 145; rights 65; World War I 160; World War II 210
Front de Libération du Québec (FLQ), 248

Gagetown, New Brunswick, 50
Galt, Sir Alexander Tilloch, 6, 36, 43, 58, 94, 318; British America Land Company 25; childhood 24; Confederation 27; death 29; father John Galt 24; Finance Minister 28; life 23–29; railways 25–26; retirement 28; Sherbrooke 25; son Elliott 27; wife Amy Torrance 27
Globe, The, (The Globe and Mail) 32, 34, 37, 64, 82, 107, 136
Goods and Services Tax (GST), 289, 290
Grand Pré, Nova Scotia, 153
Grand Trunk Railway, 26, 43
Gray, John Hamilton (of New Brunswick), 10
Gray, John Hamilton (of Prince Edward Island), 10
Great Coalition, the, 6, 11, 12, 65

Halifax, 102, 104, 112, 131, 136, 257, 281
High River, Alberta, 255, 256, 266
High River Times, 255
Hopewell Cape, New Brunswick, 193
Howe, C.D., 213, 272
Howe, Joseph, 6, 103, 126, 129–130, 131, 132
Hudson Bay Company, 66

Imperial Conferences, 146, 172
Intelligencer, The (Belleville), 115, 116, 124

just society, 247

King, William Lyon Mackenzie, viii, 149, 150, 167, 168, 171, 172–173,
174, 193, 197, 199, 200, 201, 209, 210, 211, 212, 213, 221, 226, 232, 233, 235, 239, 253, 269, 303, 314, 315, 319; background 178–179; death 191; early years 179–181; father 178, 182; Liberal leader 183; life 177–191; mother Isabel Mackenzie 178, 179, 182, 188; Prime Minister 184–191; retires 190; Rockefeller 182; spiritualism 186–188; World War II 189–190
King–Byng Affair, 172–173, 185–186, 197, 232
Kingsmere, 177, 181, 188, 190, 212; ruins 178
Kingston, Ontario, 12, 13, 23, 29, 61, 62, 63, 79, 81

LaFontaine, Louis-Hippolyte, 26, 41, 43
Langevin, Sir Hector-Louis, 13, 78, 99
Laporte, Pierre, 248–249
Laurier, Sir Wilfrid, 77, 87, 108, 110, 126, 135, 156, 157, 158, 159, 166, 168, 169, 180, 181, 182, 185, 189, 191, 205, 213, 218, 223, 253, 303, 319; childhood 139–140; death 151; early politics 142–143; journalist 141; life 138–151; Opposition Leader 144–145; parents 139; Prime Minister 146–149; wife Zoë Lafontaine 140, 141, 142, 149, 150, 187; World War I 149
Laurier House, 181, 187–188, 190
Le Défricheur (The Pioneer), 141
Lévesque, Rene, 250
Liberals, 17, 71, 83, 85, 103, 117, 135, 149, 150, 158, 168, 169, 170, 174, 181, 183, 190, 195, 204, 214, 220, 222, 223, 245, 247, 256, 260, 263, 273, 276, 281, 290, 308, 309; huge loss 224; King–Byng Affair 185; King 191; Pacific Scandal 70, 97; Riel 106; Rouges 142
London Conference, 7, 10, 18, 53, 65
Lougheed, James, 194, 195, 197
Lower Canada, 3, 4; as Canada East, 4, 5, 6, 12

Macdonald, John Sandfield, 35, 96
Macdonald, Sir John Alexander, 6, 27,
    51, 57, 58, 81, 96, 103, 105, 106,
    107, 119, 122, 131, 132, 133, 136,
    142, 143, 144, 145, 157, 166, 184,
    191, 223, 226, 227, 243, 252, 253,
    276, 301, 303, 304, 314, 315, 318,
    319; Brown 30, 32, 34, 36–37; CPR
    69–70, 71, 73, 75; Cartier 40, 44–48;
    Confederation 8, 65–66; daughter 68;
    death 78, 98, 99, 108, 120, 134;
    early politics 64–65; early years
    62–63; funeral 78–79; life 60–79;
    Mackenzie 84, 89, 90; McGee 17,
    21, 66; Mowat 12–13; Opposition
    Leader 71; Pacific Scandal 69–70,
    97; parents 61; Riel 66–68, 72–74;
    son Alexander Jr. 63; son Hugh John
    64; wife Isabella Clark 63, 64; wife
    Susan Agnes Bernard 66, 68
Macdonald-Cartier Freeway, 48, 100
Mackenzie, Alexander, 33, 70–71, 142,
    143; brother Hope 83, 85; CPR 86;
    daughter dies 82; death 89; early
    years 81–82; elected 84; Lambton
    Shield, The, 82; life 80–90; Prime
    Minister 86–88; wife Helen Neill
    81–82; wife Jane Sym 83, 87
Mackenzie, William Lyon, 33, 62, 178,
    182, 188
Manitoba Schools Question, 110, 122,
    135, 145, 146
Martin, Paul, 314
McCully, Jonathan, 10
McDougall, William, 11, 32, 67
McGee, Thomas D'Arcy, 6, 58, 66, 318;
    assassination 14, 20–21; Boston
    editor 15; Canadian arrival 16; child-
    hood 15–16; Confederation 18–19;
    daughter Peggy 21; eulogies 21;
    Fenians; 19–20; funeral 14, 22; Irish
    radical 16; life 14–22; wife Mary 16
McGill University, 93, 94, 140
Meech Lake Accord, 251, 276, 288,
    290, 313; distinct society clause 276
Meighen, Arthur, 163, 183, 184, 185,
    188, 196, 197, 207, 220, 221, 226,

232, 262; daughter Lillian, 174;
    death 174–176; early days 166–167;
    King–Byng Affair 172–173; life
    165–176; Parliament 168–171;
    Prime Minister 171–173; wife Isabel
    Cox 168
Métis, 66–68, 72–73, 132, 143, 217
Montreal, 4, 14, 16, 19, 21, 22, 43, 47,
    70, 93, 95–97, 98, 100, 115, 139,
    144, 238, 244, 246, 247, 250, 251,
    256, 271, 273, 283, 289, 310;
    Alouettes 272; Canadiens 271;
    Forum 215; Rebellion Losses riot 26,
    94; Royals 242; Trudeau's funeral 252
Moodie, Susanna, 94
Mounties (RCMP), 86, 163, 170, 176,
    247, 290
Mowat, Sir Oliver, 12–13
Mulroney, Brian, 251, 254, 255, 264,
    265, 276, 277, 298, 299, 313; Baie
    Comeau 279–280; father 279, 280;
    lawyer 283–285; life 278–290; mother
    279; PC leader 286; Prime Minister
    287–289; return to business 289–290;
    university 280–283; wife Mila
    Pivnicki 283–284, 286, 287, 288

National Energy Program (NEP), 251
National Policy, 53, 69, 88
Natives, 3, 66–67, 107; Blackfoot 2;
    Cree 2, 74; Ojibway 2; Plains 74
New Democratic Party (NDP), 174, 245
New France, 3, 319
Newtonbrook, Ontario, 230

October Crisis, 248, 274
Orange Lodge, Loyal, 116, 117, 118,
    119, 120, 122, 125
Ottawa, 13, 46, 53, 73, 90, 106, 113,
    142, 143, 156, 158, 163, 168, 177,
    180, 181, 182, 183, 195, 196, 197,
    221, 222, 227, 232, 235, 245, 251,
    256, 257, 258, 262, 268, 272, 297,
    311, 319; capital 34; Macdonald's
    death 60, 78–79; McGee's assassina-
    tion 15, 20, 318
Ouiji boards, 188

Pacific Scandal, the, 53, 69–70, 72, 85, 119, 133
Palmer, Edward, 10
Papineau, Louis-Joseph, 25, 42, 92, 139
Parliament, 12, 16, 70, 84, 85, 88, 107, 118, 122, 123, 149, 151, 165, 168, 169, 173, 174, 185, 190, 196, 199, 221, 227, 230, 239, 248, 258, 260, 263, 273, 284, 286, 309, 310; creation 7; fire 161; Macdonald 64, 77, 78; Quebec City 33; rowdiness 71; secret staircase 80; Toronto 17, 27
Parti Québécois, 250
Patriotes, 25, 42
Pearson, Lester Bowles, 190, 214, 215, 223, 226, 241, 245, 246, 272, 274, 276, 309, 310; brothers 230; death 239; diplomat 233–235; early years 230–232; External Affairs Minister 236–237; life 229–239; Nobel Prize 214; parents 230; Prime Minister 237–239; wife Maryon Moody 232, 234
pirates, 244
Plains of Abraham, 3, 204, 206, 207
Pope, William 7, 318
Prince Albert, Saskatchewan, 217, 218, 219, 220, 222
Progressive Conservatives, 221, 258, 265, 281, 284
Progressive Party, 172, 221
Protestant, 7, 116, 118, 147, 279, 317

Quebec (province), 3, 11, 76, 145, 147, 148, 151, 177, 185, 203, 207, 208, 224, 244, 246, 273, 278, 281, 283, 284, 285, 287, 309, 317, 319; Catholic Church 142; Confederation 7; English 96, 204; Meech Lake 276, 288, 290; October Crisis 274; Quiet Revolution 245, 282; Riel 74, 75; separatism 238, 247, 282, 311, 314; World War I 150, 159, 160, 169; World War II 189, 210
Quebec City, 13, 26, 47, 67, 143, 204, 206, 271, 279, 287, 308
Quebec Conference, 7, 10, 12, 18

Reach for the Top, 294
Rebellion (1837), 4; Lower Canada 12, 25, 42, 93; Upper Canada 62, 63
Rebellion Losses Bill, 94
reciprocity (see also free trade), 5, 184, 288
Reform Party (Canadian Conservative Alliance), 256, 265, 301
Reform Party (Liberal), 26, 30, 31, 34, 36, 50, 82
representation by population (Rep by Pop), 33, 34, 36, 84
responsible government, 4, 51
Richard, Rocket, 215
Riel, Louis, 87, 107, 118, 119, 122, 132, 249; Cartier 45, 47; Laurier 142, 143; Manitoba 11, 67–68, 75, 106; North-West Rebellion 72–74
Rossland, BC, 268, 269
Rouges, 139, 142

St. Alban's raid, 96–97
St. Andrew's East (St. André Est), Quebec, 92, 95
St. Jean Baptiste Society, 42; parade 247
St. Laurent, Louis, 185, 222, 223, 235, 237, 256; boyhood 204–206; cabinet 209–212; conscription 209–211; death 215; lawyer 207–209; life 203–215; parents 204, 205; Prime Minister 212–215; wife Jeanne Reneault 206–207
St. Lin, Quebec, 139
St. Mary's, Ontario, 166, 171
Santa Claus, 114
Sarnia, Ontario, 82, 83, 90
Saskatoon, 148, 217, 218, 319
Sauvé, Jeanne, 251
Senate, 7, 99, 108, 123, 191
separatism, 238, 248, 282, 311, 314; referendum 250, 311, 314
Shawinigan, Quebec, 304, 305, 307, 312, 316
Shea, Sir Ambrose, 10
Social Credit (party), 200, 256, 257, 258, 265; B.C. 295

Stanley Cup, 77
sunny way, the, 146

Taché, Sir Étienne Paschal, 11–12
terrorists, 314–315
Thompson, Sir John Sparrow David,
98, 99, 120, 121, 122, 134, 145,
154, 155; boyhood 102; cabinet
posts 106–109; daughters 107–108;
death 111–113; early career
103–105; life 101–113; Macdonald
105; marriage 102–103; parents
102; Prime Minister 109–112; wife
Annie Affleck 102–103, 104,105,
106, 108, 109, 110, 111, 112, 113
Tilley, Sir Samuel Leonard, 56, 58;
childhood 50; Confederation 52–53;
death 55; Lieutenant Governor
53–54; life 49–55; Minister of
Finance 53; Premier 51; wife Lady
Tilley 54
Toronto, 19, 26, 34, 83, 90, 113, 145,
173, 174, 175, 178, 180, 230, 232,
239, 256, 259, 275, 277; Brown 30;
Lower Canada Rebellion 4; Maple
Leafs 239; Parliament 17, 27
Trans-Canada Highway Act, 213
Trudeau, Pierre Elliott, 239, 254,
259, 261, 262, 263, 274, 275, 286,
287, 288, 303, 310, 311, 312, 314,
319; early years 241–243; funeral
252–253; life 240–253; parents 241;
Prime Minister 248–251; political
beginning 245; retirement 251; son
Michel's death 252; son Justin 253;
travels 243–244; Trudeaumania
246–247, 287; wife Maggie Sinclair
248, 252
Tupper, Sir Charles, 56, 57, 58, 99,
121, 123, 124,145, 154, 155, 156;
cabinet posts 132–134; Confederation 130–131; daughter Emma
132; death 136–137; early years
127–128; life 126–137; medical
career 128–129; Premier 130; Prime
Minister 134–135; retirement 136;

son Charles Jr. 123, 154; wife
Frances Morse 129
Turner, John Napier, 239, 287, 312,
313; business return 277; cabinet
274–275; early years 268–271; father
Leonard 268, 288; life 267–277;
Member of Parliament 272–273;
mother Phyllis Gregory 268–269,
270; Prime Minister 275–276; wife
Geills Kilgour 272
twist, the, 300
Union (party) government, 160, 170
United Nations, 190, 212, 234, 236
United States of America, 3, 4, 6, 7, 15,
86, 153, 199, 225, 234, 235, 269,
287; Annexation 94; Fenians 5, 19,
131; free trade 288; reciprocity 5,
184, 288; terrorism 315; war with 4
University of British Columbia, 258,
268, 270, 271, 292, 294, 295
University of Toronto, 167, 179, 231,
232, 236
Upper Canada, 3, 4; as Canada West,
4, 5, 6, 33

Vancouver, 136, 258, 267, 268, 270,
292, 293, 295, 297, 299; Council
295; School Board 295
Vimy Ridge (battle), 161

Wakaw, Saskatchewan, 218
War Measures Act, 249
War of 1812, 4, 41
Whelan, Patrick James, 21
Windsor Castle, 101, 111, 112
Winnipeg, 75, 134, 146, 167, 170,
232, 272; strike/riot 163, 170
World War I (First World War), 149,
153, 159–163, 169, 185, 210, 231
World War II, (Second World War),
174, 188, 194, 209, 234, 243, 249,
292, 315

Ypres (battle), 161

Zeppelins, 231